BASEBALL
The Writers' Game

Also by MIKE SHANNON

Diamond Classics: Essays on 100 of the Best Baseball Books Ever Published

Johnny Bench

Willie Stargell

The Day Satchel Paige and the Pittsburgh Crawfords Came to Hertford, N.C.: Baseball Stories and Poems

Tales from the Dugout: The Greatest True Baseball Stories Ever Told

Tales from the Ballpark: More of the Greatest True Baseball Stories Ever Told

More Than Casey: A History of Baseball Poetry

Everything Happens in Chillicothe: A Summer in the Frontier League with Max McLeary, the One-Eyed Umpire

A Guide to Collecting Baseball Books

BASEBALL
The Writer's Game

M I K E   S H A N N O N

Brassey's, Inc.
Washington, D.C.

Library of Congress Cataloging-in-Publication Data

Shannon, Mike.
    Baseball : the writer's game / Mike Shannon.
      p. cm.
    Includes bibliographical references.
    ISBN 1-57488-421-2 (pbk. : alk. paper)
      1. Sportswriters—United States—Biography.   2. Baseball.   I. Title.
  GV742.4 .S47   2002
  070.4'49796'0922—dc21
  [B]   2002074471

ISBN 1-57488-421-2 (alk. paper)

Printed in the United States of America on acid-free paper that meets the American National Standards Institute Z39-48 Standard.

Brassey's, Inc.
22841 Quicksilver Drive
Dulles, Virginia 20166

First Edition

10 9 8 7 6 5 4 3 2 1

For Kathleen Dermody Shannon.
She plays the prettiest first base you've ever seen,
but I'm the one who made the great catch.

Contents

Introduction to the Second Edition

As we ex-jocks get older, the athletic exploits of our youth become greater. That's the way our memories work. For aging writers, it's a different story. All you have to do is pick up a book and read it to see if it's as good as you remember.

As far as *Baseball: The Writers' Game* is concerned, it has aged more gracefully than I have, and I'm as happy with it today as I was in 1992, when it was first published by Jill and Jim Langford of Diamond Communications in South Bend, Indiana. The book is a fascinating look into the life of a writer and into the game of baseball, and it is still a wonderful guide for anyone who would like to follow in the footsteps of the authors interviewed in these pages. I give most of the credit for the book's appeal to the subjects themselves and thank them, again, for participating so generously in its development.

My gratitude to these authors reminds me of a matter that needs to be addressed here briefly: how the subjects were chosen in the first place. I didn't think this would be of so much interest to other people, but initial reviews of the first edition of the book proved otherwise. So to set the record straight, please allow me to clear up a few things that I didn't make clear the first time.

As I stated in the introduction to the original edition, I got the idea for this book after reading Jerome Holtzman's wonderful *No Cheering in the Press Box*. What makes my book different from Mr. Holtzman's is that while his is a collection of interviews with newspaper sportswriters, *Baseball: The Writers' Game* is a book of interviews (oral history monologues, if you prefer) with authors, specifically the authors of at least two great baseball books. That was the criterion I used to select the subjects of this book.

This criterion did disqualify some notable writers, which led to at least one complaint, but neither of the writers mentioned in one review had published a book up to that point; one was a magazine writer, the other a newspaper columnist. While both were excellent writers, their books weren't actually books, just a collection of previously published short pieces, and having such pieces bound between covers is not the same thing as writing a book. This book is about the people who have risen to the challenge of sitting down and writing a book, from beginning to end.

For anyone who would like to question why an author has not been included, I have never stated or meant to imply that the 15 subjects in the original book were the only authors of great baseball books on the face of the earth. The fact that two additional authors have been included in this new edition proves this. I have chosen the 17 authors in this book not only because they clearly deserved recognition, but also because they interested me, and they were willing to talk to me and give me a great interview.

I would first like to thank Chris Kahrl, the editor at Brassey's whose appreciation for the original book has been instrumental in bringing this new edition into being. It is a pleasure to work with such an editor, who is knowledgeable about baseball and, if anything, even more nuts about the game than I am.

I am deeply grateful to all the subjects of the original book and to the rookies in this new edition, Greg Rhodes and Dan Shaughnessy. I know few people who deserve success as much as Greg, and fewer still who share the fruits of that success so generously. The Boston Red Sox may not hit in the clutch, but Dan Shaughnessy does. He gave me a great interview under very trying circumstances, and it was a kindness I will never forget.

As always, I must recognize and thank my large and loving family. There would be no books with my name on them without my beautiful wife, Kathy Dermody Shannon. She is my treasure. And no dad could be more proud of his kids than I am of mine: Meg, Casey, Mickey, Babe, and Nolan Ryan. My parents, John and Willie Shannon, are the best people I have ever been privileged to know, and I love my brothers and sisters—Laura, Susie, John, and Tim—more than I can say. As for in-laws, they don't come any better than Vinnie Patterson (my favorite son-in-law), Jeff and Andrew Smiley, Lyle and Evan Klemmt, and Carla Gowan Shannon.

Special thanks must go to my brother John his lovely wife, Janice Vereneau Shannon, and their kids John, Rachel, and Laura, for stabling me and keeping me in oats, hay, and sugar cubes during my trip to Boston, Massachusetts, in connection with this book. When the shocking and terrible events of September 11, 2001, unfolded, John and I were on the Massachusetts Turnpike halfway between Waterbury, Connecticut, and Boston on our way to see Dan Shaughnessy. When Janice called on John's cell phone the first time, we thought a tragic accident had occurred. When she called the second time, we knew. John looked at me and immediately said, "Osama Bin Laden." Those long minutes of infamy made us even more grateful than ever for our loved ones, our lives, and our country.

Baseball is the greatest game, and it is a fitting honor that it was invented and nurtured into perfection in the greatest country in the world. I am proud to think that with this book and in conjunction with the great baseball authors represented here, I have made a small contribution to the literature of that game.

May God bless America.

1

CHARLES C. ALEXANDER

From the time he was a boy rooting for the Texas League's Beaumont entry, Charles Alexander has been an ardent follower and student of baseball. A professor of history at Ohio University since 1970, Alexander has been instrumental in gaining respectability for baseball as a subject of scholarly inquiry by authoring definitive, superbly researched and written biographies of two giants in baseball history, Ty Cobb and John McGraw. He previously established his academic reputation by writing two books on the Ku Klux Klan, two studies of the impact of nationalism on American intellectual life, and histories of the Eisenhower Era and Project Mercury. A graduate of Lamar University (1958) and the University of Texas (Ph.D., 1962), Alexander has taught at the University of Houston, the University of Georgia, and the University of Texas. He has lectured at universities across the country and abroad and teaches a wide variety of courses at Ohio University in American intellectual and cultural history, the United States in the twentieth century, and the history of American sports. His impressive and entertaining one-volume history of baseball, Our Game, *was published in the spring of 1991.*

I GOT INTERESTED in writing a book about Ty Cobb while I was organizing a course in American sports history for the fall of 1980. I had to familiarize myself with the extant body of work in American sports history, which was a lot smaller then than it is now. And it occurred to me that there were all kinds of terrific historical subjects that hadn't been touched or if they had been touched had been dealt with by journalists who have one agenda as opposed to professional historians who have another. Professional historians had done very little in this area, and I thought that one of the most appealing biographical subjects was Ty Cobb. What had been written about Ty Cobb thus far was based upon anecdotes, oral accounts, folklore. Nobody had undertaken to study the man seriously.

At the time I was quite sheepish about whether this was the direction I ought to take my own career. Sports history had not gained the kind of respect within the academy that it has since, in the last 10 years or so.

My wife, Jo Ann, and my old friend from the University of Texas, Stephen B. Oates, the noted biographer of John Brown . . . Abraham Lincoln . . . William Faulkner . . . Martin Luther King . . . Nat Turner, helped me make up my mind. Steve was visiting us, and we were just sitting around, bullshitting one night. I mentioned the idea of doing a Cobb biography and said I'd really like to do it but didn't think I ought to. Steve and Jo Ann jumped on me and said, "No. You're cheating yourself. If that's what you really want to do, you ought to do it." So they convinced me.

Still, I wouldn't have felt confident enough to do the Cobb book if I hadn't already established what I thought was a pretty solid reputation as a professional historian. So I understand the reluctance that my graduate students have when I try to steer them in the direction of sports history. Because they have this doubt: "Who's interested in this besides fans? Is this going to carry any credibility in the profession? How can I get a job teaching sports history?" Well, I try to sell it to them as part of American social history and tell them that it makes as much sense to study sports history as to study the history of American business or the history of American transportation or the history of American science. If you were working in the history of American medicine, everybody would get all excited and talk about how important and profound it is. I think you would probably learn as much or more about the development of American society from Mare Maltby's history of early professional football, which he did as a doctoral dissertation under my direction here at Ohio University, as you would from studying the history of American medicine during that period. That's the rationale I give them. But I understand their timidity on the subject because I had the same thing 10 years ago when I first started to work on Ty Cobb. I didn't have to worry about getting promoted or getting tenure, but I wondered if I would possibly hurt my reputation by doing the Cobb book. As it turned out, I think I strengthened my reputation, and I know I made myself a lot more generally known as a writer and as a historian than I would have been otherwise.

While sports history is booming, it's still true, and will be true for the rest of my life at least, that many members of the academy, who ought to know better, still regard this kind of history as frivolous, crackpot history and not as serious as studying, for example, the pattern of divorces granted by the Catholic Church in Mexico in the eighteenth century. That sort of thing is supposedly more serious because it's more traditional and presumably more involved with the serious matters that affect people's lives, life-and-death matters like marriage, children, divorce, hunger, war, suffering, and all that; whereas sports presumably have to do with fun, and thus the history of how people have fun is less significant than how they've suffered. And certainly, the history of those who have performed to provide entertainment for those who are having fun would be even less significant than the history of suffering and hardship. Or, so the thinking goes. For example, the film I showed to my class this morning, *America Lost and Found,* gives you a lot of standard documentary footage of Depression America and then juxtaposes that with all this other stuff that you don't normally associate with the Depression: people betting money on lotteries; the National Smile Contest; a group of car salesmen getting together and talking about who's going to sell the most cars this year; and the New York World's Fair and its vision of the future. When people think about the serious history of the Depression, they focus on the unemployed, the economic factors that caused the Depression, the New Deal trying to get the country out of the Depression, the politics and economics of the New Deal, etc., etc. And most people in my profession would think that studying forms of entertainment in the Depression would be less significant than studying the politics and economics of the period. And yet, as this film very cleverly brings out, most people most of the time are less engaged in suffering than they are in trying to find ways to divert themselves and have some fun and make life a little better. That's a basic truth I think historians have overlooked for centuries now.

On the other hand, I'm somewhat afraid that sports history will come to be taken too seriously by its practitioners, that it will be dealt with in such a heavy-handed manner that the fun will be taken out of it. I encounter a number of people—they tend to be members of the North American Society for Sports History, and they publish in the Society's journal—who I suspect are not real fans. They don't really like the game on the field or in the arena. They're more interested in race relations, drugs, class and ethnic origins, the relationship between the rise of the city and the rise of professional sports . . . those kinds of things. I'm interested in all that too, but I can't get away from the game on the field.

For example, this book, *Winning is the Only Thing: Sports in America Since 1945,* by Randy Roberts and James Olson, is an unrelieved complaint against American sports in the post–World War II years. What comes through is that the authors don't really like the subject; they don't like sports, and I told Randy Roberts so when he asked me to read the pre-publication manuscript. I asked him, "Where are the games in this book? Where are the athletic heroics that thrill people and give you this history to write in the first place?"

I began work on Cobb about September 1980, and I started writing the book on Labor Day 1982. I'll never forget that because Jo Ann was painting a room and I was writing this book. I said, "This is ridiculous. Here you are working your ass off painting, and I'm working my ass off starting this book, and it's Labor Day." I finished the book around the end of February 1983. I was amazed because I'd never been able to write a book that fast, and I was teaching full time. Jo Ann was amazed too, first of all because I was writing so fast, and second because I was in such a good mood the whole time. It was the first book I ever wrote that I actually looked forward to getting back to every morning and to carrying on with Cobb's life. And that's one reason I decided to do the McGraw book. And I did have the same enjoyable experience with McGraw, which also took me only about six months to write.

I was pleased with the way the Cobb book turned out and with the way it got me involved in that whole period of baseball history. Actually, it got me involved in that whole period of American history in a way I hadn't really dealt with before. Everything I'd ever published had been based in the history of the United States in the twentieth century, and in particular I had published a lot of work pertaining to the 1920s and 1930s. So even though I started out with a mastery of the general historical period in which Cobb lived, I read everything pertaining to baseball history that I could get my hands on.

Now with the John McGraw book, of course, I had to go back into the nineteenth century, into a period in baseball histroy about which I knew even less. Like most people, my own thinking had been dominated by this pre-1900 syndrome, the idea that so-called modern baseball begins in 1900. Well, one of the things doing the McGraw book left me with was the sense that that's ridiculous: there's no point at all in dividing baseball history. But if you have to divide it into two eras, it would be pre-1893/post-1893 because, once the pitching distance was moved back to 60'6" and some other rules changed leading up to that were in place, then modern baseball was really created.

Preparing for the Cobb book was a great experience, though, because, for the first time in my life, I had a good reason to read all this baseball stuff . . . all those Fred Lieb and Frank Graham team histories . . . and Cobb's autobiography, *My Life in Baseball: The True Record,* which is indispensable. As I suggest in my epilogue to the Cobb book, when Cobb's autobiography came out it was probably the best book of its kind ever published. And even with its limitations, it's still one of the best autobiographies by a major sports figure.

The Al Stump piece, "Ty Cobb's Wild Ten-Month Fight to Live," rings true, but the problem with it is that Stump gives you the impression he was with Cobb nearly all the time for a 10-month period that ended about six months before Cobb died. That's not true. Stump was with Cobb for four or five weeks accumulative time during that whole period. In fact, Cobb, who was always restless, was all over the place. He had two different homes, one in California and one in Georgia, and he lived other places at times too. I was able to retrace Cobb's steps pretty closely, enough to indicate that the part of his life that Stump saw was pretty small.

Other people who saw Cobb during that time saw Cobb in other ways. In particular, a second cousin who became very close to him in his last couple of years, a fellow who lives in Cordelia, Georgia, where Cobb was going to build his dream home on the mountain top but never did, had a very different slant on Cobb. He said, "I came to love the old man. That's the way I felt about him." So you have to be careful about the Stump piece. The experiences he describes I have no doubt were true, and they do reveal a lot about Cobb, but it's not a well-rounded picture.

Another thing is that Stump, just like John McCallum and everybody else who'd written about Cobb, didn't take the trouble to investigate the circumstances of his father's death at the hands of his mother. One of the things I wanted to do was pin all that down, and by going to the Augusta papers I was able to get a pretty full account of what had actually happened. I also talked to people who had either been small children when it happened or who hadn't even been born when it happened but for whom it was a part of the history of the small town of Royston, Georgia, where Cobb had grown up. These people had heard the facts of the case all their lives, and it is still a well-known event in the history of the town. I was able to clarify what other people who had written about Cobb were fuzzy about: why was his father's death such a monumental event in Cobb's life? And it has to do with the very questionable circumstances under which his mother shot his father and what her own personal conduct had been leading up to the shooting.

The Stump piece was very interesting, but I do know that it upset the Cobb family very much, and it also upset a lot of people in Royston, Georgia. And one of the unfortunate things about it was where it was published, in *True* magazine, a men's magazine not known for its reliability, and this gave it a sensational aspect. I also think Stump exploited this relationship with Cobb because he'd collaborated with Cobb on the autobiography, and, just as soon as Cobb died, Stump rushed into print with this tell-all story, "Ty Cobb's Wild Ten-Month Fight to Live." I think that left something to be desired in terms of taste.

In my research for the book, Cobb's children were no help to me because I never got any communication back from them at all. It was all one way. They simply would not answer my letters, and I just gave up. I'd been given to understand that I'd have this problem, so I wasn't surprised that I didn't get any cooperation from either of the two daughters, Shirley Cobb and Beverly Cobb, or the surviving son, Jimmy Cobb. Apparently, this is their standard response because I recently heard from a fellow interested in doing a movie about Cobb. He had been trying to establish contact with Jimmy Cobb, who lives in Santa Maria, California, both by letter and by telephone, and he couldn't get his letters answered nor could he get his telephone calls returned.

I think the aloofness of the Cobb offspring is a result of a combination of the fact that there was a great deal of hard feelings within the family—Cobb's marriage to their mother broke up, and they became estranged from him in the last 10 years of his life—and the fact that there's been a lot of nonsense written about Cobb. I guess if I were the son of a famous person like Cobb and there'd been some of the crap published and said about him that has been about Cobb, I guess I'd take offense as well and tend to distrust people who wanted my cooperation so they could write something about my daddy. Even though I tried to explain at length who I was and what I was doing and signed my letters "Charles C. Alexander, Ph.D.," that didn't carry any weight.

I went as far as I could go in terms of what I learned about their family affairs from other people: from Cobb's niece, a couple of cousins, and some other people in Georgia. But I didn't feel as if I could speculate anymore than I did about the kinds of troubles they had from the 1930s on. The great difficulties that Cobb had with his family seemed to have started right after he retired, which is not surprising. He always had trouble in retirement, but I suspect those early years were particularly difficult for him. You see, Cobb struggled to get to the top of his profession, and he struggled throughout his career to keep himself on top. Then, his retirement was another long struggle to find something to do because he was very rich and nobody would give him a job in baseball. So what was he going to do with his life? (By the way, I wanted to entitle the book, *The Struggles of Ty Cobb*, but the publisher said no.) Within a matter of three years after his retirement his wife filed the first of several divorce actions that she filed and then withdrew. And finally, of course, she went through with the last one.

Even without the cooperation of his offspring I think I was able to capture the main elements of Cobb's life. I don't think I missed the basic story. On the other hand, it would have been nice to have had their cooperation. You always think in terms of that trunk of personal letters up in the attic which nobody else has ever seen and that you might be able to establish contact with somebody who will be able to lead you to the trunk.

I particularly would have liked to know more about the relationship between Cobb and Ty Cobb Jr., who was the first born and from whom Cobb became bitterly estranged. They just didn't see each other for many years and finally reconciled just before Ty Cobb Jr.'s death from a brain tumor when he was only 35 or so in the early 1950s.

I don't know how much balls I would have had to push some things anyway if the three offspring had been willing to sit down and talk to me, in terms of the relationship between Cobb and their mother, for example. I'm not an investigative journalist, and I'm not habituated to prying into people's private affairs, so I think I would have been very uncomfortable trying to get very far with that aspect. Certainly, other people, journalists in particular, would have been a lot pushier. "They" might have flown out to California to bang on people's doors, but I just wasn't prepared to do that. I just don't think I could have brought myself to have been as insistent as a good journalist has to be, or at least as insistent as they think they have to be.

To be honest, I think interviewing, and oral history particularly, is very much overrated and is of little value in getting primary, factual information. You have to know the story beforehand and just use the oral history to fill in, or the oral history can give you some clues that you can follow up on. This is one of the problems I have with all the people working in black baseball history. They tend to accept what they're told uncritically, and, my god, you just can't do that. You can't do that with old people, number one; you can't do that with old ballplayers, number two; and you sure can't do it with old black ballplayers. Because these guys have a complaint, an honest gripe to be sure, but they do strive to make the exploits of themselves and of the black baseball teams as heroic as possible.

I have a similar complaint against the Society of American Baseball Research (SABR) and their *Baseball Research Journal* in that they don't have a sufficiently critical attitude toward the kind of articles they accept. If it's fun to read, they're prepared to publish it. But they're not as prepared as they should be to deal with its credibility as history. In a recent issue, for example, there's an interview with Tweed Webb, an oldtime semi-pro ballplayer in St. Louis who worked as a sportswriter for the St. Louis black press for many years covering baseball. It's an interesting interview with him about himself up to a point. Then the author is naive enough to include Webb's assertion that catcher Bruce Petway threw Cobb out stealing 16 out of 17 times in a series of exhibition games in Cuba. It never happened. It just never happened. But how do you document this? Well, you document it by saying it's true, as Webb does. You say, "I wrote about that 50 years ago, but people just wouldn't believe it."

In most places, you read that Petway threw Cobb out two out of three times. In fact, he threw him out one time. This was a matter of some note at the time, in 1910, but what was more notable at the time was that Jose Mendez struck Cobb out in that game. That was what got people really excited. I don't know what you're supposed to do with much of the black baseball history that's been written; I really don't. There are a lot of quotable quotes, but how much history is there?

I think the purpose of biography is to re-create a life. It's not just to tell history because you can write history in a lot of other, different ways, and in fact you can write it in more direct ways and you can tell more about history by not focusing on a particular individual. But in biography you're really trying to re-create somebody's life, trying to bring that person to life as far as you can, and trying to make the reader feel as if he knows the subject insofar as one can ever know another person who lived another time, who is remote from you and from your own experiences perhaps. And, of course, this is where differences in skill, imagination, insight, and whatever come into play.

I also don't think that you can write a decent biography of someone you despise. That's the quarrel I have with Robert Caro's volumes on Lyndon Johnson. It's clear that Caro just despises Johnson, he just hates him, and this comes through. What it does is create a constant doubt in the reader's mind as to whether Caro is giving us the real Johnson, as to whether anybody could be that totally unredeemably bad. Caro gives us a Johnson who starts out as a teenager with the intention to cheat, deceive, screw, and exploit everybody he comes into contact with, and I don't think that was Lyndon Johnson. I don't think that's the way human beings are in general. And certainly, I wouldn't have written about Ty Cobb if I'd had nothing but hostility toward him: "This guy's a total son of a bitch, and I have no use for him whatsoever." I couldn't write a book about somebody I felt that way about.

It is true, I think, if you're a halfway decent human being yourself, that in studying somebody else's life you will most of the time, at least in some ways, sympathize or even empathize with the subject because everybody's fallible. I think one of the qualities of a good biographer is the ability to recognize the same fallibility in himself that he can see in other people. And vice versa.

Also, I don't think I was old enough 20 years ago to write biography. I think it requires a certain maturity, maybe even a certain amount of suffering on your own part. I think you have to have lived a lot, have met a lot of people, and have had a pretty rich experience yourself in order to relate as closely to somebody else's life as you need to relate to write a good biography. And I don't think I could have done it any earlier than I did. I was 44 when I started working on Cobb, and I think that's about right to be able to come to terms with somebody's life besides your own. It's often said of mathematicians that they peak at 28 or 30, something like that. And writers of poetry peak fairly early as well, I think. Poetry seems to be a young person's art. Maybe biography is an older person's art. It is in my case anyway.

I've been influenced in the way I think about biography by Stephen Oates, who did start doing biography young and who did it well young, in his biography of John Brown, which started out as his doctoral dissertation at the University of Texas. He and I have talked about biography over the years, and I've gotten a lot of insights from him. On the other hand, I think maybe I tend to be less wrapped up in my subjects than he is and more detached from them. In his biography of Martin Luther King, for example, I personally think he was not as critically detached from King as he should have been, and consequently he was not able to see what I see as the rather sad character of King's last years, where he's taking all kinds of wrong turns and going up dead ends. But that's his book to write, not mine. I do think you have to maintain a certain detachment, a delicate tension between author and subject. You can't completely identify with the subject.

I didn't try to psychoanalyze Cobb because psychoanalysis is ultimately unprovable. It is a therapeutic clinical approach used to treat people who have neurotic or psychotic disturbances. I've never been able to understand how you can apply this clinical approach which you use on live people, on patients, to figures who are not living and whom you can never know or have personal access to. That's problem number one.

Problem number two is that psychoanalysis by definition is a theory. You're taking a theory as a model of behavior and then trying to understand the behavior of a real person in the light of that model. Of course, the tendency is always to fit the subject into the model. And the problem with the model is that human behavior is unpredictable.

Take the case of Cobb, for example. Many young boys growing up with the kind of demanding, imposing father that Cobb had would have been repressed, intimidated, and reduced to submissive, milquetoast little guys, momma's boys perhaps. Cobb, to the extent that his father tried to dominate him, seemed to rebel and to grow and to become more of a distinct, independent personality. Yet, at the same time he was constantly striving to please his father. And pleasing his father came to be his great goal in life . . . at the same time that establishing himself as an independent human being became something he strived to do.

Also, his father's death would have been a shattering experience for many people; would have caused them to become reclusive and shame-ridden; would have destroyed their lives and made them dysfunctional. In Cobb's case, it set him on a course to prove something to everybody. It made him an even fiercer, more striving, more assertive and aggressive personality than he'd been before. So how are you going to take a theory that is supposed to predict behavior and use it when the predictive behavior doesn't work out? What's the point? Fortunately, and thank god, the psychoanalysts don't have it all figured out and never will. Human behavior is too complex and too variable and too eccentric to be able to reduce to formulae. For that reason I think the psychoanalytic approach to history never carries you very far.

As far as biography is concerned, psychoanalytical biography is absolutely at odds with biography as art. You're so busy being clinical in psycho-biography that you lose the flavor, the color, the excitement of a real life being lived. Even screwed-up people don't know most of the time that they're screwed-up, and they don't live their lives in such a way that they can be studied effectively by a psycho-biographer. Now there's a difference, of course, between psychoanalytical writing and using some psychology. I think I used some psychology, what I would call common sense, experiential psychology, in writing about Cobb, and McGraw as well. I think any biographer has to do that. Any biographer looking at Cobb would have to see that his relationship with his father was very significant in his life. But you can describe how you think that relationship was significant without trying to relate it to some kind of psychoanalytical model.

In writing about Cobb I could also bring to bear certain psychological insights based on my having had a background similar to Cobb's. I grew up in a little southeast Texas town in what was still the segregation era. Race relations had not really changed all that much when I was growing up from the time Cobb was growing up 60 years earlier. My father was the school superintendent of this little town; Cobb's father was the school principal. Cobb's father was a big man in town, and people came to him for advice and looked to him for leadership in the same way they did my father. I was expected to be exemplary, in school and out of school, as was Cobb, and there is a certain amount of discomfort for a kid in that situation. I was always the superintendent's son; Cobb was always the principal's son, Professor Cobb's son. So I could relate to all that.

I could also relate to Cobb's impatience with people who are not willing to pay the price to achieve what they are capable of achieving; with people who are prepared to settle for second-best; with people who don't have any sense of excellence. I admired that about Cobb. I think the bottom line about Cobb is that he set a standard of excellence for himself that he met and that he insisted other people meet as well. And he had no patience with people who wouldn't at least try. I feel the same way. I didn't have this advantage in doing the McGraw book because my background and McGraw's were radically different. He grew up as the son of Irish-Catholic immigrants in a little town in upstate New York, and he was a New York guy most of his life. He came from a whole different cultural context than the one I came from and the one Cobb came from, so I didn't feel as personally close to the historical figure of McGraw as I did to Cobb. I think I was able to get close enough, though.

Oxford University Press didn't pay me a lot of money up front for the Cobb book. I didn't really expect them to. At that point I was happy just to get a publisher for the book and particularly one as prestigious as Oxford. But I thought they did a rather poor job promoting the book once it had been published, and if it hadn't been for Pete Rose re-awakening people's awareness of and interest in Ty Cobb, the book wouldn't have sold even as well as it has. In hardback it sold out of two printings of 2,500. In paperback it has sold about 25,000. I'm gratified that the paperback has been used in quite a few college courses over the years, not only sports history courses but also courses in biography and Southern history. People often tell me at conferences and meetings that they've used the book in some context I never thought it would be used in.

I was also told that my book had a lot to do with a revival of interest in Cobb by the people of Royston, Georgia. Cobb was the most famous person who ever came out of the town, and the townspeople had tried to establish a Ty Cobb museum there, but it had not been a success. They had given up trying to exploit Cobb as a tourist attraction, but they did decide that just as a local thing, and at the same time as a way to publicize Royston in surrounding towns and in Atlanta too, they would have a Ty Cobb centennial and that they'd have it in conjunction with the annual Chamber of Commerce Christmas dinner.

The centennial celebration didn't correspond with Cobb's birthday, which is December 18—we were down there the 8th and 9th, I think—but at least it was in December, and it was 1986, so it was 100 years after he was born, even though Cobb didn't live in Royston until he was five or six years old.

I addressed the Chamber of Commerce on Friday night, and on Saturday they had a Ty Cobb centennial parade in conjunction with their regular Christmas parade. Gaylord Perry came over from Gaffney, South Carolina, where he was the baseball coach at Limestone College. Saturday morning Gaylord signed bats and balls and I signed copies of my book at the city hall, and then we went to a luncheon at a small church college in the little town of Franklin Springs about three miles outside of Royston.

By this time my wife, Jo Ann, and I had been around Gaylord for several hours, and we were enjoying joking around with him. After lunch we started back to Royston to get organized for the parade. Jo Ann, Gaylord, and I were riding in this white stretch limousine that a car dealer in Atlanta had provided the town of Royston as a courtesy, and the president of the town's only bank was chauffeuring us around. By then people were coming into town for the parade, and traffic on this two-lane highway was really backing up. We were poking along at about 30 miles an hour, and all of a sudden Gaylord said, "Look! There's a yard sale. Pull over there." And Jo Ann said, "Yeah, pull over. I'd like to go in there, too." I said, "Guys, we really need to get back . . ." And they said, "No, no. Let's check this out."

So, this long limo—the damn thing was about 30 feet long—stopped in the right-hand lane, with cars in the left-hand lane coming by, zip . . . zip . . . zip, in the other direction. Luckily, one of the two police cars that the town of Royston owns happened by. The cops recognized the stretch limousine and saw we were having trouble making a left-hand turn, so they stopped.

The cop got out, stopped traffic from this direction, stopped traffic from that direction, and waved us across. We hinged this stretch limousine into these people's front yard. And here was this 60-ish man and woman standing out in the front yard with their mouths open, watching all this maneuvering as we pulled into their driveway. Out popped this great big guy—Perry's 6'4" and weighs about 250—in a suit and tie; I had on a sports coat and tie; and Jo Ann, a good-looking gal, was all dressed up.

Gaylord and Jo Ann said hello to the people having the garage sale and then disappeared into the house to check out the antiques. So I stood around and chatted with these people for awhile: "I'm Charles Alexander, and I teach at Ohio University. I'm down here for the Ty Cobb centennial. The big fellow is Gaylord Perry. He's a famous baseball pitcher; retired a couple of years ago."

Well, they'd never heard of Perry, but they figured that he must be important and that I must be important. So when Gaylord and Jo Ann finally reappeared, having not found anything they liked—I don't know what we would have done if they had—the owners of the place, the people with the yard sale, had us all pose on the front step while they took our picture. We got back into the limo; the cop stopped traffic for us again; and we got back onto the highway and resumed our progress back into town. Then we went through the town as the co-grand marshals of the parade. Gaylord rode in the back of one convertible, and Jo Ann and I rode in the convertible right behind him. Everybody seemed to be very pleased by the parade, and some of the people I'd met on my previous trip doing research for the book yelled and cheered at me from the sidelines. Then we went over to city hall, the ex–Cobb Museum, for the dedication of a Ty Cobb sculpture. Gaylord and I both made some more remarks, and that was about it. We really did enjoy being with Gaylord. He's a totally unprepossessing guy, just a good old boy. And he really seemed to enjoy the day too.

BASEBALL BOOKS BY CHARLES C. ALEXANDER

Ty Cobb. New York: Oxford University Press, 1984.
John McGraw. New York: Viking, 1988.
Our Game: An American Baseball History. New York: Henry Holt, 1991.
Rogers Hornsby: A Biography. New York: Henry Holt, 1995.

2

JIM BROSNAN

*Jim Brosnan was a major league pitcher for nine years, but he is better known as the author of two bestselling, "inside" accounts of the game—*The Long Season *(Harper & Brothers, 1960) and* Pennant Race *(Harper & Brothers, 1962). The former diary astonished a lot of observers who could hardly believe that a major league ballplayer was capable of composing such a witty and literate book without the aid of a ghostwriter, while the latter confirmed Brosnan as a writer of real talent and intelligence. Nicknamed "Professor" because of his un-jock-like love of books and classical music, Brosnan was mediocre as a starting pitching but found himself when he was shifted to short relief. In his best season, recounted in* Pennant Race, *he made a major contribution (10-4, 16 saves, 3.04 ERA) to the Cincinnati Reds's surprising drive to the 1961 National League pennant. Since retiring from baseball at the end of the 1963 season, Brosnan has worked as a sports journalist in radio and television and as a freelance writer of juvenile baseball books and baseball articles, profiles, and book reviews for a wide range of newspapers and magazines.*

MY KIDS will resent me saying this, but when *The Long Season* came out, when I had the book in my hands for the first time, I felt as proud as a father. That was my baby. I may have been even more proud of writing that book than of fathering my kids because the book was all mine. It wasn't a dual job.

I have always loved books and been fascinated by them. From the time I was eight or nine years old, I spent as much time in the library reading as I did playing sports. I'd walk to the library, which was about 10 blocks from my house in the Westwood area of Cincinnati, and, if it rained, that was okay with me; gave me more time to sit in the library and read.

I had eclectic tastes. I could read anything and usually did. I particularly enjoyed reading Joseph Altschuler, a children's historian who wrote several novels about American Indians. A lot of my feeling for the Indians and their culture came from his books. There were five books in the series, I think, and one of them was particularly graphic in describing how the Indians would take scalps after a battle. Being 9 or 10 years old, I would have nightmares about losing my hair. "Losing mah harr," as my wife's relatives down South would say. I must have read Altschuler's series of Indian novels three or four times. Altschuler was my fallback. If I couldn't find anything else to read, I could always go to his books.

So my ambitions as a kid were to write a book or be a doctor, something like that, and way off in the distance, maybe be a major league baseball player. In fact, I would never have gone into professional baseball if I'd had the money to go to college. And after five years in the minors and two years in the army, I almost quit baseball. I had no intention of staying with baseball because I had been 4-17 with Springfield, the Cubs' AAA team in the International League, the summer of 1953, the year I got out of the army. I figured I wasn't going anywhere in baseball, although I will say in my own defense that it was a terrible ball club that I pitched for in Springfield.

When I had gotten out of the army, early in 1953, I had taken, at the government's expense, a very thorough aptitude test. The test, which took all day, showed I had two options: write or be an accountant. Everybody knew you can't make a living as a writer. I heard that morning, noon, and night. So it looked as if I were destined to be an accountant. The government not only led me in the direction of accounting, but they also gave me the name of the school I should attend, Benjamin Franklin College in Washington, D.C. So that fall, after the baseball season, I enrolled at Ben Franklin. There were only 22 people accepted into the accounting program for the first semester, and there were only eight of us left for the start of the second semester. It was a tough school, but, if you made it through, they guaranteed you your CPA and a government job, for very good money.

It looked great, but right after Christmas I got a letter from the Cubs saying they were inviting me to spring training with the big club. And damned if I didn't go. Well, they offered me a major league contract, worth $5,500, which was a lot of money to my wife and me then, if I stayed with the ballclub. I went to spring training and made the club, which shows you how little the Cubs had in their minor league system. If I had belonged to any other organization, (a) I would not have been invited to spring training, and (b) there was no way I would have been picked for the major league club. Tommy Lasorda, whom I pitched against on several minor league levels, couldn't believe the Cubs were going to keep me, since he had had some terrific years as a minor league pitcher but couldn't make the jump to the majors.

Unfortunately, I wasn't ready. I couldn't pitch in the big leagues; I didn't know how. And they soon found out. But I finally got some good instruction in Chicago, from veteran pitcher Howard Pollet. After the Cubs sent me down to the Texas League, I went 8-1 for the last two months of the season. Then the next year in 1955 with Los Angeles in the Pacific Coast League I was 17-10. I had learned how to pitch.

In 1956, when I made the majors for good, I didn't have good stuff yet, but I knew how to pitch. By 1958 I had improved enough that I was the opening day pitcher for the Cubs against the Cardinals.

Making the big leagues was partly due to my having a big league arm. I always had a big league arm, although I didn't have a big league head or a big league attitude. I once asked Don Osborn, who was my minor league manager in Macon, Georgia, and Nashville, Tennessee, why he put up with me considering all the trouble I was. It was sometime in 1977 when I was doing a story on Willie Stargell. He said, "We always knew you had it here," and he touched his arm. "We were just hoping you'd get it here and here," and he touched his head and his chest over his heart. He meant that in the beginning I didn't have the desire, and he was right. I wasn't driven to be a professional baseball player. When I finally got a real competitive urge, I got it from handball. I loved playing handball, and I hated to lose. Of course, you lose a lot in handball because the only way you improve is to play somebody better than yourself. And one day it occurred to me, "Hey, why don't I feel this way about pitching? Why don't I hate losing the contest between me and the hitter?" I mean, if I made a good pitch and the batter hit the ball out of the ballpark, I'd shrug it off: "The guy was better than me on that pitch." By 1958 I began to hate to lose at pitching; I hated it even when somebody got a hit off me. The competitive urge in baseball finally came to me, but when it came I was already in the big leagues.

I also had some clout. I worked as an advertising copywriter in the off-season for an agency run by a guy named Art Meyerhoff, who was on the board of directors of the Cubs. Meyerhoff was involved in bringing Wid Matthews over from the Dodgers as the new general

manager to inject new life into the Cubs organization, and Meyerhoff didn't have any conpunction about building me up to Matthews
as one of the best prospects in the Cubs organization. Wid's wife and
Meyerhoff's wife played bridge together, and, since I loved to play
bridge, I was soon invited to play bridge with the general manager
and his wife. I had that kind of influence working for me. I was in a
bad organization that had hardly any prospects, I had the good arm,
and I had some clout; so a lot of things contributed to getting me to
the big leagues that weren't solely mine, weren't solely in me. Writing the book was. The book was my first born. My daughter Jamie
was my wife's first born or rather "our" first born. That's what I
mean when I say I was as proud as a father for having written *The
Long Season.*

I got the chance to write *The Long Season* through my friendship
with a guy named Bob Boyle, who was an early member of the *Sports
Illustrated* staff. Boyle was here in Chicago one winter doing a profile
of P. K. Wrigley for *Time.* He wanted to talk to somebody who had a
player-owner relationship with Wrigley, somebody who had talked
to Wrigley face-to-face. Since I was with the Cubs at the time and
lived in Chicago year round, Boyle was directed to me. I didn't know
Wrigley well, but I had met him a couple of times since the advertising agency I worked for handled the Doublemint chewing gum
account and the accounts of a number of other Wrigley businesses.

Boyle asked me how I felt about Wrigley, and obviously I had
good things to say about him. Mainly, that he wasn't cheap like a lot
of owners were and that he was a friendly, curious man, curious
about many, many things. He made you feel as if he were interested
in you, and he did that with everyone, not just ballplayers. Ballplayers who had never even seen an owner before would have thought
that Wrigley's interest in other people was an exceptional thing
about him.

Anyway, Boyle and I got to be friends, so much that our families
would get together and go out. Boyle knew that I was working as a
writer for an advertising agency, and one night when we were out
having dinner he asked if I was interested in writing about baseball.
I told him that I already had written about baseball, off and on. I
had kept a journal my first year in the minor leagues, and I kept one
the year before I went into the army. I said that I'd surely like to
write about major league baseball if I ever did anything, or if anything happened to me, that was worth putting down on paper

because, at that point in my career, I was still suspect as a major leaguer.

The next year, in 1958, I got traded from the Cubs to the Cardinals. Boyle called and said, "Alright. Something happened to you that's worth writing about. Will you do it?" So I wrote a piece about being traded and sent it to *Sports Illustrated*. They liked it, printed it, and said to do another piece.

What I wrote about next was my relationship with a new manager, Fred Hutchinson, whom I admired a lot. Hutchinson made me a relief pitcher. He decided that's what I was going to do, and he thought I could be a success at it. He needed somebody to do the job in relief that Larry Jackson had been doing because he wanted to make Jackson a starting pitcher. I wrote about all that, the relationship between a player and a manager, from a player's viewpoint in a way that had never been done before.

So here are two pieces for which I got national recognition. Actually, the first thing I ever published was a review of Mark Harris's *Bang the Drum Slowly* in a little semantics magazine called *Etc.* My immediate boss at Meyerhoff was helping the editor of *Etc.*, S. I. Hiyakawa, publish the magazine here in Chicago, and they asked me to review Harris's book. So that was the first time I was ever in print until *Sports Illustrated*. I went from *Etc.* to *SI* without a rejection slip, something I came to learn all about in future years.

The idea to do a book about my experiences occurred to Boyle. I was in New York talking to Bob Creamer of *Sports Illustrated* about a third piece I had done for the magazine, on the Cardinals's recent trip to the Far East. There were problems with the story, and it wasn't going to work out. Creamer, as all good editors do, was trying to explain the problems with the piece so that I wouldn't repeat them, and Boyle came in during this writer-editor conference. Boyle said, "How about going over to Harper & Row—it's right down the street—and talk to Evan Thomas, the executive editor?" Evan Thomas was the son of Norman Thomas, the former Socialist candidate for president a couple of times. So I went over to talk to Thomas, who was a devoted baseball fan. He had read one of my *SI* pieces, and he asked me, "Do you think you can do this for a whole season?" I said, "Sure." He said, "Okay. Spring training starts in a month or so. Send us something after the first six weeks." I said okay, got up, and walked out of his office, with a book contract. Of course, I had no advance and no guarantee of any kind, but I had a shot at it. A lot of things happened in spring training that year. I had no trouble sending them 50 pages, and they loved it. They said, "You've got the start of a good book here. Now finish it."

In gathering material for the first part of *The Long Season*, I didn't try to record everything I saw or heard. I would only put down things that interested me, and I'd work with that. It really wasn't the right way to go about doing it. As I learned later, you ought to collect an awful lot of material, sift through it, keep some things, and throw out others. Of course, the journal style is the simplest way to write anything. And I always had a sense of humor about what I saw. For instance, in regard to coaching, I had enough experience in the game to know what was bullshit and what was informative and helpful teaching. In the spring training I described in *The Long Season* there was a lot of the former in Cardinals manager Solly Hemus and some of the latter, good coaching that is, in hitting coach Harry Walker and pitching coach Howard Pollet. I knew the difference between bullshit and teaching, and since there was a whole lot of bullshit in the Cardinals camp, it was easy for me to pick out things that illustrated the bullshit. At the same time I was looking for things that illustrated the big league experience, as if to say, "This is how it's done in the big leagues." So it was only those kinds of things I was looking for and only those kinds of things I would write down.

Since I was living on the beach during spring training, I probably wrote most of the incidents up between the time I showered, got in the car, and drove to the beach. I found it's easy to write in the car. I'd actually write out a sentence while driving and then edit it and have a better sentence. And I could remember whole paragraphs I'd composed in my mind by writing down the best line so that when I got to the beach house it only took me 30 minutes to cover the day. I'd ask myself, "What was the best of the day? What was the most interesting thing that happened today?" I'd write that up each day, and the days piled up.

In some cases the most interesting thing of the day was not something that happened on the field but in the clubhouse or totally away from the ballpark. For instance, I wrote some about my friendship off the field with Phil Clark, who was also living on the beach near me and my family. Phil had been a highly successful pitcher in the Cardinals's minor league system for years, but he was having a rough time, and it looked like he wasn't going to make it. I never had his experience. I got sent down to the minors from the majors, but I never had the feeling, "My god, I'm giving them my best, but it's not good enough, and I'm not going to be around much longer." Phil was a good example of the type of guy who establishes great minor league credentials but comes up a little short for the big leagues. In Clark's case, he couldn't throw quite hard enough, and his breaking ball was too flat and not fast enough to be a slider. So he had the kind of pitches he could get away with in the minors because he could mix them and he had good control; but when he got to the majors, guys hit those pitches. Even if he made a perfect pitch, if he threw that fastball that wasn't quite fast enough over the inside corner, guys with quick bats would hit it out of the ballpark. He was finding that out, realizing that he didn't have stuff quite good enough for the majors, and he'd bitch and moan about it, in a very distinctive Georgian accent. He and his wife were from Albany, Georgia. I spent a lot of time listening to their voices and writing about them and the way they felt about the game, most of which never got in the book. I couldn't find a way to describe this with humor, and I wasn't a good enough writer to use pathos to illustrate the point that ballplayers often find the business of baseball, at the top, too much for them. I kept the notes about Phil Clark for a long time, thinking I could use them in the baseball novel I've never written. They're gone now; I lost them in one of the five floods our neighborhood has had over the years. You know, "the once in a century rains"; we've had three of them in the last 10 years.

Once the season began, I seldom took notes in the clubhouse out in the open, although I could have. I was always reading, writing, and working crossword puzzles anyway, so the players wouldn't have thought anything of it.

If I didn't want to forget something said in the clubhouse, I'd go into the john and write it down in a notebook. But those occasions were rare because, as I said, I wasn't trying to record everything that happened but just those instants, those moments that struck me as being of interest. And if I had to put dialogue to an incident, I'd do that as soon as I got back to the hotel or back to the house. I obviously missed a lot of good things, but I could hardly have sat around acting like a reporter, recording every conversation.

For *Pennant Race* I kept a notebook in the pocket of my warmup jacket because, by that time, I wasn't trying to hide anything. In the bullpen I was anxious to get stuff down right away. It would have been far better to have had a tape recorder to get the entire dialogue because, if you're taking notes and four or five guys start talking at one time, each getting a zinger in, you're going to forget a lot of them. And I knew that. But with *Pennant Race* it wasn't unusual for me to pull out the notebook and record something somebody said at the time he said it.

Except for the first scene of *The Long Season,* everything in that book is almost exactly the way I put it. There were a couple of things changed in *Pennant Race* where I might have been a little harsh in my opinion of somebody, and the Harper libel lawyers suggested I either soften them or take them out. In both cases I said, "Let's just take them out." But as a general rule there were hardly any changes at all.

The first scene of *The Long Season,* the one that did get taken out, was about the trip the Cardinals took to Japan. The scene was set in a Japanese inn, a Japanese inn which could even be referred to as a brothel. Two of the bachelor players, Joe Cunningham and Don Blasingame, were involved in a very funny incident at this inn where they got drunk and left their shoes behind. I thought, "This is the way I'm going to write about the big league experience . . . with a sense of humor." This was one of the funniest things I could think of, and I thought it would have made a great lead-in. Buz Wyeth, the editor of the book, said, "Yes, it's very funny, but our lawyers say you can't use it. What if these two players want to get married? What would their fiancées think? This scene would cause a scandal, and we'd be subject to a libel suit and so would you." He also asked me if I had Cunningham's and Blasingame's permission to put them in the scene. I said, "No. I don't need their permission. I was there, and I saw what happened." Nevertheless, we cut it to what you have in the book now. That was alright with me. It wasn't alright with Cunningham who not only got married shortly thereafter, but also became a born-again Christian. He thought I had no right to put as much of the incident in the book as I did. Blasingame didn't mind. He said, "I'm just glad you didn't tell the whole story."

I wasn't that comfortable with the sexual angle to begin with. Len Schecter, who wrote *Ball Four* with Jim Bouton, was incensed that I'd left all the sex out, especially the voyeurism. It may not be now, but back then voyeurism was a staple of big league life. Everybody did it. If they'd wanted to, the Zeist people could have gone around to training camps and sold a lot of their best binoculars every spring. Schecter said, "You only wrote half the story." Then he went around trying to find somebody who'd tell him the other half of the story, and he found Jim Bouton. There's a lot of sex in *Ball Four,* of course, and it caused at least three divorces.

Bouton has never been forgiven by the baseball establishment. I thought that I wouldn't be forgiven either, but I was never really ostracized. Two years ago I played in the Equitable Old-Timers Game here in Chicago, and it was clear that ex-players think of me as an ex-player, not as a writer. Which is good. Because they think of Bouton as a fink, which has to hurt him because he was a player longer than I was.

I suppose the fact that Harper quashed the Japanese scene told me that I should be very discreet about the sexual activities of players. There are some hints in both books that players on the road were not celibate, but I didn't push it.

My editor tried to put the kibosh on martinis. Buz called one day and said, "Broz, there's just too many fuckin' martinis in the book. If you don't take some of them out, we're going to lose the entire children's market." I said, "What do you mean, 'there's too many'? I already cut most of them out."

A couple of weeks later Wyeth sent me a note saying, "We've made a deal with *Sports Illustrated* for the serial rights." *SI* was going to publish a chunk of the first part of the book about spring training. Dick Johnston, who was then the editor of *Sports Illustrated,* was supposed to be a notorious martini lover, and he told Harper & Row, "What do you mean you're going to take out some of the martinis? Put more in!" At that point Harper & Row finally realized, "Maybe we have an adult book here, and we don't have to worry about the juvenile market." So I heard no more about an excess of martinis. There are probably more martinis quaffed in *Pennant Race* than there are in *The Long Season,* and I never heard a word about it for the second book.

There were about 100,000 copies of *The Long Season* published altogether. *Pennant Race* had an initial printing of 10,000 and then Harper printed another 10,000, but didn't sell many of the second 10,000. *Pennant Race* was as critically well received as *The Long Season,* and it spent a week or two on the bestsellers list, but after its initial burst it just died. It was out of stock by 1964. Buz Wyeth apologized about it. He said, "I'm sorry. We have to take *Pennant Race* down. We're not making any money on it. We're recalling books. Would you like 100 copies?"

I always liked *Pennant Race* better than *The Long Season.* I was more satisfied with it, I guess because I had a better feel for what I did in *Pennant Race* than for what I did in *The Long Season.* Simply because I didn't know when I started the first book if the journal method would suit the material or suit me or allow me to say as much as I wanted to say. After *The Long Season* met with approval and I reread it, I could see that I was much more comfortable with the journal mode than I realized I was, and I knew with *Pennant Race* that I was going to be comfortable right from the beginning.

One thing in particular that I wrestled with when I started *The Long Season* was whether or not I should include material about my minor league career to establish why I was in the position I was in; that is, a big leaguer writing about his game. I wondered if I needed to explain "How did I get there?" I wittingly decided, "No, I can't go back and do all that because it'll take up too much time." I realized that flashbacks wouldn't fit the journal method; in both books I was describing events in one particular year. Also, I think I have more good lines in *Pennant Race,* and I had a better story to work with. The Reds were a Cinderella team in 1961. We won a pennant we weren't supposed to win. The press kept asking, "Are the Reds for real?" Yes, we obviously were for real.

The critics, thank god, loved *The Long Season.* I couldn't tell if they were writing as secret fans or as actual fans who realized that the fluff they usually found in the baseball books of the time did not represent anywhere near the truth. It was a real sham . . . ghostwriters essentially writing the same story over and over again, no matter what the player they were profiling was really like. Even as a kid I had this feeling when I read the typical baseball biography.

Red Smith liked the book. When I read his column about the book, I thought, "I've arrived." No writer in the business has ever impressed me more as a sports aficionado and sports expert than Red Smith.

Jim Murray was a friend, and I knew he was going to write something nice about the book, so his praise didn't count. But then I found out that Rex Stout had read the book. That was a big kick because I had read every Nero Wolfe book that Rex Stout ever wrote, and I continued to look forward to more Rex Stout books. And Peter DeVries, whose style I admire so much, liked the book. I later wrote him a fan letter, and he wrote one back saying, "I should be writing you a fan letter because I read your book when it first came out and loved it. I only wish I could throw a fastball as well as you can." A very short note, but it's one I'm keeping.

So the reaction from word people was almost universally good. Harold Rosenthal of the *New York Times* said my grammar was not always proper, but he was really picking nits.

On the other hand, the players were looking at me very strangely.

They thought I was odd anyway. Now they were much more cautious in talking to me. Larry Jackson, a friend of mine and a pitcher on the Cardinals, was quoted as saying that I didn't pitch well enough to write a book about baseball, which I thought was a strange comment. What did my pitching ability have to do with my writing ability? Jackson later said what he meant was that if I'd had more experience I could have written a better book. Ken Boyer, another friend of mine on the Cardinals, seconded Jackson's opinion. He said there were a lot of things I shouldn't have said and there were a lot of things I missed. Boyer and others thought I stepped over the line in making caustic remarks about Cardinals manager Johnny Keene and general manager Bing Devine. If you were an organization man, like Boyer, you wouldn't think of telling tales that belonged inside the family. It would have been okay for me as a Cardinal to write about the Cubs or for me as a Cub to write about the Cardinals, but as a Cardinal I couldn't write about the Cardinals. Notwithstanding the fact that I was with the Reds at the time the book was published.

Those two players, from whom I might have expected total silence if not support, were the least outraged and the least critical. More typical was the reaction of Joe Garagiola who went on the air and ripped my ass. And Gino Cimoli, a Cardinals outfielder, was heard to say that he'd punch me in the nose the next time he saw me. Joe Reichler of the AP went after me, saying that I was a traitor to the game and that I ought to be kicked out of baseball by the commissioner.

The Cardinals organization was very upset, and they wondered if something shouldn't be done to stop this sort of thing. They were acting as if there would be dozens of confessions from inside the game if something weren't done right away to make an example out of this rebel Brosnan.

Well, nothing came out of the commissioner's office. I did have a long conversation with Gabe Paul, who was general manager of the Cincinnati Reds and an influential member of the establishment. He said, "I have only two things to say to you. One, that was a funny book. But, two, you should not have written that you'd throw Ernie Broglio a high fastball if he'd throw you one because the least hint that there might be collusion between opponents in a scheduled event would be bad for the game." He was the one member of the establishment who at least privately said he liked the book. Publicly, nobody in the establishment liked the book. So there was a good deal of criticism within baseball and a good deal of praise without.

The net result for me was to give me more confidence as a pitcher, as a player. For some reason or another the book made me feel as if I belonged. I felt as if my teammates totally accepted me. And I felt as if I had more reason than ever before to prove that I could get batters out.

And I got better, from the time the book came out right up to the end of my career. Only right at the end, in 1963, when I was with the White Sox, did I realize I was losing my stuff, and if I didn't come up with a new pitch I wasn't going to be around very much longer.

Early in 1963 the Reds traded me to the Chicago White Sox, partly because I'd worn out my welcome and partly because the Reds simply didn't want to pay my salary. After my good years for the Reds in 1960 and 1961 I had been rewarded, and I was making more money than any other pitcher on the team besides Joey Jay. The Reds felt I had a bad year in 1962 and wanted to cut my salary for 1963. I held out, and they traded me just to get rid of me. Hutch called Al Lopez, the White Sox manager whom he was good friends with, and told him he could get a very good pitcher for whatever the White Sox would give the Reds.

The White Sox were a good team, and they really welcomed me as a veteran pitcher who could help them in the bullpen a lot more than the guy they traded for me, a kid named Dom Zanni. And I pitched very well in the beginning, getting five or six saves in my first eight or nine ballgames. Later on though I started getting hit hard. The pitches I should have been getting guys out on weren't getting guys out. J. C. Martin and Sherman Lollar, the White Sox catchers, kept pumping me up. They'd say, "Hey, just keep pitching like that, and we'll win. We'll get that pitch for you." See, American League umpires, to this day, won't call the low outside pitch a strike, and I had to have that pitch. That was my out pitch, a low slider on the outside corner. I'd been getting hitters out for years with that pitch, and I could still throw it with good stuff. But when the umpires wouldn't call it a strike, the batters would take it for a ball, I'd have to come in with something else, and I'd get hurt.

The next spring the White Sox wanted to cut my salary, so I held out again. This time I wasn't traded; I was released. Any club in the league could have picked up my contract for a dollar, but there were no takers.

Had I been able to stay with the White Sox another year and been able to enjoy it, I might have done a book about them—because that was an interesting ballclub. There were a lot of interesting guys on that team, like Hoyt Wilhelm and Dave DeBusschere. And if the White Sox had made a run at the Yankees, I might have had an interesting story to tell. Buz Wyeth wanted to know if I had any interest in doing another book. The way he put it was that if I found anything different enough about the two leagues that was worth my writing about, it would have been worth their while to publish it. But I wasn't in the American League long enough to do a book.

After the White Sox released me, I didn't really try to find a job with another team because I had great doubts as to whether I could survive another year. I didn't want to be killed with a line drive or be embarrassed, as I sometimes had been, like the night the White Sox had their father-son game. My son Tim played in the game, had his little White Sox uniform on, and was very proud. Then in the real game against the Minnesota Twins I came in in relief. I walked two and messed up the sacrifice bunt to load the bases. Then on a 3-2 pitch Earl Battey hit the ball out of the ballpark. There were 35,000 people in the park, and Tim says he's never forgotten the feeling he got when he heard all those people booing his daddy. He still remembers it, and he's never liked baseball since.

BASEBALL BOOKS BY JIM BROSNAN

The Long Season. New York: Harper & Brothers, 1960.
Pennant Race. New York: Harper & Brothers, 1962.
Great Baseball Pitchers. New York: Random House, 1965.
Great Rookies of the Major Leagues. New York: Random House, 1966.
Little League to Big League. New York: Random House, 1968.
Ron Santo, 3rd Baseman. New York: G. P. Putnam's Sons, 1974.
The Ted Simmons Story. New York: G. P. Putnam's Sons, 1977.

3

ROBERT CREAMER

After a stint in the Syracuse University School of Journalism and a brief career as an advertising copywriter, Robert Creamer went to work for Sports Illustrated *at the magazine's inception in March 1954 and stayed until January 1, 1985, when he retired with the rank of senior editor. Creamer ghosted* The Quality of Courage *(Doubleday, 1964) for Mickey Mantle; co-authored* The Yankees *(Random House, 1979), and did three collaborations; with Jocko Conlan (*Jocko, *J. B. Lippincott, 1967),* Red Barber *(Rhubarb in the Catbird Seat, Doubleday, 1986), and Ralph Houk (Season of Glory, Putnam's, 1988). The book that made Creamer famous was* Babe: The Legend Comes to Life *(Simon & Schuster), which Jonathan Yardley of the* Washington Post *called "The best biography ever written about an American sports figure." Published in the year Hank Aaron broke Ruth's home run record (1974), Creamer's biography exploded many myths about the Babe yet inspired renewed admiration for him and his accomplishments. Creamer's encore to* Babe *was another superb biography of a monumental baseball figure,* Stengel *(Simon & Schuster, 1984), and his latest (1991) is a book about the 1941 season entitled* Baseball in '41: A Celebration of the Best Baseball Season Ever—in the Year America Went to War *(Viking, 1991).*

I WAS BORN a mile southwest of this house. I've lived almost all my life here in Tuckahoe. I'm a real local boy. As a boy I loved to play baseball. I wasn't very good, but I liked playing it, and I liked reading about it. I liked to write too. I always wrote. When I was about 11, we had a neighborhood team in this section which is called Gifford Park where I grew up, and we played a game that we won 11-10. I went down to my father's real estate office in the village and typed out a story of the game. I was an avid reader of the sports pages. I knew all the clichés, and I wrote an account of this game in great detail. I even had a very meticulous boxscore.

I went around to the offices of the *Tuckahoe Record,* our weekly paper, and put my story through a slot in the door. Next week the paper came, and I looked through it, looked through it, looked through it, and, by god, there was my story. I know now that I was a true writer even then because I got mad at the editors. There was a headline on the story that said, "Gifford Aggregation Cops Close Decision," and when I saw the words "Aggregation" and "Cops" and "Decision" I thought, "Those dumb clucks. They put the wrong headline on my story." I thought it was the headline for a story about some police action or something. I'd love to go back and find that story if I could.

I wrote in high school for the *Tuckahoe Record,* covering basketball and stuff. And I did a little writing at Syracuse University. It was just part of me. I never said to myself, "I want to be a writer." You just do it. If you know how to play the piano, you play the piano.

I graduated from Tuckahoe High School in 1940 and enrolled in the School of Journalism at Syracuse. I've always heard schools of journalism mocked and derided by people of my generation, but I learned a lot in that one year I was there. But I wasn't a good student—I goofed off a lot—and I flunked out. I started over again at Fordham and stayed there until I went into the army during World War II. After the war I went back to Fordham for a year or so, but I never graduated. They didn't call it "dropping out" then. I left college to go to work. And I got married.

For about four years I worked in ad agencies as a copywriter, and I was probably the worst advertising copywriter in the history of the country. I just didn't know how to do it. I could write the long, institutional ads, but I was dreadful at the short punchy selling stuff. I got fired by a very nice man named Bill Bernbach, who later helped to found a famous ad agency called Doyle, Dane, Bernbach. They're the ones who did the "You don't have to be Jewish to like Levy's Rye Bread" ad. Bill fired me, but he fired me gently. He said, "You're in the wrong business. You're a good writer, but you're not an advertising writer. Look for another job."

I didn't pay any attention to what he said at first. I got a job as an ad manager for a weekly newspaper; I was terrible at that and got fired again. I went to another paper as an ad man and quit that job; then got a job with another ad agency in New York City as an assistant account executive for about three months, and I got fired after that.

Early in 1950, married, with one kid and another one on the way, I started to pay attention to what Bernbach said. I got an editorial job with Crowell-Collier and went to work for *Collier's Encyclopedia*. I worked there for four years and became the de facto sports editor of the *Encyclopedia*.

One day near the end of 1953 a girl named Constance Urdang, whom I worked with, walked by my desk; dropped a clipping on it; said, "If you don't look into this, you're a damn fool"; and went on. The clipping said, "TIME Incorporated to Start Sports Magazine." I thought, "Gee, this is something I should jump on." As I've said, I'm a terrible salesman, but I knew this was what I wanted to do, so I started selling myself. I asked everybody I knew if they knew anybody at TIME Inc., and it was amazing how many people did know somebody. I wrote a letter or two, and people starting writing letters for me. TIME Inc. must have gotten 20 or 30 letters about "This Creamer fellow."

Finally, about two or three months later, a man named Henry Romney, who was screening applicants for the new magazine, called me and asked me to come over to talk to him. So I did, and after a long talk he asked me, "Do you know sports? I mean, do you really *know* sports?" And I said, "Oh, yeah, sure, I know sports." And then I left.

I got back to the office and thought, "Well, that wasn't a very convincing answer." So I wrote him a letter showing that I really did know sports. For instance, I told him that I knew what it was like to get knocked out boxing. I remembered boxing at camp one summer, and all of a sudden there was this electric flash, and I was on the floor of the ring, waking up, realizing I had been knocked unconscious, and listening for the referee's count, wondering what it was up to. I saw the ref lift his hand and bring it down and say, "One!" I'd been knocked out but only for that instant. I wrote things like that in that letter, and I guess it made an impression because I next went to talk to Sid James, the first managing editor of *Sports Illustrated*. I was nervous, but after about 15 minutes I realized he was talking as if I had the job.

He wanted me to start right away. I told him I'd have to give two weeks notice at my other job, but I was thinking, "I've got the job! I've got the job!" I was making $85 a week at Crowell-Collier, and by that time we had three kids: Jim, Tom, and John. We had two more

later, Ellen and Bobby. Eighty-five dollars a week wasn't very much,
and I was moonlighting as a kind of bookkeeper for a neighbor
named Charlie Terwilliger, who was an advertising space salesman
for MacFadden and had a clock repair business as a hobby. Before I
had gone for the interview with Sid James, Connie Urdang had
come by again and said, "What are you going to ask for in salary?" I
said, "I don't care . . . $86.50 . . . I'd just like to get that job." She
said, "I have a friend who knows something about TIME Inc.; I'll
talk to him." She came back and said, "My friend says you have to
ask for $150 a week." I said, "$150 a week? Are you crazy? I'd take
it if they gave me $90." She said, "He says if you don't ask for that
much they won't pay any attention to you."

So now I'm in this interview, and I've got the job, and Sid James
says, "Oh, one more thing. How much do you want?" I thought,
"Here it comes," and I started to squirm. I was thinking, "$125?
$110? $105? What should I ask for?" I hemmed and hawed and
finally said, "Well, I was sort of wondering about $150 a week?" And
he said, "I was thinking more about $175." And I said, "That'll be
fine," and walked out, more or less on air.

That night I went over to my moonlighting job, and Charlie Terwilliger, who had written one of the letters for me, said, "How'd it
go?" I said, "I got the job." He said, "How much?" And I told him
the story: I asked for $150, and they gave me $175. And he said,
"Those sons-of-bitches! We would have knocked you down $25 . . .
they put you up $25!" But that's what TIME Inc. was like. It was a
great place to work, and it was so much fun. So I was there at the
very beginning in March 1954, five months before the first issue of
Sports Illustrated came out.

When the magazine began in August 1954, I was a staff writer.
Maybe a year later I became an associate editor, and then that whole
rank of associate editors became senior editors. I was called an "editor," but I was a writer too. I moved back and forth. I was articles
editor for a while, and I wrote and edited different sports: baseball,
track, football, basketball, hockey, golf, horse racing. It was a pla-
toon system in that people moved in and out of writing and editing
positions like playing third base for a while and then right field. I
loved working for *Sports Illustrated,* and I stayed there for more than
30 years, until I retired on January 1, 1985.

My first book was one that I ghosted for Mickey Mantle called *The
Quality of Courage.* A lot of sportswriters didn't like Mantle, but I
thought he was fun to be with. You had to know that Mickey doesn't

come on strong, and he doesn't like people to come on strong to him. He didn't have many stories though, so I had to use a lot of other material.

I did *Rhubarb in the Catbird Seat* with Red Barber, which was a tremendous experience because he's such a decent man and a great storyteller. He's a writer, too, and his sentences came out perfectly formed, yet he never criticized my writing.

Jocko Conlan was a lot of fun too, and he had great stories to tell, although some of his political and social comments put me off a little bit. Jocko had more suggestions about my writing than Red Barber did, but Jocko was okay. He was very pleased with the book, but he never could understand why *Jocko* didn't sell more. Maybe the book was too anecdotal; I don't know.

Even though I've done four collaborations, I don't like to do them. That's why, as much as I like Ralph Houk, I really wish I hadn't done *Season of Glory*. A collaboration is not your own book. You have to do what somebody else thinks or what you think they think. If Roger Kahn, for instance, could have done a book *about* Pete Rose, I think it would have been much more interesting and exciting for him, instead of difficult as it was. When you have to do the other man's book, it's hard, especially if you're conscientious, as Kahn is, and as great a reporter as Kahn is.

Anyway, after the first three collaborations, I wanted to do a book of my own, and I wrote a note to Peter Schwed at Simon & Schuster suggesting a book on Babe Ruth. I don't know why it occurred to me to want to write about Ruth because this was way before Henry Aaron was threatening his record. Peter was interested. He said, "Why don't you see if any other books on Babe Ruth have been done recently." That's how casual baseball book publishing was then. So I wrote him a note about what had been done, and he said, "Okay, let's go ahead with it."

I called up Sterling Lord, the literary agent whom I knew from being articles editor at *SI*, and said, "Sterling, would you represent me?" Literary agents always seem to back away from taking on anybody new, and Sterling didn't seem very interested. I said, "Sterling, I've already sold the book to Peter Schwed. I just want you to handle the contract." And he said, "Oh! Fine," and he's been my agent ever since. We signed the contract in the summer of 1969, and it took me five years to go from contract to book.

For one thing, I did a lot of research, and for another I had a full-time job with *Sports Illustrated*. During that time I did a lot of traveling for *Sports Illustrated*, to Switzerland, England, Ireland, Australia. But a big reason the book took so long was that after I'd written 70,000 words, I still was only up to 1919. Ruth's career for most people didn't really begin until 1920, his first year with the Yankees, and I had 70,000 words on his life and career before then. I was really in anguish, and at first thought, "I've got to get rid of all this." But then I decided, "I can't. I love this stuff. *I* think it's fascinating, and I'm going to go with what interests me." So I wrote it the way I wanted to.

I learned it's not that a writer is necessarily the best judge of what he writes, but he has to be *the* judge. If you start to warp what you're writing to fit the desires or what you think are the desires of an editor or the public or somebody else, you distort it. You can't help distorting it. You have to do what you believe in. If you're a good craftsman, the thing you make will be good. If you're not a good craftsman, then it won't be good. But making it the way someone else wants it won't help a bit.

I showed the first six chapters to Andy Crichton, a great friend of mine at *Sports Illustrated.* I expected him to say, "Golly, this is really great, terrific," but he said, "This is very good, Bob; however, I think you have a little too much baseball stuff in here." I snatched the chapters back from him, but he was right. I still have a lot of extraneous detail. Andy made me realize you have to have a balance. Write what you want but think of the reader too. So I kept enough baseball to get people to stay with me in those early years, but I tried not to wear them out with every base hit and every fielding play.

Editing is so important, like the editing Herman Gollob did on *Stengel.* I told Herman to watch out for my "cutesies." We were reading over the manuscript, and at page 87 or something he said, "Is this a cutesie?" I read it, and it was some pompous reference to James Joyce that I'd dragged in by the heels in order to say that listening to Stengel talk was like reading James Joyce. I thought it was great when I wrote it, but when Herman mentioned it I realized I'd been showing off. I felt myself redden, and I said, "Yeah, that's a cutesie." So we took it out. That's good editing when a guy can find those things. P. G. Wodehouse was writing to his friend Bill Townend one time when he was about 75 years old, and he said, "I think I've finally found the secret to writing. The secret is to go through your stuff and find something you particularly like and take it out." E. B. White said much the same thing: "You have to kill your darlings."

Anyway, in the spring of 1973 I told Peter Schwed I'd have *Babe* done by the end of the summer. So he called me on the 31st of August. I said, "Peter, summer doesn't end until the autumnal equinox. I still have three weeks." On Friday, September 21, the phone rang. I said, "Hello," and a voice said, "Bob, today is the autumnal equinox." I said, "No, it isn't, Peter. It's tomorrow at 11:14 A.M." ... or whatever it was, and he started laughing. I said, "Peter, I'll have the thing finished over the weekend." I was off Tuesday and Wednesday because those two days were my weekend from *Sports Illustrated.* He said, "You've really got it done?" I said, "I'll bring it to you on Thursday." I still had a chapter to do, but I worked on it at night and all day Tuesday and Wednesday and took the manuscript into him on Thursday morning. So it was the autumnal equinox plus a few days.

Ford Frick has often been maligned as a do-nothing commissioner, but I liked him. He was always nice to me. He told me some wonderful stories about Ruth, and he gave me the ending of the book. He told me about going to see Ruth when he was dying. I ended the book with a paragraph quoting Frick verbatim about going in to see Ruth, seeing Babe's wife and daughter across the hall in the hospital, and being shocked at how thin Ruth was. He said, "After a while I left. I went across the hall to say goodbye to Claire and Julia. Then I went home, and the next day he was dead." I was working on the last chapter, and I thought, "I've got to get that in." I typed it out just that way, and when I typed the last phrase, "and the next day he was dead," I stopped. I said, "Oh. That's the end of the book." It was the funniest feeling. People have said, 'Why didn't you put the funeral in?" Well, the Babe's funeral was ornate and elaborate, and everyone has heard the stories about Babe and the beer and about Cardinal Spellman and his teary prose and all the rest. I thought, "He's dead. That's the end of his life, and that's the end of the book. Period." I thought it was a good ending. It was Frick's ending, but it was almost like Hemingway, it was so tightly done.

With Stengel, I did use his funeral because I thought it was so much a part of his story. Harold Rosenthal told me how the mourners waiting for the funeral to start in the chapel out there in California started telling Casey stories, and the laughter kept bubbling. That seemed to fit the man, so I put it in *Stengel.*

Peter praised the Ruth book, and Sterling called up a few days later and said, "Bob, this is wonderful." I thought, "That means it's not bad." I didn't really know how good or bad it was, but I remem-

ber feeling good that it was acceptable, that it was going to be published; that was the main thing to me at the time.

I like *Babe*, and I'm very proud of it; however, I was tremendously
lucky to have Ruth as a subject. You can't find a better subject than
Ruth. He was a fascinating man. When I did that book, almost 20
years ago, I wrote that almost every day you hear his name mentioned, you hear people talk about him. Well, 20 years later, it's the
same thing. He was one of the great characters in American cultural
history.

Joseph Bottner did a 2,000-page biography of William Faulkner,
and if you love Faulkner then you undoubtedly find that a fascinating book. But it must have been a tedious book to write and, I think,
to read. I could have written 2,000 pages on Ruth. I mean that.
There were so many stories I didn't use, so many areas I didn't
explore in detail. Rich, rich material. You almost can't write a bad
book about Ruth, but maybe you can write too much. I think what I
did right was to realize that I couldn't be encyclopediac, that I had
to stop. To quote Samuel Johnson: "To pursue perfection is to chase
the sun."

And after I got rid of the excess in my first six chapters, I wrote it
straight; I let it be Ruth's story. When you're writing a biography,
you can do it like Blottner did with Faulkner, getting every possible
detail in, which is important to scholars. But I didn't think about
Ruth scholars. I thought, "This is a story, and it's a story about an
entertaining man, so tell the story to entertain people."

I recognized fairly early that Ruth was perfect material for this
approach because his life was so melodramatic. I don't envy anyone
doing a biography of Henry Aaron. Aaron was a great baseball player
and a very nice fellow, but his life is a straight line. There were very
few crises, very few ups and downs. That's all Ruth had was ups and
downs! That was Ruth's life constantly. And with these crescendos
and fallings-off throughout his life, you have a natural pace to work
with.

Stengel also had crises in his life, the ups and downs. In fact, he
said, "I'm a man that's been up and down." I found a marvelous
quote of his from 1923 when he hit the two game-winning homers
in the World Series. A woman reporter interviewing him for a New
York paper asked him if his success in the Series was turning his
head, and he said no because he knew that nothing lasts, neither the
good nor the bad. And I thought, "This is existential." Stengel had
a very philosophical attitude toward the world, and it was fascinating

to watch him go into these crises and handle them and go through them again.

I'm convinced you could do 2,000 pages on Ruth because the stories and anecdotes about him go on and on. Since the book was published, I've heard of many new sources for stories about him. For instance, I talk in the book about Ruth being a sexual athlete and all that stuff, but I never found any woman that he'd actually slept with except for Claire, whom he was married to. After the book was in print, somebody said I ought to go talk to old Charlie Weber, a local man who'd been friends with Bill Terry back in the 1930s and was sort of a baseball groupie. So I paid him a courtesy call, and it turned out that he knew one of Babe's extra-curricular girlfriends. But it was too late then. I wanted to cry because I missed her. I hadn't gotten to her. And I'm sure an old lady would have boasted a little bit, very delicately, about this sort of thing.

And there was a story about Ruth playing at a local golf course named Leewood which I'd heard as a kid and which people my age absolutely believed to be true. According to the story, Ruth was playing at Leewood when he missed a putt, got mad, and gouged a big divot in the green with his putter; and they barred him from the club. I checked the story out with Ben Curry, who had been the Leewood club president at the time, and he said, "Gee, I never heard that story, and as president of the club I would have known about that. I've never heard that story, and I just don't think it's true." So I didn't use it. Years after the book came out I ran into an old boyhood friend named Jimmy Meyer, and we started talking about the book and Babe Ruth. Jimmy said, "Babe Ruth was something. I remember I was caddying the day he smacked that putter down on the green at Siwanoy," which is another local golf club. I said, "What?" He said, "Yeah, I wasn't caddying for him, but I was in the foursome. He got mad, and he just took that club and went 'zing!' right into the green." I said, "Did they ban him from the course?" He said, "Yeah, I think they did. I never saw him over there again." I looked at him thinking, "Why didn't I run into you 10 years ago when I wanted this story?" So it was the wrong golf course, but a true story. All the lies about Babe are true, Waite Hoyt told me.

And I would have liked to have had more in the book about Claire, Babe's second wife, but at the time I had to be careful because she was still alive. People told me a lot of stories about her that I couldn't use. My own dealings with her were not pleasant. She wasn't any help at all. She wasn't going to talk with me unless there was money on the line, and I didn't have any money to offer. I asked several people about her because I didn't want to misunderstand her. I talked to Bill Slocum Jr., for instance, and he described her in an unprintable way. He didn't like her at all, and he did a book with her. With one exception, Alan Snyder, I never found anybody who had a good word to say about her.

So I wondered, "Why did Ruth take to this woman when he could have had any woman he wanted?" It was partly because she was so beautiful and partly because she was so smart. You see, she'd known other ballplayers before Ruth, but when she spotted him, she knew that he was the main chance, he was the money, he was the big guy. And she handled him beautifully because he couldn't get to her right away. She played him on a string. She was one shrewd woman.

But there was something else that drew Ruth to Claire, and that was the fact that she had a family. Her mother had come up to New York from Georgia to live with her and one of her brothers, I think, and she had her daughter from her first marriage; so she had a home life. And Ruth never had a home life; even with Helen, his first wife, he hadn't really had a home life. So now he's coming to Claire's apartment and playing cards with Claire's mother, who always got along with him. These were some of his wild nights out!

I didn't want to get into a diatribe against Claire, though, because I didn't want to write that kind of a book. Besides, she wasn't that important; I mean, the fact that she was a difficult woman wasn't important. Well, in a sense it was, in that Babe lived with it, but she was good for him too: she solidified his life, she gave him balance, she gave him a family, and she controlled his spending. I wrote that, but I didn't get into the unpleasant stuff about Claire. Even if I had the license writers have today, I don't know if I would want to get into all of it.

The thing I was proudest of with *Babe* was finding original material, particularly the stuff about Ruth and Ed Barrow back in 1918. All the baseball myths have it that Barrow was the guy who turned Ruth into a hitter, and it's accepted as gospel. I found out that it was totally the opposite: Barrow didn't want Ruth to switch from pitching to hitting. Ruth fought for it, got into furious arguments with Barrow over it. When I wrote that, I thought I'd made a great contribution to baseball history and that people would say that Babe Ruth fought Ed Barrow to switch from pitching to hitting. And, you know, it hasn't made the slightest bit of difference. People still credit Barrow. The subtitle of the book was "The Legend Comes to Life," but once a legend or myth is set, it never changes, no matter what you do to get the actual facts on record. You ask baseball people today about Ed Barrow, and they know exactly who he was: the guy who made Babe Ruth a hitter.

Stengel and the grapefruit story was the same thing. Dodger manager Wilbert Robinson was going to try to catch a baseball dropped from an airplane at Daytona Beach during spring training in 1915 except that a grapefruit was dropped from the plane instead of a baseball. The substitution probably saved his life because the grapefruit hit him in the chest. It burst open, and he said, "Oh, I'm dead, I'm dead!" And then he finds out it was a grapefruit, and he says, "Who done this?. . . Stengel!" So everybody assumed Stengel did it. But I went back and checked it out. It's amazing how detailed the newspapers were in talking about the woman flyer, Ruth Law, who had the airplane, and the ballplayers who went up with her. Never once was Stengel's name mentioned, and the papers went into great detail about who went for the flights and who didn't. And that was the year Casey was sick all spring with typhoid. So Casey was not involved with the grapefruit incident in any way. I told the story and figured, "Now people will know it wasn't Casey." Made no difference. Of course, Casey often said he *was* involved. Harold Rosenthal asked him about it once, and Casey said, "We tied a kitchen chair to the wing of the plane, and I sat in the kitchen chair and dropped a grapefruit." Harold, being a very good reporter, wrote to Ruth Law, and she wrote back and said, "I was considered crazy but not that crazy! You couldn't have flown one of those old planes with a chair tied to the wing."

So you have myth, then you debunk the myth, and the myth goes on again. You can't change it: it's astonishing. There's a vanity in writing where you think, "Now I've told it. Everybody knows it. That's it." But it doesn't work like that. You're just a little pebble that's thrown into the stream, and all you can hope is that you change things a tiny bit.

I've seen *Babe* referred to as a bestselling book, but it was never technically a bestseller. I like to think it was because the *New York Times* had only 10 books on its bestsellers list back then; now it's 15. I know that Simon & Schuster printed 35,000 copies in the first printing and another 10,000 in a second printing, and they sold almost all those copies. It went to the Book-of-the-Month Club and was a good seller there for quite a while. Jerry Holtzman put it in his "Sports Classics" series, and I keep getting a small royalty check from Jerry every year. Pocket Books did very little with it in paper-back, but Penguin did better with its paperback, and it's still in print with them. Near as I can figure, it's sold somewhere between 75,000 and 100,000 copies all told.

When the publisher finished with the manuscript, they sent it back to me. I put rubber bands around it and stuck it away some-place. I went down to the Babe Ruth Museum in Baltimore after the book was published to speak at a celebration of Ruth's birthday, and somebody said, "Do you suppose we could get the manuscript of your book for the museum?" I said, "Sure." So I sent it down, and they have it in a case with a lot of artifacts and stuff. It's a nice feeling to know it's there.

While I was down there that time, I also met Mamie, Ruth's sister, whom I'd spoken to several times before on the phone. She was a charming lady, a little tiny lady. I asked her how tall she was, and she said, "Four eight. I used to be four ten, but I shrank." She looked like Babe, and she had the Ruth personality. She was a delightful woman, a very quiet, conservative, gentle lady, and it was a pleasure talking to her. That same day I found myself talking to a rather nice-looking, dark-haired girl who looked something like Susan St. James, the actress, and I had the same sense of enjoyment. I asked her who she was, and she said, "I'm Mamie's granddaughter." I thought, "There it is again." It's the personality that Ruth had, an engaging thing: you enjoyed him.

I don't think Ruth would have given a damn about my book. You know the story about him finding out that he was a year younger than he thought he was when he applied for a passport in 1934? He always thought he was born on February 7, 1894, but they found a birth certificate that said "Baby boy Ruth" was born February 6, 1895. I mention in my book that there is no total proof that that was Ruth's actual birth certificate. Anyway, in Babe's own mind he was 40 years old in 1934, and now they said he was 39. He didn't change his age. He still used the old birth date and the old birth year. He said, "What the hell difference does it make?" That's the way he was. It was inconsequential to him, and I think that's how he would have regarded the book.

But that's assuming you'd transport me back in time to the 1940s or whenever, when Ruth was still alive. If you were to transport Ruth to this era, then you'd have a whole different set of values. Now, everything is money, everything is worth something, and Ruth had a great sense of his own value. So now, maybe he'd think, "God, if a book's gonna sell, I should get some of the money." Ruth wasn't penurious; in fact, he was often quite generous. But he definitely understood his worth. And he liked money. It meant something to him, so maybe his attitude would be entirely different now. You can't tell.

I'd love to talk to Stengel about my Stengel book because I think Casey would read it, and he'd have some very strong opinions about it which he'd want to start talking about. In *The National*, the new daily sports newspaper, they have a little feature which I think is a disaster, and they've got to get rid of it. It's a paragraph of fictional Casey Stengel commentary, a Stengel monologue on current topics. I don't know who's doing it, but it's awful. It has no validity because it doesn't have Casey's unique thinking processes behind it. What made Casey so fascinating was not just his funny way of talking, but also his way of seeing beyond the obvious.

I can tell you a story that illustrates this. Carl Furillo showed off his arm making a great throw to home plate during the first out-of-town Brooklyn Dodger game ever telecast back to New York. Everybody in New York watched the game, and the next day a bunch of writers were in the Yankee dugout talking about Furillo's throw. I think there was no one out with men on first and third, the Dodgers ahead by two, and the runner on third made a move to go home on a fly to Furillo but changed his mind and went back to the base. Furillo's throw came in on a line to the catcher, and the writers were debating whether the guy could have scored if he'd gone in.

Casey sat there just listening, but all of a sudden he says, "Yes, but where should Furillo have thrown the ball?" Walter Bingham, a friend of mine at *Sports Illustrated*, was a young writer then, and he was sitting quietly on the other side of Casey, away from the writers. Without hesitation he said, "Second base." Casey swung around and pointed at him and said, "Right!" The other writers looked puzzled. What happened was that the runner on first went to second on Furillo's throw home, so that Milwaukee ended up with the tying run on second in scoring position, and the Dodgers were no longer set up for the double play that could have gotten them out of the inning.

So while all the other sportswriters were raving about Furillo's arm and arguing about whether the runner should have tried to score from third, they missed the more obscure play that Stengel saw, which Bingham was aware of too. But that's the way Casey's mind worked. He saw things that other people missed.

I'm very pleased to have written *Babe* and *Stengel*, but I was lucky to have two such subjects. I simply had tremendous material to work with. The other day I read that when writers get past a certain age, they come to realize that what readers want is 90 percent content and 10 percent style. It's what you have in the book that's important, not your great skill with words. If the most marvelous writer in the world doesn't have something to write about, it's nothing. Who cares about these very introspective books? That may be one of the reasons I don't care for Faulkner or Virginia Woolf: I find their prose tedious and tiresome, and I don't care about their murky insides. I much prefer Joyce or Hemingway where people are doing things. Hemingway may have been a great fraud as a human being, but at his best he was a marvelous writer. The content is there in Hemingway. And it's there in Joyce. And Ruth had content, and so did Stengel. They were very easy to write about. And they were fun to write about.

I came away from both books with great admiration for Casey and Babe. For all their faults, they were *plus* people who made the world a lot more palatable place.

I got into a sort of a bad habit when I was working at *Sports Illustrated* and doing books at the same time because I'd write the books when I could find the time at night, and I'd squeeze them in on weekends and vacations. I didn't work on them steadily. It wasn't my primary job, and I'm a slow writer. Actually, as Roy Terrell used to say to me, "You're not a slow writer. It's just that you don't start working until two in the morning when your deadline is at six, and then you work like mad and get it all finished." That's true. And I did the Ruth and Stengel books that way, in bursts, tremendous bursts. And that's a bad habit.

Now that I'm retired from *Sports Illustrated*, I have to rev myself up and say, "Writing is a 9 to 5 job; you've got to do this five days a week." It's difficult for me to do it that methodically because I was used to working under pressure and doing it in those bursts. It's harder now to get into that rhythm and that routine which are so important for a writer.

I think essentially I'm lazy. Laziness is inertia. You don't do anything; then you start moving and all of a sudden you do a whole lot. You don't rake the yard for three months; then suddenly you do the whole thing in one day. Whereas the intelligent man does a certain amount each day, gets into a rhythm, and gets it done properly.

Paradoxically, I didn't like *Season of Glory* because I had to do it too quickly. I didn't get a chance to do all the things I should have done in that book. It was a patchwork book.

Ralph Houk was fine. I taped him, got a lot of stuff. But Ralph, in his very pleasant way, has an acute sense of public relations. He knows what he's saying and what he doesn't want to say. He never said a bad thing about anybody. Everyone was a great guy, a great guy, and Roger Scholl, my editor at Putnam, said, "There's an awful lot of great guys in here."

I knew from what others had told me that Roger Maris had gotten angry at Ralph Houk when Houk was the Yankees' general manager. I guess Roger was mad about being traded, but I never could get the specifics from him because Maris had died by this time. I asked Ralph why he and Maris had had a falling out, and Ralph said he was never aware of it. Clete Boyer was another guy who got mad at Houk. When I asked Ralph, he said, "Clete's a great guy. I see him in Florida, go golfing with him. I didn't have any trouble with Clete." Was Ralph lying or dissembling? I don't think so.

Then I figured something out. Here's a man, Ralph Houk, who grew up on a farm in Kansas during the Depression, before electricity came to the farms. It was a hard world. It was a big thing for the Houk family when Houk's mother got an electric stove to replace the wood stove she'd used for years. Houk played three or four years of minor league ball starting in 1938 or 1939 when it was really a scramble. He went into the army early in World War II, fought in combat across Northern Europe, beginning shortly after D-Day, had friends of his killed in this arena of constant death, had a sniper's bullet go through his own helmet. He's been through a depression and a World War, and he's going to worry about a ballplayer not liking him? Houk was a tough man, a strong man, and these things were nothing to him.

But it meant that he couldn't provide me with the conflict that you need for a book. Also, it was understood that this was not to be an autobiography. So there was a blandness that you couldn't get away from, and that's why Houk talking is only part of the book. I think his quotes are the best part of the book, but there weren't enough of them. So I was disappointed. I thought it should have been a better book.

Right now I'm working on a book about the 1941 baseball season. I remember 1941 as being the best baseball season ever. It wasn't just the DiMaggio hitting streak or Ted Williams hitting .400; it was also the Dodgers who were tremendously exciting. Before this they were bums with a small *b*, but Larry MacPhail came in and turned things around, and now everybody rooted for the Dodgers. And, oh, what a pennant race between the Dodgers and the Cardinals!

And, of course, at the same time everyone knew the war was coming. When you say "1941," the first thing anybody thinks of is Pearl Harbor. But Pearl Harbor didn't happen until December, so that means for 11 months 1941 was not the first year of war; it was the last year of peace, though a very precarious peace.

The danger in writing a book like this is that you start to drag things in: "As Pete Reiser rounded second base, Winston Churchill said . . ." It's a terrible way to write a book, I know; I've done it myself. But I was 19 that summer, and the pressure of world events was there. It was real. It was part of my life. I was at Syracuse from September 1940 to June 1941, and I remember that the father of a friend of mine named Harry Schmidt came up from Philadelphia to visit in late May. We were in Mr. Schmidt's hotel room when Roosevelt made this great speech declaring "an unlimited national emergency," taking the United States as close to war as he could without war actually being declared. So it was a vivid moment. I remember listening to the speech; it's not something I read about in books. At the same time, people like me sort of shoved these world events aside and paid attention to DiMaggio and the great National League pennant race. Anyway, that's what I'm working on now.

I've also got three non-sports book projects I'm working on. I want to write a historical novel, and I have it all pretty well plotted out. I want to try a detective story based on an interesting murder case I read about in the newspaper. And I want to do a book on James Joyce, a common reader sort of thing. Everybody always gets that look when I mention him: "Ugh, James Joyce!" But look . . . I do not have a college degree, I'm not an English professor, I'm not particularly well read, I've never read Henry James or Dostoevsky, but I love James Joyce.

And he's accessible. I read and reread *Ulysses* and find myself laughing. I think it's the most delightful book I've ever read. It takes a while, of course. It's difficult at first, but all of a sudden things just jump off the page at you. It's the most rewarding book. So I want to write a book with a title like "Joyce without Tears" or "How to Read *Ulysses* without Being Bored or Feeling Stupid." It's simple if you approach the book without feeling that you have to understand everything in it when you read it. It's like listening to music: at first you might not like or understand it, but the more familiar you become with it, the more you appreciate and enjoy it. The only thing is that you've got to accept the fact that you'll have *Ulysses* next to you on the bedside table for the rest of your life.

BASEBALL BOOKS BY ROBERT CREAMER

The Quality of Courage (ghosted for Mickey Mantle). Garden City, NY: Doubleday, 1964.

Jocko (with Jocko Conlan). Philadelphia and New York: J. B. Lippincott, 1967.

Rhubarb in the Catbird Seat (with Red Barber). Garden City, NY: Doubleday, 1968.

Babe: The Legend Comes to Life. New York: Simon & Schuster, 1974.

The Yankees: The Four Fabulous Eras of Baseball's Most Famous Team (co-author). New York: Random House, 1979.

Stengel. New York: Simon & Schuster, 1984.

Season of Glory (with Ralph Houk). New York: G. P. Putnam's Sons, 1988.

Baseball in '41: A Celebration of the Best Baseball Season Ever—in the Year America Went to War. New York: Viking, 1991.

4

CHARLES EINSTEIN

No one has a greater knowledge of baseball literature than Charles Einstein, the man who defined the baseball anthology by assembling the three original volumes of The Fireside Book of Baseball *series (1955, 1958, 1968). Despite being out of print and routinely stolen from libraries, the* Fireside *books have stood the test of time and constitute the cornerstone of any serious baseball library. Extremely versatile and prolific, Einstein has published more than five million words as a newspaperman, columnist, novelist, screenwriter, and prize-winning author.* A Flag for San Francisco *(Simon & Schuster, 1962) and* A Pitcher's Story *(Doubleday, 1967), a biography of Juan Marichal, are among the best of Einstein's baseball books; but the jewel is* Willie's Time: A Memoir of Another America *(J. B. Lippincott, 1979), which was a finalist for the Pulitzer Prize in biography. Formerly the Giants beat man for the* San Francisco Examiner, *Einstein is a lifetime honorary member of the Baseball Writers' Association of America and lives in semi-retirement in Mays Landing, New Jersey, where he writes an entertainment column for the* Newark Star-Ledger.

PETER SCHWED had the idea for the first *Fireside Book of Baseball*. Peter's retired now but eventually became chairman of the board at Simon & Schuster. He had read a baseball novel of mine called *The Only Game in Town*, which was serialized in *Collier's*. He got in touch with my agent in early 1956, and the book was completed before we moved from Westchester County, New York, where my wife, myself, and our four children were then living, to Scottsdale, Arizona, at the beginning of the summer.

At the time, the people at Simon & Schuster were talking, optimistically, about a sale of 15,000 copies, and my agent and I just accepted that figure out of hand. The thing just literally took off, though, and to this day I have no idea why. I suppose that maybe it was the fact it was the first true baseball anthology. There had already been collections of this stratified part of baseball and that stratified part of baseball, but this was the first one that lumped everything together and didn't care what it was.

It got enormous reviews. I mean, not just in terms of acclaim, but also in terms of where the reviews appeared: John Chamberlain with a full column in the *Wall Street Journal*; Charles Poore, the entire daily review of the *New York Times*; the Sunday book review section of the *New York Times*; so forth and so on.

Within a year I proposed a second *Fireside Book of Baseball*, and here we went again. One of the interesting reasons I proposed it was the fact that there was one piece I could not get for the first *Fireside* that I was absolutely aching to have. It was a piece on Little League baseball written by Shirley Jackson, who wrote "The Lottery." She had just come out with this piece in *Harper's* magazine, and it was going to be part of a book she was doing for Alfred Knopf, I believe. She wrote back and said, "No, I can't give you permission to run it because Knopf doesn't want me to and I don't want to make waves with them." And I was thinking, "If you can do it in *Harper's* magazine, why can't you do it here?" But the answer was no, and the first thing I did when they said, "Yes, let's go ahead with *The Second Fireside Book of Baseball*" was get in touch with Shirley Jackson and say, "Now, can I have this piece?" And, of course, we got it, and it's in the second *Fireside*.

The first *Fireside* came out in late 1956, and Peter Schwed said to me when the contents came in and I delivered the manuscript, "Is everything here? Have you touched on the major points in the history of baseball?" I said, "Yeah, pretty much we have. There's always someone who's going to come along and pitch a perfect game in the World Series, but 'til that happens I think we're alright." And on publication day that's exactly what happened. (Don Larsen pitched the first and, to date only, World Series perfect game on October 8, 1956.) Which is a lesson: baseball is no respecter of publishers.

The first book sold over 80,000 copies. I lost track of the editions, but I saw a 15th printing. By that time all three books were out, and they were selling them in boxed sets. One of their problems was that each book was in a different supply of warehouse copies. The books were in demand, were still selling, but they just stopped printing them because the publishing costs of the 1970s would simply have placed them out of the market. Or so they felt. The second book topped out at about 40,000, and the third was somewhere around 25,000.

Simon & Schuster refused to title the fourth book *The Fourth Fireside Book of Baseball* because somebody there didn't think the book would sell with that title. They believed that somebody seeing that title would be put off by the fact that he didn't have the first three, and therefore, why start a collection with the fourth of anything?

So what they wanted to do was call it *The Fireside Book of Baseball, Fourth Edition*. That's simply incorrect, but I will get back to that. In terms of the decision not to call it *The Fourth Fireside Book of Baseball,* the reason they gave me was that a person walking into a bookstore would ask for *The Fireside Book of Baseball* and when the clerk would tap the computer, the computer would come back saying, "There is no such title" because the computer would have *The Fourth Fireside Book of Baseball.* And I said, "Why don't you have your computer list it both ways?" Their answer was "Our computer can't do that." So they called it *The Fireside Book of Baseball, Fourth Edition.*

I said to them, "That's got to be the worst title in history because nobody will review it." At that point it had also been made clear that it was not going to be a hardcover book as the first three had been but was going to be a softcover. So I said, "If you come out with a paperback and call it *The Fireside Book of Baseball, Fourth Edition,* people are going to think it's an updated version of an earlier book. Who's going to review it?"

They decided to take that to heart, and they printed a little belly band, a diagonal strip on the cover, which said, "All New Material," which is interesting because the last thing an anthology is "All new material." There's a story in there by Ring Lardner that he wrote in 1914; you'd hardly call that "All new material."

Of course, what they meant to say was *The Fireside Book of Baseball, Volume 4* because "volume" means "book"; "edition" means "version." And it should have been not "All new material" but "All new collection."

In any event, the book got exactly two very brief reviews: one in *Kirkus* and one in the *Sporting News.* The first *Fireside* book got more than 100 reviews. So when I'm told about the prevailing wisdom of publishers, I have trouble believing in it. The publishers have lost everything, in my judgment, except the will to make money.

When I started out, I had great faith in publishers and was willing to leave all sorts of things up to them, such as the blurb copy on the flyleafs of my books. The last four hardcover books I've had I've done the blurb copy myself. Not because I have become any better at this than I ever was, but simply because the publishing world itself has lost the kind of talent it used to have. Either by attrition or by the fact that talented young people aren't coming into it.

For instance, here is the blurb copy on the back cover of the fourth *Fireside Book of Baseball*: "What may be one of the longest running literary anthologies in American letters . . ." And it goes on. "What may be one of . . ."; in the first five words there are two qualifying phrases! So why'd they write it at all? They could have left the page blank for all the selling that it does.

In some respects though I think the fourth *Fireside Book of Baseball* is the best of the four, I really do . . . certainly in terms of the fiction and poetry. Each book has a strength, and in the fourth I think the fiction is just stunning. Because there had been 19 years since the third book, and there'd been an accumulation of great stuff: Chaim Potok's chapter from *The Chosen* on that softball game; and that long section from Will Kennedy's *Ironweed* on the guy who played third base for the Senators; and that ballgame in the insane asylum from Philip Roth's *The Great American Novel*. You read this stuff and your mouth just drops open. And Robert Coover and Irwin Shaw and on and on, one great piece after another.

And yet interspersed there's something in there I'm not sure I like. And that is more pieces than maybe there should have been on, or more references in pieces to, what makes the game: (a) so great or (b) so different. And I'm wondering what there was in me that tugged at me and said, "Gee, we'd better have this piece saying what it is that's good about baseball." There's almost an element in there sometimes of the writer wanting seemingly to be credited with what is good about baseball. And, you know, this is the rooster taking credit for the dawn. Baseball can get along fine without it; it really can.

The first book almost produced itself simply because at that point the entire previous history of baseball literature was open. I got some guidance from various people . . . mostly old-time sportswriters who would say, "Well, so-and-so was famous, and you ought to have something of his" . . . but I really didn't have to do all that much in the way of investigation. I was sitting there saying, "'Alibi Ike' . . . yes. Heywood Broun, 'The Ruth is mighty and shall prevail' . . . yes." And so forth and so on. And after I said "yes" 104 times, I turned it off and that was the book.

In the first book there was very little in the way of discretionary trivia; probably for that reason the first book lacked a little something that did come along once that monkey was off the back. To hearken back to what Peter Schwed said, "Have we got everything in it?"—it got to a point where that was not that much of a pressing concern, until the fourth book, and then after 19 years you start worrying again, "Do I have everything important that happened in those 19 years?" That's a long time. So that came back at you. For instance, for the fourth *Fireside* one way or another I had to find a piece on Nolan Ryan and his fifth no-hitter. That belongs in the *Firesides.* By then they'd established that certain things are being covered by this series. So you are a victim of that.

But the first *Fireside* had a couple of off-trail things in it. One was the psychiatrist's case history of the girl who shot Eddie Waitkus. Waitkus was shot just before the 1949 All-Star Game, which I covered. He was now recovering in the hospital; he was out of danger. He had been leading the fan voting for starting first baseman on the National League team, but his place was taken by the runner-up who was Johnny Mize. Mize made two errors, and the American League won. And I had a lead that said, "Ruth Ann so-and-so shot the wrong first baseman." And the old INS (International News Service) which I worked for would not put it on the wire . . . the best lead I ever wrote. That case history was in there, and it was the result of my newspaper work because I had covered the shooting for the INS and had covered her arraignment afterwards. At the arraignment they had a table and here were copies of this psychiatrist's report, unsigned, and I just lifted one off the top and took it with me. I never found a use for it until seven years later, and that was one of the relatively few pieces I didn't have to get a permission for because it was a public document.

And there was a short story called "The Spitter" by Paul Fisher, which had never been published before, although Paul had it privately printed for some friends of his. He had sent it to the *Saturday Evening Post,* and they wanted to publish it, but he had used some language in it which today would be so tame—some reference I think to "the walking young and the suckling young"—and the *Saturday Evening Post* did not want the word "suckling" in their pages. They asked him if he would change the word, but he said no. Somebody put me on to it, I met Fisher, he gave me a copy of it, and I put it into the *Fireside.*

A certain amount of the second one was what got left out of the first one, like the Shirley Jackson example I gave you. But you could begin to have some fun with the greener fields. One little segment in it was a collection of editorial cartoons showing how editorial cartoonists use baseball to illustrate what's going on in the world they cover. I will never forget one by Burris Jenkins Jr. of the Hearst newspapers who had been championing Douglas MacArthur for president of the United States. In this cartoon the United States is playing world communism in a game of baseball, and you can see the scoreboard, and it's very late in the game. And here comes MacArthur out of the dugout swinging four bats, and the title of the cartoon was "Time for a Real Pinch Hitter." and then you look at the cartoon again, and you look at the score, and the United States is losing 87-0. There were 12 runs in the first inning, 14 in the second, 17 in the third, and so forth and so on. It's 87-0, and now it's time for a pinch hitter!

The Third Fireside Book of Baseball uncovered what is something of a find, and that was the first newspaper photograph taken by Brian Lankar, who has become a world-renowned, Pulitzer Prize photographer. And it's an absolutely great photo, showing a fielder and a baserunner at second base. The baserunner is touching the bag with his hand and looking up not at the umpire but at *two* umpires because the two umpires had arrived, one from first base and one from third base. And one of the umpires is signaling "safe," and the other is signaling "out," simultaneously.

There are any number of pieces in the four books that don't have any prefatory note by me at all. None. They simply did not need one. But some of the pieces did require exegesis. For instance, in the fourth *Fireside* book we have the brief that was filed by Bowie Kuhn's lawyers in answer to Charlie Finley's suit against him in 1976, and that has to have some kind of introduction, not only to set it up for the readers who if they ever knew what the suit was about might have forgotten by now, but also to get people to want to read the piece because you can intimidate people with a lot of footnotes and legal stuff. And here's a marvelous story once you get into it. It's beautifully written, and it's what won the law suit for Kuhn as a matter of fact. A brilliant piece of legal work.

I had a strange problem—and this is by way of confession—in the first *Fireside* book, and it was with "Who's on First," the routine as Abbot and Costello did it. Incidentally, I believe that was the first time it had ever appeared in written form. I wrote it out by listening to a recording that I had. Incidentally, also, there were long versions and short versions; mine was one of the shorter ones. I'm glad of that because a lot of what's funny is simple repetition. It's funny when you hear it, but it loses something on the printed page. But I was going to list the author's name simply as "anonymous." But my problem with that was "anonymous" starts with *a*, and I'd already reached the decision to organize the pieces by authors in alphabetical order. That made more sense than anything else. And I was damned if I was going to start the first great collection of baseball works with "Who's on First?" I mean, my god, there must be something that could come ahead of this. So, it wound up at the back of the book, and the author was listed as "unknown" which starts with a *u*. A four-line poem, a grave little item of historical interest, appeared at the front, under *a* for "anonymous" because nobody knows who wrote it. And so I had this note of clarification in the way of a prefatory note in the front of "Who's on First?" in which I said something to the effect that "'anonymous' differs from 'unknown' in that 'anonymous' presumes that somebody wrote it, you just don't know who; 'unknown' doesn't know if it was ever written at all." So out of the mud grows the lotus.

When you ask me what my favorite pieces from the *Fireside* series are, read the contents of *The Baseball Reader,* which is a *"Best of the Fireside"* anthology, and that tells you what they are. At least for the first three books . . . because that really was what did the deciding, my own favorites. When you read the two pieces by Ed Linn and John Updike on Ted Williams's last game side by side, you say, "Did these two guys go to the same game?" It's not only possible that both the Linn and Updike pieces on Williams were right, I think that that is it: they were both right. What is it T. S. Eliot says in *Prufrock*: "There will be time to prepare a face to meet the faces that you meet." Williams had one face for Updike, and he had one face for Linn. And he had reasons for both those faces. Sure. There's a shattering line in the Linn piece—when Williams is asked, "What did you feel out there, hitting a home run in your last game and running around the bases?" And Williams says, "I felt nothing." It's just a shattering line. Of all the things that can happen in baseball there's got to be room for that too, but you wonder how much of that is what he felt at the moment and how much of that was what he was going to tell Linn that he felt. I don't know the answer to that. Another of my favorites is the Al Stump story on the dying Ty Cobb, which is just an unbelievable piece of writing.

I suppose there's always a certain amount of fun in—and you have to watch out for it if you're editing an anthology—in letting your own background and experience do some persuading on its own. That may be dangerous. For example, not everybody in the world fell in love with Elbie Fletcher, the first baseman of the Pittsburgh Pirates, the way I did when I was 12 years old. Perhaps I've let that color my imagination too much in the years since. I did a novel in which one law partner said to another one, "You remind me of Elbie Fletcher." Well, I'm having fun with that, and I want this guy to keep on talking, which he did. I couldn't shut him up; he was wonderful. But I wondered, "What's this doing for the reader?" I don't know.

Another problem which confronts a baseball anthologist is the degree to which newspaper, magazine, and book writing feasts on the New York teams. It's a fascinating exercise for me to go through the indices of the four *Fireside* books and see who has the most mentions. The margin isn't that great, but inevitably DiMaggio has more than Williams, Mays has more than Musial, and Rizzuto has more than Luke Appling, who was four times the shortstop that Rizzuto was. And yet there's nothing you can do about it. Number one, it's a reflection of the literature as it stands because the better the newspaper writers were, the better the chances they were going to gravitate to New York. Look at Red Smith; he wound up in New York. And number two, the fact is, the Yankees have won more pennants than anybody else. And when you write about baseball and collect literature about baseball, you are liable to find that your subject matter has more to do with winners than with losers. Once in a while there's an exception. Two of the *Fireside* books have pieces by Jack Orr about failure in Philadelphia. One of them about the Phillies team that had all the hitting and no pitching, and the other one was about the Phillies team that had all the pitching and no hitting. Failure in Philadelphia, that was Jack's specialty.

But you have to look out for it, and once in a while I would find myself consciously reaching out not for one non–New York piece but for a selection of eight of them so that I could pick one of them. And authentically, some of the great pieces do come from outside New York, and there's no way what it describes could have happened in New York. For instance, there's a piece in the first *Fireside* about the ballpark in Nashville called "Sulphur Dell," which had a hill in the middle of right field. The right fielder couldn't see over the top to see who was hitting. That's as much a part of the game as anything else. And finally you get to the point of questioning what location means anyway because Cooperstown is where the Hall of Fame is because it was the birthplace of baseball except that baseball was not born there.

I'm proud of the first three *Firesides* and proud of the contents of the fourth, but the looks of it are a disaster. The "bottom line" has won. It looks like a Crazy Eddie catalog. They have a picture on the cover about which I told them in April when they sent it to me, "It's too big. You've got to take three-fourths of an inch off the top and half an inch off the bottom." And they said, "You're right." Then the book came out, and they hadn't done a thing to the picture. I said, "I thought you told me you were going to do this." And they said, "It would have cost $700." So that's the answer.

I don't mean to talk only about Simon & Schuster because the problem is industry wide. It's what happened to automobiles in the 1970s and to electronics in the early 1980s: the regard for quality is gone. They see profit instead, and the consequences of this they do not see. What will happen is that the good publishers are going to be found among those publishing houses that are owned by foreigners, not by Americans. And it's already happening.

The introduction of *The Ultimate Baseball Book* calls the *Fireside* series "baseball literature's greatest monument" and goes on to say that their being out of print is "baseball publishing's greatest shame," and other people have had very nice things to say about the *Fireside* books. In a sense I think they were the precursor of the anthology style you've seen in other baseball books that have come along. So, sure, I'm proud of that. But that would apply to the first three books because those nice things which were said about the books were said then, before the fourth one came out.

Also, I have to say that I'm an accidental party to some of that because the formats, the looks of the dust jackets, and so on were the doings of the publisher. As I've said, in those days I was very happy to leave that kind of thing to them. I was content that they knew more about that kind of thing than I did. I haven't learned all that much over the years, but that doesn't mean that they still know more than I do. Because they don't now.

So when you ask me how proud I am of them, I have to say in all honesty that if I could have stopped with the first three, I'd be prouder than I am. As a matter of fact, I told Simon & Schuster; "We're going to have to have a fifth *Fireside Book of Baseball.* They said, "Why? Why do you even want to talk to us after the way you've been screaming and complaining?"

I said, "Because the only thing that will make the fourth one look intentional is to have a fifth one looking exactly like the fourth one. Make it look as if we deliberately switched the format."

Yes, I would agree that *Willie's Time* is the best baseball book I've authored. *Willie's Time* was conceived in 1975. I wrote a three-page outline, and it sold right away. I think it did a little over 30,000 in hardcover, but unfortunately it was pigeon-holded as a baseball book.

Willie's Time went in for the Pulitzer in biography. It could as easily have gone in for the Pulitzer in history. It was a calculated thing. It was a horseshit year for biography, so we thought we'd take a run at it; *Willie's Time* was short-listed but did not win the Pulitzer. The winner, which surprised me, was Morris' biography of Theodore Roosevelt. The reason it surprised me was that a biography of Theodore Roosevelt had already won in 1934 or something like that.

But the thing that my book had going for it was a clause in old man Pulitzer's will which not everybody knows about, which says that the winner in the field of biography can only be a book on an American subject. If I had written about Bocce ball in Italy, that could not have gone in. Such a book is banned. But I'm saying to myself, "Here is the civil rights revolution, here is Willie Mays, and here is baseball. All between the same set of covers. What could be more American?" And I rather think that's what got it as high as its finish.

The only thing in this book I don't like—and I mean the "only" thing because I like this book—was not my idea. There's a preface in there of just a page and a half, saying what this book is. The editor, who was a freelancer hired by the publisher, insisted on it. Everything in me cried out, "Don't do this." But I was fighting them about six other different things, and I figured that maybe if I did it for them I could win on the other six. And that's exactly what happened. I wound up doing it for them, and I've regretted it ever since because if a book doesn't tell you what it's about, then a page and a half up front or 80 pages ain't gonna help you. It was totally meaningless, and I think it hurt the book because it was so damn self-conscious.

The table of contents is set up with five different presidents because Mays' career spanned five presidents of the United States. And now here I am in the preface saying, "Mays' career spanned five presidents of the United States . . ." Why do I have to say that? I already told you in the table of contents. So this same editor said he wasn't sure *Willie's Time* was that good a title. I said, "Why not?"

He said, "Well, people may not know who you're talking about."

I said, "What other 'Willie' did you have in mind?"

He said, "People used to call the Kaiser that."

Another reason I didn't like that preface was that it made it sound as though I was making Willie the owner or proprietor of that period, which is not the purpose I had. I meant this no more than "The Age of Jackson." Jackson didn't own "The Age of Jackson." The reason I like the title so much, besides the fact that it's short and easy to remember, is that you can't say *Willie's Time* and be mad. You can't get angry when you say *Willie's Time*. There's something that bubbles over right in the title itself, and it was so much like the man himself.

It was set up from the beginning that *Willie's Time* would bridge five presidents; that would be the structure of the book, the presidency of each one, from Truman to Nixon. And then the second decision—and I think this is the one that actually did more for the book than any other in terms of its structure—was that whereas Mays' career and the events that surrounded his career in public and everyday life would be followed chronologically, events that affected Mays personally could fall anywhere. Mays' boyhood took place before Truman was president, so I figured it didn't have to be part of the chapter on Truman. As a matter of fact, much of his boyhood is told in the last chapter, in the one on Nixon. And it worked. And the reason it worked was that it was a way to blunt the disappointment, the chill in the air that comes at the end of the career when he's not playing anymore. I mean, of all things I did not want to do was to go out on a down note, and yet you can't come to the end of a ballplayer's career and not go out on a down note. It's impossible to do, unless you can cushion it in some way that ordinarily wouldn't be thought of, and that's what I was doing. And so I had the fun of reporting some boyhood things . . . Where? At the very end.

Willie's Time was a memoir, so it included some of my own autobiographical memories: you know, the menu on the train, the Polish jokes, so forth and so on. As a matter of fact, Chris Lehman Haupt in reviewing it said, "Some of these things I don't know what they're doing in here, but it is a memoir, so I guess he's got the right to put 'em in." It's anfractuous as hell. Joel Oppenheimer reviewed it in the Sunday *Times* and was very kind. He said that the book was all over the place, but "it always lands me someplace I want to be," which was the kind part. And the book does jump around a lot, but by the same token it was done with great care. I wasn't hopping just for the sake of hopping.

For instance, in the opening pages of the book we have gambling in baseball, but not the gambling of the Black Sox. Instead we have the gambling of the nineteenth century when the umpires used to throw games. And the idea is to trace a history that was mirrored because Willie Mays' grandfather was a pitcher in Tuscaloosa, Alabama, so you have roots in the presence of change.

The book opens with a train called "The San Diegan" going from Los Angeles to San Diego. This is in 1951, and all hell breaks loose for the next 23 years. Someone called it "the most turbulent period in the history of this country." And the last page of the book has the same train running from Los Angeles to San Diego.

The interesting thing is that on the day the last steam engine was phased out, made its last trip, people standing there and waving at the steam engine could look up and see the contrails of jets at the same moment. And yet what was Mays doing? He was playing center field. Here was a man who won the MVP award twice, but he won them 11 years apart, which is 12 seasons. And you look at his figures which were 12 seasons apart, and they're interchangeable. He literally made time stand still. Nobody else in history has won the MVP award 12 years apart. People have won it more often but never with that kind of time span.

That's number one. Number two, I have no hesitation at all in saying that my subject was the greatest player who ever lived. And I mean *the* greatest. I had something to work with. Harvey Kuenn had played against Mays in All-Star Games and exhibitions, but when he was traded to the Giants he got to see him day in and day out, he just walked around talking to himself, "My god, I can't believe what he does." And people would say to him, "Are you a believer now?"

"Yes, now I'm a believer."

Tommy Henrich and Joe Gordon, who played with DiMaggio, saw Mays on a regular basis and said, "He's just something else." And he was. Even his detractors, when they were leveling, were just as much in awe of him as anyone else. Lefty O'Doul, who was filled with the derring-do of DiMaggio and the old San Francisco Seals and so on and was the first to scoff when the Giants came west, never had anything good to say about Mays. He didn't walk around saying he was a bad ballplayer, but he wasn't one of his champions. And yet I can remember being at Candlestick Park on a real cold night, and it's the last of the seventh inning and the game's over—the Giants are way ahead and everyone's leaving—and I remember O'Doul bundled up in one of the boxes in the mezzanine. And someone says, "Why don't we get out of here, Lefty?"

And Lefty says, "Alright." But he gets to the door and he turns and says, "Wait a minute. Lemme watch Mays hit." He stayed to watch Mays hit, and then he left. When he was leveling, he didn't want to miss this either.

Mays had the game not only in the physical ability to play it, but had it in his head too. He was talking to Aaron—this is not in the book—when Aaron was zeroing in on Ruth's record, and he said, "You must hit it at home. Ain't gonna look right if you hit it on the road."

And Aaron says, "I can't take myself out of the lineup."

Mays said, "You don't have to."

It was not just "You have to lay down on the road and make sure you don't hit it out of the park." It was far more sophisticated than that. What he was saying was, "Here is how you can pick a spot at home when you know who's going to be pitching, and this is the time you're going to hit it."

And he did that himself. I mean, here is a man who played for the Giants all his life and finds himself traded to the Mets; the Giants go to New York and play the Mets' and in his first game as a Met Mays hits a home run. Now the Mets go to San Francisco; first game in his old ballpark he hits a home run. Also, when Al Dark was having that trouble as manager, and he was about to be fired by Horace Stoneham, Mays is sick. Dark writes his name out of the lineup because he can't play. Mays takes the card, writes his name back in, and hits two home runs and saves Dark's job. I mean you can sit here all night and say, "This was one accident after another." It was not one accident after another.

He had an utter sense of theatre in him, just as Ruth did. You take what he did in the 1962 season, his last time at bat in the regular season, his last time at bat in the playoffs, and his last time at bat in the World Series, with the Giants either tied or behind each time, game on the line. Home run, single, double! I mean, what the hell's that! Tell me anyone else who's ever done that. So did I have something to write about? You bet I did.

There was something special in Mays, a dimension that guys like Musial, Aaron, and Pete Rose, for all their accomplishments, didn't have. Rose got plenty of adulation, sure, when he was on his hitting streak and when he was chasing Ty Cobb's record; but, my god, on the best day he ever had, when he walked into Shea Stadium, they booed him. That would never have happened to Willie Mays. The dimension was simply different. Rose was hated. Ruth was hated. But not Mays. It sounds sappy to say it, but there's only one player I could have written such a book about. I mean that. I couldn't have written this book about Ted Williams, for instance.

You know, Jackie Robinson criticized Mays for not speaking out on behalf of blacks. This reminds me of a politician I knew named Jess Unruh who ran for governor of California against Ronald Reagan. Jess was a Civil War buff, and I remember saying to him once, "Jess, if you were in the Civil War, every day would be Shiloh." And for Jackie Robinson every day was Shiloh. But like it or not there have to be the other people too, and Mays was one of the other people. He did some things that Robinson couldn't do. For instance, in 1966 when they thought that the blacks were going to riot in San Francisco, the Giants were in the pennant race playing Atlanta in September. So they got the idea, "Let's televise the game and keep people at home." But it was only seven hours to game time, and how are you going to let the people know? So what they did was cut a radio announcement, and they had Mays do the talking. He got on a microphone in Atlanta, and they got it back to San Francisco 20 minutes later, and it was on every radio station in town the rest of the day: "Stay home and watch us play." And, yes, they stayed home, and, no, there was no riot.

There was a real dichotomy there. One time he addressed a Black Hall of Fame banquet and said, "I've been told, 'Willie, you're ashamed of your people.' But that's not true." So he heard it. There's no question about it. On the other hand, some of him was apolitical. There wasn't that much conscious decision-making half the time anyway. He liked money, liked playing ball . . . who the hell are we to judge?

He has a terrible reputation for not keeping appointments. Why is he like that? I don't know. Somebody might say he's showing you who's boss, his independence or whatever, but who knows. Somebody wanted to show him a site for a restaurant that would have borne his name, and he just didn't show up. And somebody was going around saying, "Why?" There is no answer.

When Mays was coaching for the Mets, Donald Grant liked him to come down to the board room on Wall Street so he could introduce him around: "Joe Blow, I'd like you to meet Willie Mays," you know. Well, is that coaching the Mets? I mean, he wasn't supposed to be a

PR man with the Mets; he was supposed to be a coach. On the other hand, he was supposed to show up too, and he didn't always do that.

It's interesting that when Kuhn made that ruling on him with Bally's, I think the Mets were just as glad as not: "Will nobody rid me of this turbulent priest," you know. And, after all, the Mets employed Kuhn. They helped pay his salary. And it didn't hurt Mays any. He made $50,000 a year for the Mets; he made $100,000 a year for Bally's.

Mays wasn't witty with the press, but he was with his teammates. He really was. One time when Mays was tying his shoe and Don Mueller walked by, Mueller said, "I hear you're the best center fielder in the National League." And Mays replied, "Best right fielder too." Another time we were on a plane and Stu Miller, the junkman who threw a real flutterball, was saying, "When I was in high school I was a catcher." And Mays said, "What'dja throw to second, the change?"

And he was sharp too. He said an interesting thing about a month after President Kennedy was shot. We were at some kind of benefit, and somebody was talking about how great Lee Harvey Oswald's aim was. And Mays said, "Yeah, if that's who he was shooting at," which is fascinating because a book just came out theorizing that Connally was the real target. Oswald had a gripe against Connally who had been secretary of the navy when Oswald was trying to get out of the Marines. He had written to Connally and didn't get the result he wanted. And the more you think about it, the more sense it makes. The guy's riding in the front seat . . . well, if you miss him, the car's going forward so the bullet hits the guy in the back seat, that's all. And it's the one thing nobody can acknowledge, whether they have a conspiracy theory or not: that the president was killed by mistake. Nobody can acknowledge that. The Warren Report wouldn't even go into it. And I remember when Martin Agronsky had the first interview with Connally in his hospital room, the first thing out of Connally's mouth was: "Martin, I know he wasn't shooting at me." In other words, he was beating that one down before it even surfaced, or he was gonna try to. But Mays said, "If that was who he was shooting at."

And there's a wonderful story in *Willie's Time* illustrating his baseball sense. Warren Spahn threw the first home run Mays ever hit, and now 14 years later he's Mays' teammate, and he's in his last season. He's riding the bench; they don't even use him in the bullpen; he's through. They're in Houston, and Mays hits his 500th home run. Spahn is weeping, and when Mays gets back to the dugout, he puts his arms around him and says, "I saw the first one, and now I've seen the 500th. Tell me, was it the same feeling?"

And Mays says, "Yes." He looks away for a second, then looks back and says, "Same pitch too."

William Goldman had the best description of him, and it's in *Willie's Time*: "I fell in love with him that afternoon and watching him then I realized unconsciously that it was about time he arrived on my horizon. He was what it was all about. He was the reason. In my head there was a notion of the way things ought to happen but never do. Not until Willie came along, and I could finally sit there and say, 'Oh, sure, that's it.'" That says it all.

BASEBALL BOOKS BY CHARLES EINSTEIN

The Only Game in Town (fiction). New York: Dell, 1955.

The Fireside Book of Baseball (editor). New York: Simon & Schuster, 1956.

The Second Fireside Book of Baseball (editor). New York: Simon & Schuster, 1958.

A Flag for San Francisco. New York: Simon & Schuster, 1962.

Willie Mays: Coast-to-Coast Giant. New York: G. P. Putnam's Sons, 1963.

Willie Mays: My Life In and Out of Baseball. New York: E. P. Dutton, 1966.

A Pitcher's Story (with Juan Marichal). Garden City, NY: Doubleday, 1967.

How to Coach, Manage, and Play Little League Baseball. New York: Simon & Schuster, 1968.

My Ups and Downs in Baseball (with Orlando Capeda). New York: G. P. Putnam's Sons, 1968.

The Third Fireside Book of Baseball (editor). New York: Simon & Schuster, 1968.

Willie's Time: A Memoir of Another America. New York: J. B. Lippincott, 1979.

The Baseball Reader: Favorites from The Fireside Books of Baseball (editor). New York: Lippincott & Crowell, 1980.

The Fireside Book of Baseball, 4th ed. (editor). New York: Simon & Schuster, 1987.

5

PETER GOLENBOCK

A graduate of Dartmouth ('67) and the New York University School of Law ('70), Peter Golenbock gave up careers in law, publishing and journalism to become the author of a string of bestselling baseball books, beginning with Dynasty: The New York Yankees 1949–1965 *(Prentice-Hall, 1975) and including* Number 1 *(Delacorte Press, 1980) with Billy Martin and* Balls *(Putnam's, 1984) with Graig Nettles. The book that fungoed Golenbock to fame was* The Bronx Zoo *(Crown, 1979), the hilarious inside account of Sparky Lyle's purgatorial year in the Yankees' bullpen while New York staged a great comeback to swipe a pennant from Boston, despite the shenanigans of Reggie, Billy, and George. Much less humorous but equally absorbing in its depiction of the emotional bonds between a team and its community is* Bums: An Oral History of the Brooklyn Dodgers, *which won the 1984 CASEY Award. The Golenbock canon also includes:* Guidry *(Prentice-Hall, 1980);* Bats *(Putnam's, 1986) with Davey Johnson;* Personal Fouls *(Carroll & Graf, 1989) about the North Carolina State basketball program; and* Teammates *(Harcourt Brace Jovanovich, 1990), a children's book about Jackie Robinson and Pee Wee Reese. In 1991 Golenbock published* The Forever Boys *(Carol Publishing), a behind-the-scenes look at the St. Petersburg Pelicans of the Senior Professional Baseball League, and in 1992 Putnam's released his* Fenway, *an oral history of the Boston Red Sox.*

IT WAS THE SUMMER of 1989 when I got the idea for *The Forever Boys.* I read a short blurb in *USA Today* which said that a new league composed of former major league baseball players over the age of 35 was going to begin play in the state of Florida. It occurred to me that if one of those teams would allow me to travel with it, to ride the buses with the players and sit in the dugouts during the games, it would give me the opportunity to write a book about what baseball on a professional level is really like. I'd be able to capture the flavor of what these fellows say to each other, how they relate to each other, how they feel about the game. A major league team would never allow a writer to do that. But here was a league which needed as much publicity as it could get. I also thought that if one of those teams would allow me to be its amanuensis each player would then be willing to talk to me about what really happened to him in his major league career. I suspected that many Senior League players felt that their major league careers had, for various reasons, ended prematurely and that other players felt that they had not been given a fair chance to establish themselves in the majors in the first place. That's what I was interested in more than anything else.

I called Jim Morley, the founder of the Senior Professional Baseball Association and owner of the St. Petersburg franchise, and he invited me to come down to the league meetings about 10 days before the beginning of the season to talk to all the owners. I went down to the magnificent Coral Gables Biltmore Hotel and made my pitch about what I wanted to do. The team I wanted to write about was the Miami team called the Gold Coast Suns because Earl Weaver was going to manage it, and I thought it would be a lot of fun to spend a season with Earl. The general manager of the team, who was also an announcer for the University of Miami basketball team, a guy named Sonny Hirsch, was apparently upset over *Personal Fouls*, my book that detailed the wrongdoings of Jim Valvano, the former basketball coach of North Carolina State. When I said I wanted to write the book with the Gold Coast team, Hirsch's immediate response was, "Gold Coast passes."

The owner of the West Palm Beach Tropics, whose name was Don Sider, spoke up and said, "You can come with us." That was fine with me because Dick Williams was going to manage West Palm Beach, and I thought he would be an interesting guy to work with. By the end of the day, however, I got a message on the answering machine of the friend I was staying with: "All bets are off. Forget it." Apparently, Sonny Hirsch managed to convince Don Sider that I was going to write something negative about his team.

I went back to Connecticut where I was then living and called Morley again to tell him what was happening. Morley said, "Don't worry about it. Come down here, and you can write about my team, the St. Petersburg Pelicans." I got in the car with my family, we drove down to St. Pete in two days, and we rented a house on the beach.

On our first day in St. Petersburg, I drove over to Miller Huggins

Stadium, which has this old wooden clubhouse where Babe Ruth and Lou Gehrig used to play. I said hello to Morley, and Morley introduced me to Bobby Tolan, a former Cardinals and Reds star who was going to manage the St. Petersburg team. Then Morley said, "Peter, we've got a problem. Bobby loves the idea of your book and so do I, but there isn't a single player on this team who wants you here."

The players were reluctant to work with me because they felt they'd often been double-crossed by sportswriters during their major league careers. For so many of them, their worst enemy had been the local sportswriters, and their distrust of anybody with a pen and notebook was very great.

I'd already plunked down a couple of months' worth of rent money for this house on the beach, and panic was beginning to rise inside me. I had to do something fast, so I said to Bobby, "Will you give me five minutes to talk to the players about what I want to do?" Tolan said sure, so I went into the Pelicans' locker room to plead my case.

Because of my previous collaborations with ballplayers, I knew that you must, in some way, show the players that you can be trusted. In all the years I've been doing this I have never gone back on my word to a ballplayer. If I tell a player I'm going to do something, I do it. If I tell him I won't do something, I don't do it. You want to be absolutely up-front with them about what your goals are, and once you establish those goals you follow through on them. That's very, very important. If your field is baseball, you establish a reputation, and that reputation gets around. So I told the Pelicans about the players I had worked with on my previous books, and I explained to them what I wanted to do in a book involving them. Fortunately, I was able to convince them that my motives were pure and that I wasn't interested in spying on them at night or in doing some type of exposé. In fact, by the end of the five minutes they were volunteering information to me about some of the things that had happened to them during their major league careers.

And thank heaven I was able to win them over because it was one of the great experiences of my life, to spend that winter with that baseball team. What made the experience all that more exciting, for me and for the purposes of the book, was the fact that St. Pete won, first, the divisional championship and, then, the league championship. It was a wonderful ending to a magical season. It would have made some difference if the Pelicans hadn't won but not a great dif-

ference because the book is really about how major league baseball
treats its players.

You see, when you write a book, you have to be aware of your readership. You have to ask yourself not only "Is this interesting to me?"
but also "Will this be interesting to the public?" I knew, for instance,
that the buyers of baseball books would much rather read about
what happened to these players during their major league careers,
how they related to and fared against the Jim Palmers and Mike
Schmidts and Reggie Jacksons and Steve Garveys, and so forth than
anything that might happen in Senior League games. And my sense
of this was proved out because yesterday, in the middle of its second
season, the Senior League folded. If I had pegged this book on the
viability of the Senior League, what would I have been left with when
the league folded? But since I pegged the book on major league
baseball, the folding of the league doesn't invalidate the information in the book. Actually, it's more accurate to say that play was
"suspended" because the league may come back next year.

I'm very pleased with the way *The Forever Boys* turned out. When I
started the book, I didn't know if I'd be able to fit all the hundreds
of jigsaw pieces of the story together, but I pulled it off. I think it's
the best book I've ever done.

My wife and I fell in love with St. Petersburg, and after I finished
the book we decided to stay here. We sold our house in Connecticut
and moved back here. We don't miss the cold and snow of Connecticut at all.

Yes, it is a shame the Senior League folded, but I think it'll be
back next year. I was doing the color for the Pelican's radio broadcasts when the season ended. Dick Bosman began the season as the
color commentator, but he was also designated as a pitcher on the
team so that if somebody got injured he would come out of the
broadcast booth and join the pitching staff. He'd sort of pull a Dizzy
Dean. About a third of the way through the season it turned out that
the Pelicans did need Bosman to Pitch, so I volunteered to take over
for him for no compensation. I felt a lot of gratitude toward Jim
Morley, and I was going to all the games anyway. I'd had some radio
experience on WOR in New York, and I thought I'd be able to hone
some skills doing the Pelicans games. Plus, I figured that working
with the play-by-play man, Jack Wiers, who had broadcast Baltimore
Orioles games in 1987, would give me the opportunity to learn how
to do it right. All of which turned out to be the case.

During our broadcasts Jack and I tried to let people know how terrific Senior League baseball really was. For instance, the Pelicans had a catcher named Butch Benton who had once been a number one draft choice of the New York Mets. For one reason or another he had never made it in the big leagues, but in the Senior League he was a star. And Luis Gomez, the Pelicans shortstop, a very, very quiet guy, was as good a fielder as anybody. Jack and I stressed the talents these players had so that when the fans came out to the ballpark they would watch carefully and see that these players really were exceptionally skilled.

You know, I've never understood why sportswriters are so fascinated by how much money the ballplayers are making. Even when I was a kid the writers would dwell on Mickey Mantle's $100,000 salary. And I remember one spring training when Jim Bouton was holding out. The year before when he had won 21 games he had made something like $12,500. Now he wanted $22,000, but the Yankees would only give him $14,000, and they finally settled it at $18,000. The newspapers were full of the entire negotiations. I always wondered, "Who cares?" and "Why is it anybody else's business anyway?"

Today, of course, it's much worse with baseball's show business atmosphere. If you pay a player $3 million it will definitely boost your box office, merely because people want to come out to see the team's new $3 million ballplayer. The problem is that if a ballplayer makes $200,000 one year and $3 million the next year, he's still the same ballplayer, but people tend to look at his salary first and his skills second. You can argue, "The guy's making that much money; he's going to have to live with $3 million expectations." But his salary really doesn't have a lot to do with the game itself. The guy has certain skills, and whether he's making X number of dollars or Y number of dollars, he has the same skills. People should appreciate what he can do and not judge him by his salary.

I think part of the reason the Senior League had to suspend play this season is that the salary cap limited the amount of money the players could make to $15,000 per player per month. You can't write $1,000,000 headlines about that. So fans said to themselves, "They're not making $1,000,000 salaries . . . it's not worth going to see them play"; which I thought was a terribly narrow-minded attitude. The people who didn't come to watch the Senior Leaguers play missed out on some really wonderful baseball. And the part which I found to be most frustrating was that some of the writers who covered the Senior League felt the same way. Some of the writers complained that the teams they covered didn't have "great stars." But why should it matter that the player's name is Marty Castillo or Ron Washington or Lenny Randle as long as when you go to the ballpark you're seeing great baseball. So that was a disappointing revelation to me, that some of the fans and some of the writers were disappointed because they were looking at the name on the back of the uniform and not the quality of the play on the field.

Who's had the biggest influence on me professionally? Probably a man named Dr. Joseph R. Kidd, who was the headmaster at St. Luke's School in New Canaan, Connecticut, when I began there as a sixth grader. Dr. Kidd was not only an Episcopalian minister, but he was also head of the English department. He was a stern fellow who made you write a composition every Monday so he could teach you how to use punctuation properly, how to write sentences, and how to think. Those things were important to him, and somehow he made them important to me. I often think about him. He's gone now, but he was alive when I published my first book. I sent him a copy of it. He never said anything—just sort of gave me that wink of his—but I knew he was proud of me. He never made a fuss over anything his students accomplished because he always wanted to make you try just a little bit harder.

Personally, my parents had the biggest influence on me. They taught me to differentiate between right and wrong, to take a strong stand, and to do what is right. My dad is the owner of the Regency Gallery in Stamford, Connecticut, and his gallery supplies art to a lot of major corporations. I didn't grow up particularly enriched in an appreciation of art because of my dad's business, but I did always have a kind of artistic bent. I took some art lessons as a kid, but I was never any good until I got to college when I discovered I had an aptitude for non-representational art. I bet I sold more than 50 paintings when I was going to law school in New York City, and for some pretty good money too.

When I was a kid I wanted to grow up to be center fielder for the Yankees. For a while I thought I'd make it too. One day when I was about 13, however, a little right-handed kid named White threw me a sharp-breaking curveball. When the ball came toward me, I stepped in the bucket. The umpire called it a strike, as he should have, and at that point I knew that my idea of a baseball career was over. But my interest in baseball never waned. If anything it grew because I was able to appreciate more those people who could successfully stand in against the tough curveball pitchers.

Giving up my dream of playing center field for the Yankees wasn't any big adjustment because I've always been a pretty self-aware person. I've never been delusional about my abilities. Once I saw that I could no longer be the best at something, then I sought to do something else. That's why I practiced law only eight weeks after graduating from law school in 1972 before going to Prentice-Hall to become an editor. I saw there were people out there who loved being lawyers. They wanted to spend the rest of their lives researching cases, being shut up in little rooms with piles of books. I knew that I would never want to do that badly enough to be able to compete with them, so I got out of it.

I started at Prentice-Hall as the assistant editor of a service that was mailed to banks and other institutions concerning President Nixon's wage and price controls. Every week these detailed rules and regulations came out, and my job was to rewrite them into understandable English so that anybody involved in either prices or pay could know what they could or could not do.

One day, at the end of my first six weeks on the job, I was browsing through one of Prentice-Hall's catalogs. I read the descriptions of the sports books Prentice-Hall was publishing, and I wasn't impressed. I thought, "I can write a book that would be better than these books." What I had in mind was a book about the 16-year period in Yankees history during which they won 14 pennants and nine world championships.

Being totally ignorant at the time about the nature of the publishing business, I decided that I would go downstairs during my lunch hour to the office of the trade book editor and talk him into letting me write this book for him. It was a totally foolish notion, except for the fact that Prentice-Hall's trade book division was not as important to them as their legal services, so that in fact I could go and knock on the trade book editor's door. In most places you're got to get past at least two secretaries to see an editor.

Nick D'Incecco was sitting in his office when I knocked on his door. He said to come in, and he asked me what I wanted. I told him I was an employee from upstairs and that I had this great idea for a book on the Yankees. He said, "I'll tell you what. You write me a proposal, and then we'll talk about it." Fine.

I figured what he wanted to hear was that we'd sell a lot of books. So I added up the Yankees' home attendance during that 16-year period. It came to something like 20 million, and I told D'Incecco in my proposal, "If one percent of those 20 million people buy this book, you'll have a bestseller." Well, he bought it . . . and he gave me a contract. And that's now *Dynasty* got started.

The thing that amazes me today is that up until I handed Nick the finished manuscript, he didn't have any idea whether or not I could write an English sentence. So I guess I sold it to him on the marketing concept, that there were all these Yankee fans out there waiting to buy a book on the Yankees.

This was 1972 and the last history of the Yankees, written by Frank Graham, had been published in 1943 and updated in 1948. As a kid I thought that Graham's history was one of the most wonderful books I'd ever read, but I still felt that I could somehow do it better. My feeling was then, and it still is today, that what people want to read about is not what the writer has to say but what the ballplayers have to say. If you can keep the ballplayers at the forefront, you'll always have a readership.

When I first got the idea for *Dynasty* I went to the Yankees to see if they'd cooperate. The Yankees' director of publicity, Bob Fishel, may he rest in peace, said to me, "If you get a contract to write a book on the Yankees, I'll give you a desk here in Yankee Stadium and you can sit here as long as you like going through our files." So after Nick D'Incecco gave me a contract and $2,500, I spent the next year in Yankee Stadium. I was one of them, part of the family, as I sat there day after day, reading and taking notes on these thousands of files they had. It was wonderful.

The problem I discovered after sifting through all my notes was that there were often two or three different versions of the same story. The accounts didn't mesh. I called D'Incecco and said, "I can't possibly write this book without getting to know all these people. I'm going to have to visit them." He sent me another check for $2,500 and off I went. After I went through that money doing the first round of interviews, I told him whom I had seen, and he sent me another check for $2,500. And after I did some more interviews and I told him whom I had left to see he sent me a fourth check for $2,500 for a total of $10,000.

Altogether I went to see about 75 players, all over the country. I saw everybody from Johnny Lindell who was living in a mobile home overlooking the Pacific Ocean to Mickey Mantle in Commerce, Oklahoma, to Enos Slaughter who was living on a farm in Roxboro, North Carolina, where if you ask for directions they tell you, "Well, you go to the third oak tree and make a right." I went to Sumter, South Carolina, where Bobby Richardson's wife tried to convert me.

And I flew into Milwaukee during a blizzard to see Tony Kubek. I had a lot of memorable experiences doing that book.

It took me three years to write *Dynasty*. As I said, I spent the first year doing research, the second year interviewing, and a third year writing. And this was before computers. I wrote three drafts of that baby and typed each one on a little Smith-Corona. When I handed it in, it was 1,100 pages long and must have weighed six pounds. Nick D'Incecco and his assistant Frank Coffey just sort of laughed and said, "We can't publish this!" So we took a month and cut it in half. Prentice-Hall published it and darned if it didn't become a bestseller. I guess there were indeed a lot of Yankee fans out there waiting for an updated history of the team.

Oddly enough, *Dynasty* was the only book I intended to write. After it came out I joined the *Bergen Record*, first as a reporter and then as an editor, and I thought my career would be in journalism. I never thought I'd write another book, until one day in 1978 when I got a call from a man by the name of Doug Newton. Doug was Billy Martin's agent, and his question was, "How would you like to write a book with Billy Martin?" Apparently, Bill had read and liked what I said about him in *Dynasty*, that he was just as important a figure as Mantle or Whitey Ford because of his attitude, his combativeness.

Of course I was interested, but before we got going on the project, Newton called back and said, "Billy's too busy. He can't do the book right now. But I've got another client whose story you might like to write."

He said, "It's the Yankees relief pitcher, Sparky Lyle." Sparky had won the Cy Young Award the previous year. I said, "No . . . I'm really not interested in doing the Sparky Lyle story."

Newton, being the very persistent man he was, said, "Look. It's February. The Yankees are in Ft. Lauderdale. Go on down there. Meet him. You'll like him."

Well, I decided, okay. Why not? Newton was going to foot half the bill for the plane fare, and back then the airlines were running $99 roundtrip specials.

I went down to Ft. Lauderdale, met Sparky, and discovered not only that this man was glib and personable but also that he had a great memory, and most importantly that he was funny. He could make me laugh. A day or so later I was sitting in the Yankees' clubhouse with Sparky, and as I looked around I saw players such as Mickey Rivers and Reggie Jackson and Thurman Munson and Graig Nettles. And I knew, of course, that Billy Martin was the manager and that George Steinbrenner was the owner. Great, great material right?

So I said to Sparky, "How would you like to write a diary about the upcoming season?"

He said, "Fine. Let's do it."

I said, "Look. I'll go over to your house three or four times a week during the season and we'll talk for an hour a pop. That's all you have to do. Let me worry about the rest."

Now, originally, Sparky thought he was going to carry a tape recorder around himself and talk into it. When I showed up at his house for our first session, he said, "I just can't do it. I'm too self-conscious to talk into this tape recorder." So I said, "Don't worry about it. I'll ask the questions. You talk into *my* tape recorder." Once we started doing that, Sparky became very comfortable with it and we had no problems from there on in. The book, which we called *The Bronx Zoo*, became our shared venture, and we really had a good time doing it.

Luck is involved in every publishing venture, and we had some good luck with *The Bronx Zoo*. As you know, 1978 was the year the Yankees were 14 games behind the Red Sox, only to come back and tie them at the end of the season and have Bucky Dent hit that dramatic home run in the playoff game to win the American League pennant. Just like I would with the Pelicans, I had a terrific ending to this very funny book. And I think what made *The Bronx Zoo* such a hit, more than anything else, was the fact that it was such a funny book. Sparky had such a funny way of telling stories that the humor sort of percolated throughout the entire book. For a long, long time, up until George Will's *Men at Work*, *The Bronx Zoo* was the number one bestselling baseball book.

After Billy got fired for punching out the marshmallow salesman, he and I finally went to work on a book. *Number 1* was a very honest account of Billy's life, which included some not-very-flattering stories about George Steinbrenner. By the time the book came out Billy was managing the Oakland A's. There was an excerpt from the book in the *New York Daily News*, including six items which the *News* bulleted because they thought they would be controversial. Billy immediately got a letter from Steinbrenner saying that if Billy didn't take the first four bulleted items out of the book Steinbrenner was going to get him fired. Well, it was more important to Billy to keep his job than to maintain the integrity of the book, so he and I had a negotiation, shall we say, which allowed him to take those four items out of the book. This was done right after the first printing, which was about 100,000 copies. But, of course, once Billy acknowledged taking those four items out, that became a news item unto itself. And once people saw that Billy was backing away from what he'd said the sales of the book were stopped cold. *Number 1* should have sold triple what it sold. But George is a master manipulator, and he knew how to compromise the book. *Number 1* still made the bestsellers list.

And so there I was: three books, three bestsellers. The funny thing was I still didn't think of what I was doing in terms of a career because, if you look around, you see that nobody writes baseball books for a living. I mean, it just isn't done. To make a career out of it, you'd have to produce a successful book almost every year, and nobody can do that. But then I talked Graig Nettles into doing a book called *Balls*; I talked Davey Johnson into doing a book called *Bats*; and I wrote a book called *Bums* about the Brooklyn Dodgers. And now, 15 years after my first book came out, I'm still writing baseball books, so I guess I have made writing baseball books my career. It's incredible to think about it, and I feel like a very lucky guy.

By the way, the reason I wanted to do a book with Nettles had nothing to do with his having a great sense of humor like Sparky Lyle. I wanted to do a book with Nettles because he was angry, and I thought it would be interesting to see what would happen when the captain of a major league ballclub would vent his anger. Graig and I thought that what *Balls* would do would be to get Steinbrenner to understand the nature of the game of baseball. We thought that we would be educating him, along with the rest of the public, as to what had to be done to make the Yankees great again. We honestly believed that we could do that. But, as you know, some people think that they are bigger than the game. The outcome of *Balls* was that very soon after the publication of the book Nettles was traded, and the mess that Steinbrenner had created with the Yankees merely continued.

At first I was reluctant to do *Bums* because I knew from my experience with *Dynasty* that it would be an extremely time-consuming project. However, part of what you do when you pick options in life is try to anticipate the possible joys involved in a particular project, and the opportunity to analyze a team as great as the Brooklyn Dodgers and to meet all those great former Dodgers was too attractive of an idea to pass up. And I'm certainly glad I decided to do *Bums* because I think it turned out to be a wonderful experience and a good book, in large part because I had such a fabulous story to

work with. All the hopes and dreams I had for that book materialized.

Sure, I'm aware of Neil Sullivan's book, *The Dodgers Move West*,
which, contrary to *Bums*, at least partly absolves Walter O'Malley of
the blame for taking the Dodgers out of Brooklyn. In fact, I periodi-
cally get telephone calls from radio sports talk shows which want
Neil and me to debate. Neil's entitled to his opinion, but I haven't
changed my opinion of O'Malley one iota.

Besides the fact that I truly despise what O'Malley did, I had a
sound reason from a craftsmanship point of view to come down so
hard on him throughout the book as I did. And that is, you've got
to take a perspective. If you don't take a perspective, what you write
winds up being rather wishy-washy. And the perspective I wanted to
take in *Bums* was that of the Brooklyn fans. So the fact that O'Malley
acquired $200 million worth of real estate or whatever it was by mov-
ing to Los Angeles doesn't cut much ice with me, the Brooklyn fan.
What I see is that he took a thriving franchise in the heart of a thriving community, moved that franchise in the middle of the night for
personal financial gain, and cut the heart of the community. Brooklyn has never been the same. Now, if you want to tell me that he *had*
to do it, go ahead and make your argument. I just don't buy it. You
want to tell me that he was a great visionary for expanding major
league baseball to the West Coast, go right ahead. I just don't buy it.
I side with Pete Hamill who said that the three greatest villains in
history were Stalin, Hitler, and Walter O'Malley. I think that's closer
to the truth because O'Malley didn't care about the fans. He just
didn't care.

Have I gotten the credit I think I deserve for my books? Yes, I
think so but it's something I had to fight for because co-authors
didn't always get much recognition. For instance, if you look at the
dust jacket of *Ball Four*, you'll see that it says the book was written by
Jim Bouton. The fellow who helped him write the book gets a tiny
8-point byline that says "Edited by Leonard Shecter." From what I
know about him, Shecter was a decent, kind of shy person but also
one of those reporters who made most of the ballplayers uncomfortable because he asked the tough questions. I don't think he antici-
pated the tremendous impact that *Ball Four* had. If he had, he might
have wanted more credit for the book. But I don't think so. Lenny
was a newspaperman, and I don't think getting credit for doing a
book meant very much to him. I'm not a newspaperman. I write

books, and the only way I can continue to do so is to keep my name in the public eye.

When I did *The Bronx Zoo*, one of the demands I made was that my name be the same size on the cover as Sparky's name. I wanted parity. I did not want to be invisible. As a collaborator, your job is to be invisible and to make the work sound as if it has been written from the first page to the last by the subject himself; however, if you want to make a career out of coauthoring books, you can't let your persona be invisible. Sparky agreed to my demand for equality, and, if you look at the dust jacket of *The Bronx Zoo*, you'll notice that my name is just as prominent as his. In fact, it's more prominent because my name is longer!

I don't know if it's fair to say that I started the trend of collaborators receiving equal billing with their subjects, but I probably had something to do with it. I do know that Billy Martin disliked the fact that I wanted my name the same size as his. That really bothered him. But my attitude was, "Why shouldn't I receive equal billing? I'm doing 85 percent of the work." Plus, I knew that after the book Billy would go back to a paying career in baseball. I didn't have any other career waiting for me, so I wanted to be known as the writer behind the book. And I think that worked out for me. I think people realize that I actually, physically wrote *Number 1* and *The Bronx Zoo* and *Balls* and *Bats*, and it's because I did not let myself become anonymous.

I should also say that I have always gotten rave reviews from non-sportswriters but either lukewarm or negative reviews from sportswriters. I don't know why, except perhaps that I'm not a member of the club, but newspaper sportswriters usually don't seem to like me and they usually don't like my books. In the first review I ever got, a sportswriter for the *Bergen Record* said, "*Dynasty* was a waste of the writer's time." That's about the most scathing thing you could say about a book a person spent three years of his life on. Obviously, I don't think that was a fair assessment of the book because today in 1991, 16 years later, you can still buy *Dynasty* in a paperback version from Berkeley. That makes me think there must have been something to that book.

On the other hand, I've always received tremendous appreciation from radio and television people. When *Dynasty* came out, John Sterling said on the radio that it was the best baseball book ever written. Certainly you take comments like that more to heart than the negative reviews. Two of my biggest fans are Larry King and Howard

Cosell, radio and TV guys. Why I've never gotten as much respect from the writers I can't say.

I do know there's an awful lot of jealousy among the people in the sportswriting business. Some writers, including my own friends, like to make a game out of ripping apart the work of other writers. I don't understand that. Everybody does something different. If you don't like a fellow's book, then don't review it. Just decline. If you like it, say something nice about it. But to take great glee in ripping apart another writer's work? I don't understand that. You'd think that people working in this sporting business would be sports, *good* sports, wouldn't you?

I love what I'm doing, and I'm so grateful to be in this business that I've always been happy to help anybody who's come to me for help or advice. I've never forgotten how somebody helped me when I was a nobody first starting out. When I was working on *Dynasty* one day Roger Kahn walked into Yankee Stadium. I introduced myself and asked him if he would consent to my interviewing him about the Yankees. Even though Roger had covered the Dodgers as a reporter and was famous for *The Boys of Summer*, I knew that he had been around baseball enough to know some interesting things about the Yankees. Well, not only did Roger consent to an interview, but he also was extremely encouraging and supportive and he tried to help me in every way he could. His generosity has always been very, very dear to me, and I've tried to treat people who've asked me for help the very same way. Some kindnesses you can't really repay. All you can do is pass them on.

BASEBALL BOOKS BY PETER GOLENBOCK

Dynasty: The New York Yankees 1949-1964. Englewood Cliffs, NJ:
    Prentice-Hall, 1975.
The Bronx Zoo (with Sparky Lyle). New York: Crown Publishers, 1979.
Guidry (with Ron Guidry). Englewood Cliffs, NJ: Prentice-Hall,
    1980.
Number 1 (with Billy Martin). New York: Delacorte Press, 1980.
Balls (with Graig Nettles). New York: G. P. Putnam's Sons, 1984.
Bums: An Oral History of the Brooklyn Dodgers. New York: G. P.
    Putnam's Sons, 1984.
Pete Rose on Hitting. New York: Putnam Publishing Group, 1985.
Bats (with Davey Johnson). New York: G. P. Putnam's Sons, 1986.

Teammates. San Diego: Harcourt Brace Jovanovich, 1990.

The Forever Boys. New York: Carol Publishing Group, 1991.

Fenway: An Unexpurgated History of the Boston Red Sox. New York: G. P. Putnam's Sons, 1992.

Wild, High and Tight: The Life and Death of Billy Martin. New York: St. Martin's Press, 1994.

Wrigleyville: A Magical History Tour of the Chicago Cubs. New York: St. Martin's Press, 1996.

The Spirit of St. Louis: A History of the St. Louis Cardinals and Browns. New York: Spike, 2000.

Hank Aaron: Brave in Every Way. San Diego: Gulliver Books, 2001.

Amazin': The Miraculous History of New York's Most Beloved Baseball Team. New York: St. Martin's Press, 2002.

6

JOHN B. HOLWAY

*John Holway has spent a good part of his adult life researching the history of
the Negro Leagues and its players, an effort for which he received the prestigious 1990 Bob Davids Award from the Society for American Baseball
Research. While researching a newspaper article on legendary catcher Josh
Gibson, Holway began interviewing old Negro Leaguers, and his collection
of the best of these interviews was published in 1975 as* Voices from the
Great Black Baseball Leagues *(Dodd, Mead). Holway's* Blackball Stars
(Meckler) won the 1988 CASEY Award; Black Diamonds *(Meckler)
appeared in 1989; and the capstone to his work on the Negro Leagues, a
dual biography called* Josh and Satch *(Meckler) was published in 1991.
One of the true gentlemen of baseball literature, Holway nevertheless has continually rebuked the establishment for not giving the Negro Leagues more recognition, once telling curator Ken Smith, "You have only half a Hall of Fame
here. It won't be complete until the great black players before Jackie Robinson
are admitted." A graduate of the University of Iowa and Georgetown University, Holway has worked for the U.S. Information Agency since 1956.*

THERE'S A THEORY that you form lifetime attachments to the players
that you picked out as your heroes at the time of puberty. My idol
was Ted Williams, but I was also interested in Josh Gibson and Satchel Paige. In 1944 when I was 14, I went to Griffith Stadium in Washington—I took the bus and then the trolley by myself—to see a game
between Satchel Paige and the Kansas City Monarchs and Josh Gibson and the Homestead Grays.

I don't remember a whole lot except Satchel Paige warming up
in front of the third base dugout before the game. He had a wind-
mill windup which nobody uses anymore. I went down to the railing
and waved my scorecard with a lot of other kids, all of them black.
Satchel pitched about three innings, which he usually did in those
days to draw a crowd, and then he left.

And Josh, I remember, was across the field, warming up his pitcher on the first base side. He was a jolly kind of guy, and he was laughing. I think the score was 2-1, the Monarchs, but I don't remember any details of the game. I knew Buck Leonard's name; he was considered the black Lou Gehrig. But I didn't know the names of any of the other guys. Now I know that Cool Papa Bell must have been playing and that Hilton Smith probably came in to relieve Satchel. And Sam Bankhead, who is the model for Troy Maxson in the play *Fences*, was probably playing shortstop or outfield for the Grays. So, my interest in the Negro Leagues stems from that game.

There's also the fact that I am a member of the transitional generation. Many of the other Negro League historians and I grew up as kids under the pre–Jackie Robinson segregated baseball, and then we came to adulthood and lived the rest of our lives under the present integrated baseball system. So our generation kind of made the transition. If you're a little older than me, you spent most of your formative adult years living under segregated baseball. If you're younger than me, you never saw segregated baseball; all your experience is with integrated baseball. So those two things, I guess, formed the foundation of my interest in the Negro Leagues.

Incidentally, I saw another Negro League game a couple of years later in 1946 after Jackie had been signed and was playing for Montreal. They were advertising, "Come to the park and see some more Monarchs who are just as good as Jackie and might go up to the major leagues." Herb Souell and Barney Sorrell, two infielders, were being touted. Neither of them made it, but I did go back to see that game.

Then I more or less forgot about Negro League baseball until 1969 when I decided that I'd like to do a story on Josh Gibson, a newspaper article. I kept waiting for somebody else to do it, but it hadn't been done so I started working on a story. I found an old man here in Washington who knew a little about Negro baseball, and he said, "Why don't you go talk to Buck Leonard, who lives down in Rocky Mount, North Carolina?" So I went down there, took my boys with me, and Buck was very nice. And Buck suggested I go out to St. Louis to see Cool Papa Bell, so I did, and again I took my boys along. Cool Papa was very nice too, and I remember that Mrs. Bell took the boys into the kitchen for ice cream so that Cool Papa and I could talk. And then Cool Papa suggested I go talk to Hilton Smith, the pitcher, in Kansas City. One thing led to another, and after several years I'd talked to about 70 guys.

Anyway, when I completed the Josh Gibson article, I submitted it to the *Washington Post*, and the manuscript came back to me with the editor's notes on it: "No, no, this is wrong. That's impossible," referring to some of the things I'd written about Josh's accomplishments, his long home runs, and such. This incredulous editor was finally overruled by his boss, the editor-in-chief, and the story did run, as a cover story of the *Washington Post Magazine*. Now that I reread it, 20 years later, I see a lot of errors and things we now know were not true, but at that time that was where scholarship stood. So I guess it was important in its time although it's way out of date.

A couple of years later I was up in Cooperstown, at the Hall of Fame, and I asked Cliff Kachline, the curator, "What have you got on Negro baseball?" And he said, "We've got a lot on Negro baseball." He led me down this long bank of filing cabinets, and we came to one marked *N*. He pulled the drawer out, flipped through the files, and pulled out one called "The Negro Leagues." He opened it up, and what they had in there was one boxscore for the Indianapolis Clowns, one short clipping of some sort from some newspaper, and my article on Josh Gibson. That was it. That's all they had in the National Baseball Library. I will say this for Cliff: He did a very good job in correcting that. He sent out questionnaires to every living player he could find and got all sorts of demographic data on them. And I mention this just to show that, again, that's where things stood at the time. Now I think Cooperstown has a very good collection of Negro League things.

A lot of guys I talked to have died since then, and I'm glad I got their stories because otherwise they'd be gone forever. And I think, "Gee, why didn't I start five or ten years earlier? I could have gotten some of the older greats like Pop Lloyd, Joe Rogan, Dick Lundy, and so on." But I'm glad I started at least when I did because I got a lot of great stories that couldn't be obtained today because the people who told them are gone.

Originally, I was thinking only about Josh Gibson for my newspaper article. I was asking Buck Leonard only about Josh, but eventually Buck started telling me things about himself, and I thought, "Wow, Buck's career is pretty interesting too." Then I went out to Cool Papa's, and the same thing happened, and I began to realize that all the players had interesting stories, every one of them.

And I found out things I didn't expect to find out. I didn't start out in order to prove that the Negro Leagues were great leagues or in order to prove that the Negro League players were as good as the

whites or in order to prove that the best Negro Leaguers ought to
be in the Hall of Fame.

I thought I was doing a footnote, an interesting sort of footnote
in the overall story of baseball—as if today you were going to do a
book on the Brooklyn Bushwicks or the House of David. They will
be interesting footnotes when someone gets around to doing those
books. That's what I thought I was doing.

And I myself didn't believe the evidence at first. It took a while
before I realized: "Hey these guys *were* just as good as the blacks
who've been playing since Jackie Robinson. They were just as good
before him too." And I resisted: "No, no no. If they were that good,
we'd have heard about them, I'm sure. You can't keep it a secret if
somebody's that good."

As a kid I grew up believing that there may have been one or two
who were freaks, like Satchel Paige or Josh Gibson, but in general
they were mostly AAA or AA ballplayers or good semi-pro ballplayers. I thought, "They can hit the ball hard, but they can't hit a big
league curve." Those were the rationales given in the *Sporting News*,
of which I was an avid reader, to explain, if any explanation were
ever necessary, why none of these blacks should ever be taken seriously. I assumed all this was true, and I grew up believing it. But I
was finally forced to admit to my own shock that, "Gee, they were as
good as the white stars of their day."

That's why I kind of sympathize with readers of mine who say,
"Oh, this is impossible. You keep saying Oscar Charleston was so
great. But he was only playing against whites when the whites were
loafing, and that doesn't count." I understand the mindset out
there that resists the evidence we've uncovered because I went
through the same mental resistance.

I didn't set out to be a Negro baseball historian, but nobody else
was doing it at the time, except for Bob Peterson who beat me to it
with *Only the Ball Was White*. And I had a pretty hard time getting
Voices from the Great Black Baseball Leagues published because of his
book. Publishers would say, "Well, you've got a good book but
there's already a book on the subject, and we don't think there's
enough of an audience out there for two books."

I had an index card file of publishers, and I went through the file
from *A* to *Z* looking for a publisher. And then I started back on the
As again. By then enough time had passed so that the editors had all
changed, and so they were reading my material for the first time.
Finally, on the second time through the alphabet, I made it on the

Ds with Dodd, Mead. Actually, I got two acceptances at the same time and went with Dodd, Mead.

Writing's like asking a girl to dance: you've got to be ready for rejection. Or like selling insurance: you've got to ring a certain number of doorbells to get a sale. And if you can't take rejection, you might as well not be a writer. Eileen, my wife, was talking to the mailman the other day. I was upstairs and overheard her. He said, "Oh, boy, I don't know why, but you get more mail than anybody on my route." And she said, "Oh, that's because John's a writer. Those are all his rejections."

Voices came out in November, which is a bad time for baseball books. The critics were kind and said nice things, but we didn't sell that many copies. It was kind of an off-beat subject, although we've created a better market by now. You could expect better sales than we got 20 years ago, so progress has been made in that respect.

Voices was a first-person book. Naturally, I did a lot of editing because the material was raw. But I don't think I put words into the mouths of the subjects. Occasionally I'd correct grammar, fix up double negatives, and make the verbs and nouns agree, but not always. Sometimes I put it down exactly in their own language. These men generally did not have much formal education, but I think they were educated in another sense. They learned things in life that you can't get in a school room, so they were more educated in that sense than some people who know life from books only. Anyway, to spare them embarrassment I'd fix up some of their grammar, but generally I let them tell their own stories in their own words.

It's kind of like a "found poem." Sometimes people say things not knowing they're being poetic, but if you choose to look at what they say as poetry, then, by gosh, it is poetry. A lot of their language is poetic, and I wanted to preserve that.

After a while I had lots of material on all these great players whom I'd never met, players whom I discovered were giants of the North American game: Oscar Charleston, Smokey Joe Williams, and those guys. I almost despaired of ever getting out a book on them. Publishers simply didn't see it as a book they could make money off of. So I went into the samizdat business: I self-published. I put out three little pamphlets, on Smokey Joe Williams, on Rube Foster, and on Bullet Joe Rogan and the Kansas City Monarchs. I sold them for $5 a piece, and now they're going for $65 each, so I'm told.

I didn't give up though. I still tried to find a commercial publisher, and Meckler Books finally said okay. By and large, the players in

Blackball Stars were the great giants of the Negro game: the Ty Cobbs and Babe Ruths and Walter Johnsons and Honus Wagners of the black half of baseball history. The book was something I had long long wanted to do, and thank goodness Meckler did it. And thank goodness *SPITBALL* magazine recognized it, because its winning the CASEY Award whetted Meckler's appetite for another one, and they did *Black Diamonds*. At first, they wanted to bring out *Voices* again. I said, "Alright, that's nice, but first let me show you some all-new material. I can give you all new players who weren't in *Voices*, and their stories are just as interesting and they should be better because now I know a lot more about the subject. I've been able to ask better questions." And for that reason I do think *Black Diamonds* is a better book overall than *Voices*.

The stories of these players are so great that someday I want to do a movie script on an amalgamation of all their stories. *Bingo Long* was good fiction, but the black players don't recognize it as being their story. They say, "No, we didn't do that. No, it wasn't like that." I'd like them to make a film that would be really accurate so that any story in the film will be a real story that happened to a real guy. And I think such a film will be better than any story you could invent.

Josh and Satch will probably be the capstone of my work on the Negro Leagues. I've done a dual biography of the two players because their careers intermingled so much. They started out on different teams, then they came together on the same team, the Pittsburgh Crawfords, in the early 1930s. Can you imagine a battery of Satchel Paige and Josh Gibson? Lefty Grove and Mickey Cochrane is the closest analogy you can come up with in white baseball. Here's these two super-duper stars in the same battery! And then their careers diverged again; they went to different teams and became rivals. In Latin America they became rivals, and then they played together in Latin America. Then they returned to the States, went to separate teams again, and they faced each other in the black World Series a few times. And the rivalry when these two met was always electric.

There's a great story about their rivalry which I thought was apocryphal but apparently is true. Josh said down in Puerto Rico, "Oh, I can hit Satchel any time; he's easy for me to hit." When word of that got back to Satchel, he filed it away in the back of his mind. And then during the 1942 World Series between the Grays and the Monarchs, they met each other again. Satchel had a 3-1 lead late in the game, and he walked three guys on purpose so Josh would come to bat. The Monarchs were going crazy: "You can't do this, Satchel; you're walking the bases loaded and Josh is coming up!" Satchel says, "Don't worry. I know what I'm doing."

And Satchel struck Josh out. He psyched him out really. Josh kept thinking Satchel was going to throw him a curve because by that time Satchel had a dinky little curveball. But he didn't. He just whistled those fastballs past him. The story illustrates that these two guys were not only great teammates but great rivals as well. And those two guys really tell the whole story of the last 20 years of black baseball. Their experiences, the people they played against, the places they went, and the teams they were with really summarize all the highlights of black baseball in the 1930s and 1940s, just at the end of the era of the Negro leagues.

I felt a great deal of satisfaction in doing that book, but now I want to go on to other interests. I don't think there's much left untold now. I guess I'll always be identified with the Negro Leagues—and I'm glad—but I never thought it would turn out this way. I always thought my interests in baseball were more catholic than that.

As a matter of fact, it strikes me as being ironic that most historians of black baseball are white. There a few exceptions like Larry Lester and Phil Dixon, who are black, but the fact is that if whites hadn't done it, it wouldn't have been done. Because a lot of the guys that I've interviewed are gone now, and if we're waiting for a black man to interview them and write their stories, it's too late. I think it's too bad that more blacks are not interested in preserving this history of their own experience. As it stands now, the history of black baseball has been pretty well covered. I wish we had more details, but what we don't have now, we just won't have. We've done the best we could.

The Negro Baseball Hall of History was a good idea, and I applaud them for making the effort. But being located in Ashland, Kentucky, made it off the beaten track. They ran out of money and had to give it up. Ironically, it also made it harder for Negro Leaguers to get into the Hall of Fame in Cooperstown.

I've always felt that the great black players should be in the Hall of Fame on their merits. They earned the right to be there on the field. They beat Babe Ruth, they beat Ty Cobb, they beat Walter Johnson, and they beat Lefty Grove. And you're mistaken if you think Lefty Grove was just fooling around and not trying to win when he pitched against blacks. I talked to Lefty Grove and said,

"What about this game when a black team beat you in 1929 . . ." And he looked me straight in the eye and said, "I've never played a black team." And I have the boxscore proving that he got beat by a black team! What I'm saying is that the white players are defensive about having lost to the blacks, they're embarrassed about it, and to argue that they would not have been equally embarrassed on the field when it happened before a grandstand full of fans, black or white, in the middle of the Jim Crow era, is nonsense. Of course, they didn't want to lose and get shown up.

So the blacks deserve to be in the National Baseball Hall of Fame; it's part of our common North American baseball heritage. We're not doing it as a favor to them; they've earned it. They've played, and they've won. The losers are in the Hall of Fame. I think the winners ought to be in the Hall of Fame right next to the losers. And, of course, they're not. They put in a symbolic all-star team of nine blacks, and then they were going to end it. But I made a stink about it, and they reluctantly let the Veterans' Committee add two more, Rube Foster and Ray Dandridge. But the odds are stacked against them. There are 15 whites and three blacks on the Veterans' Committee, and you can't get three-fourths of them to vote for the blacks; with rare exceptions. The last generation of whites which kept them out of the game is now keeping them out of the Hall of Fame; when that generation passes on and is replaced by today's generation, maybe things'll be different.

I'm always writing to the Hall of Fame—they're sick and tired of hearing from me now—saying, "Let this guy in; let that guy in." And they have 101 excuses why they can't let another Negro League player in, but one of their excuses was, "They've got their own Hall of Fame in Ashland, Kentucky, so why do they need to get into this one?. . . We don't need to put them in this Hall of Fame because they've got their own." There's going to be a new Negro baseball Hall of Fame in Kansas City [it opened in January 1991], and again, it's a good idea, but I'm afraid it's going to give Cooperstown an excuse to say, "Well, they've got a Hall of Fame, why do they want to get into our Hall of Fame?"

When I get together with other black baseball historians like Dick Clark, Jim Riley, Jerry Malloy, Bill Plott, and Paul Doherty, we love to speculate on how many other Negro League players should go into the Hall of Fame. I would say that a minimum of 12 more could go in, and you'd still be in the giant category. All the giants of white baseball are in. The present Veterans' Committee has long since named all the excellent players of white baseball and even the very goods, and now they're down to the pretty good players, such as Red Schoendienst. So if you want to get down to the Red Schoendienst–level of black player, you could put in another 30 or 40 and still be very comparable.

Leaving them aside and concentrating only on the great giants of black baseball who should be in, there's at least a dozen left. Willie Wells definitely should be in. He just died too. It's too bad they didn't let him in before he died. I'm not so sure anymore that Willie Wells was the greatest black shortstop of all time because we've recently found out that Pop Lloyd is the all-time batting champion of the Negro Leagues. It's hard to choose between Pop Lloyd and Willie Wells, but Wells should be in along with Lloyd, who is in already.

Turkey Stearnes should definitely go in. Cool Papa Bell once told me, "I don't know of anybody who hit more home runs than Turkey Stearnes." I thought that Cool Papa was just trying to be nice by saying that, but, by golly, it turns out that Cool Papa was right. We've counted them up now, and we know it's true: Turkey is the all-time home run leader of Negro baseball. On a per-game or at-bat basis Josh Gibson is still number one, but on total home runs Turkey Stearnes is the Hank Aaron of Negro League baseball. He is not only number one in home runs, he is also number one in triples and total bases; he's number four in stolen bases; and he's in the top 10 in batting average. So how are you going to keep him out of the Hall of Fame? As Cool Papa says, "If they don't put him in, they shouldn't put *anybody* in."

Then there's Smokey Joe Williams, Bullet Joe Rogan, Dick Lundy, Biz Mackey, Oliver Marcelle, Jud Wilson, Cristobal Torriente, and possibly Louis Santop. Bill Foster, the number one winningest pitcher of all time, should be in. And so should the number two winningest pitcher of all time, a rather obscure guy named Andy Cooper. When we were doing the statistics for the Negro League section in the latest *Macmillan Encyclopedia* we kept running into surprises, and Andy was one of them. Another guy who we found, to our surprise, ranks very high was Bill Byrd, who is 82 years old and lives in Philadelphia. He is number four in victories, with only three or four fewer wins than Satchel Paige and about the same as Joe Rogan. Here's a guy who has no charisma, never says funny things like, "Don't look back; something might be gaining on you," so he gets no ink from the newspapers. But there he is pitching good ball, winning games, quietly doing his job, being a good craftsman. Satchel's getting all the attention, but Bill Byrd is quietly going along winning almost as many games. So he should be in. Finally, I would put in J. L. Wilkinson, the owner of the Monarchs and the father of night baseball; Cum Posey, who developed some dynastic Homestead Grays teams; and maybe Gus Greenlee, the owner of the Pittsburgh Crawfords, the founder of the second Negro National League, and the founder of the East-West All-Star Game.

As I said, I do have baseball interests that are not black baseball–related. For instance, right now I'm working on a book about Ted Williams and the 1941 season. There's a lot of history to be rewritten about the 1941 season, just as there's great history to be rewritten about the Negro Leagues.

For one thing, I think Joe DiMaggio's hitting streak was a complete myth. Joe did not hit in 56 straight games.

In the first place, no one cared about hitting streaks before Joe. Nobody knew or cared about Willie Keeler's streak in Baltimore before DiMaggio; they had to go back in the record books to find it. Ty Cobb hits in a long streak, but he's in Detroit so nobody cares. Sisler hits in a long streak, but he's in St. Louis. Who cares how many straight games you hit in if you play in St. Louis? George McQuinn has a long streak going in 1938 for St. Louis. Who cares? George went to his grave saying, "Nobody gives a darn about my streak."

Well, now you've got a New Yorker who's got a streak. This is different; this is entirely different. When a New Yorker has a streak going, now it's news. And the New Yorkers make sure you know it's news. The New York newspapers created that streak, and I think one reason they did is that Ted Williams was hitting .400 that summer. And New Yorkers don't like it when New Yorkers are not the number one story. They had to do something to counteract this guy from Boston who was stealing the headlines. So they latched onto DiMaggio.

Another reason I say Joe did not hit in 56 straight games is that he got some very questionable hits to keep the streak going. In Game 16 he's 0-2 in his last time up. He hits an easy can of corn; Pete Fox, the right fielder, loses it in the sun; and it falls for a double. By the scoring rules you have to call it a hit, but it was a pretty cheap hit. I don't know whether Pete Rose got any hits like that during his streak; as far as I know he didn't. Okay, so we'll call that one a hit.

Now we're in Game 30 in Yankee Stadium. Now it's big news, and the New York writers are telling the world about their boy who's got a hitting streak going. He's 0-3 in his last time at bat. He hits a bounding ball to shortstop. It hits Luke Appling in the shoulder and bounces into left field.

All the players run to the dugout steps, crane their necks, and look up to the press box. Dan Daniel, a New York writer, is the official scorer. Is the streak over, or is it not over? They can't wait for Dan to make his decision. He lifts one finger: a hit. The Yankee players cheer. The streak goes on. I call it the "DiMaggio-Daniel hitting streak."

The next day Thornton Lee has DiMaggio going for the collar. Joe is 0-2 going into his last at bat. He hits another bouncing ball to Luke Appling at short. This time Luke fumbles it, drops it, picks it up, throws, and Joe beats the throw out. Is this going to be a hit? I have a friend who was at the game and doesn't want to be named because he claims to be Joe's friend. He says, "I called it an error on my scorecard." They didn't put hit and error on the scoreboard back then, and there was no public address announcement made about it either, so you scored the play the way you wanted to score it. And my friend says, "I thought the streak was over until I picked up the newspaper the next morning and saw they'd given him a hit."

The streak goes on. Again, Dan Daniel comes to his rescue. If that had been any other game, any other player, any other city. . . I don't think Joe would have gotten a hit on either of those groundballs.

In Game 54 he gets another cheap hit. He swings with all his might and tops the ball. It rolls about 30 feet down the third baseline, and he beats it out. Alright, you give him a hit.

So I don't think Joe really hit in 56 straight games. They say it's impossible for anyone to break that record. Of course, it's impossible; it was impossible to *set* it too! He never set the record. That's why it's impossible to break it.

Game 57 really intrigues me. We know that Ken Keltner made two great stops on balls hit by Joe; we know that Al Smith came in and pitched good relief and stopped Joe; and we know that Lou Boudreau made a great stop on Joe's last bid for a hit and threw him out. The streak seems to be over.

The Yankees are winning, 4-1, as the Indians come to bat in the bottom of the ninth. They get a couple of guys on, and Larry Rosenthal, a backup outfielder, pinch-hits a triple to score two runs. Now it's 4-3. If the Indians can bring Larry Rosenthal in from third, Joe gets to bat in the 10th. Another pinch hitter, Hal Trotsky, grounds out to first, and Rosenthal holds third. Soup Campbell, a third pinch hitter, bats next and hits back to the pitcher, Grandma Murphy, who traps Rosenthal off third. Rosenthal tries to stay in the rundown long enough to let Campbell get into scoring position at second. The Yankees put Rosenthal out, and Campbell hasn't moved off first. He's been watching the rundown with fascination.

Ordinarily, with Campbell on second, Johnny Sturm, the first baseman, would be off the bag, but he's playing close to the bag with Campbell on first. The next batter, Roy Weatherly, drills a grass cutter right inside the bag at first. Normally, it would be a hit, most likely a double, but because Sturm's playing close to the bag he spears it for the third out, the game is over, and Joe does not come to bat in the 10th. So Joe's luck finally runs out.

What really interests me though is that when Rosenthal hit that triple, he hit it to right-center between DiMaggio and Henrich. Now somebody threw that ball in and held Rosenthal to a triple. Earlier in the game the Indians' Gee Walker had hit a ball in the same place and had legged it out for an inside-the-park home run. This time the runner held at third and does not score. Who threw that ball in?

I have asked Tommy Henrich; he can't remember. I wrote DiMaggio a letter—he won't talk to you—asking him, "Who threw the ball in holding Rosenthal? Do you remember?" Weeks went by, and finally my own letter came back to me in my self-addressed, stamped envelope with a one-word reply: "No"; meaning he didn't remember.

So, although I haven't documented it yet, it just might be that Joe himself ended his own streak. And as Tommy Henrich told me, "We could have easily let them score that run to tie the game so that Joe would have come up again." The Yankees had about a six-game lead, so the game wasn't very important. Henrich said, "If you ever want to write about the integrity of baseball, write about that game."

Ted Williams, by the way, played that season, hit .400, with a broken ankle. He broke his ankle in spring training sliding into second base. He said, "I taped that ankle every damn day of the season." He was out for most of spring training and missed the first few games of the season and rebroke it later on after the All-Star Game in which he hit that dramatic ninth-inning home run and was out for a couple of weeks.

The other interesting things is that Ted hit .429 against lefthanded pitchers that year. He only hit .398 against righthanders. It should have been the other way around. However, of his league-leading 37 home runs, only one was hit off a lefthander. He said he shortened up against lefties and just tried to hit the ball up the middle. And you wonder . . . if he had shortened up and tried to hit the ball up the middle against righthanders, he might have gone down in history as the last, and first, of the .500 hitters!

And, of course, Ted should have won the MVP that year, not DiMaggio. First of all, the Yankees were picked to finish first, and they finished first, by 20 games or something like that. So what's so great about the Yankees winning the pennant? Secondly, the Yankees also had another streak that year: for 18 consecutive games they hit at least one homer, breaking the old record held by the Detroit Tigers. So the *team* was hot, and this was during DiMaggio's hitting streak. They say it was DiMaggio who ignited the Yankees, but the Yankees as a team were ignited by this home run streak.

On the other hand, the Red Sox were picked to finish fourth; they finished second. They could not have finished second without Ted Williams that year. Ted made the difference. Without Joe the Yankees were still a formidable team. They had good pitching, and they had the best hitting team in the league. They'd have won without Joe.

Joe was hot for one-third of the season. During those 56 games, whether he really hit safely in all of them or not, he hit .412. For two months Joe hit over .400; for the whole other two-thirds of the season he hit .322. Ted hit .406 for the whole season! Ted also led the league in home runs, and if he hadn't been walked so darn much he'd have led the league in RBIs too. The problem was that Ted didn't have an "NY" on his cap.

I saw Ted play, by the way, in 1941. He went 1-4 against the Yankees. It was only my second big league game. At my first game I had sat in the left-field mezzanine in Yankee Stadium, and the players had looked like ants. This time, my father had box seats, a rare treat after 10 years of Depression, and as we walked up the ramp to field level, there was Jimmie Foxx framed in the ramp, muscles bulging and jaw bulging with tobacco. I almost fainted. Lefty Grove was pitching, and after every inning he walked right up to where we were sitting, looked over our heads into the stands, spat, and disappeared.

I also saw Joe that year; he singled his first time up against Virgil Trucks to either tie or pass Rogers Hornsby's record for consecutive games hit in by a righthander.

The next year, in 1942, Ted's the Triple Crown winner and doesn't win the MVP award! How about that? Ted leads the league in home runs, batting average, RBIs, and total bases. Joe Gordon leads the league in two categories: most times struck out and most errors by a second baseman. Now which of those two players deserves the MVP? Which of the two has an "NY" on his cap?

Later on Ted lost by one vote to Joe D. when a Boston writer either named him ninth or not at all, so that's three times he should have won the MVP when he didn't. And that's not even mentioning the years he lost in the service when he might have hit .400 again or might have hit 60 homers.

He'd have somewhere between 650 and 680 lifetime homers without his wartime service. He would have improved his lifetime batting average, too, because those were his best years. In those three years, ages 24, 25, 26, Ty Cobb hit .420, .410, and .390. Maris hit 61 home runs, when he was 26 and Hornsby won his first Triple Crown when he was 26. Those are the big years.

Ted's the youngest .400 hitter in history, he wins the Triple Crown, then . . . Whammo! Three years are gone, missing. To my mind he was the greatest of all. Ty Cobb didn't have his power; Ruth didn't have his consistency. And Joe was a good player, a .325 life-time hitter, but he wasn't a Ted Williams.

Ted once told me, "Well, Ty Cobb was a great player . . . but he played for Detroit, and Detroit ain't New York." And I think Ted struggled with that all his life: Boston ain't New York.

You know, I saw Ted hit Rip Sewell's blooper pitch in the 1946 All-Star Game. I'll always remember, he took two little hopping dance steps and uppercut it. I was sitting in right field and figured, "Oh, oh, a pop up." But it kept going up, and the right-fielder drift-ed back, and it finally came down in the bullpen a few feet away from me.

That fall I was going to the University of Iowa and hitchhiked down to St. Louis for the World Series. I slept on a bench in the train station—a cop would come by and wake me up every hour or so—and stood in line for standing room tickets for $3.50. In the first game the Red Sox tied it in the ninth, and Rudy York slammed a homer to the last row of the bleachers in the 10th inning to win the game. It's still my greatest thrill in baseball.

Unfortunately, I couldn't cut classes to see the seventh game, the one in which Enos Slaughter scored the winning run from first on a base hit into center field. But I've seen the films of the game, and Johnny Pesky never held the ball, as he's been accused of doing all these years. He took the relay from center, turned, and threw home, all in one motion. I have a standing bet with anyone who sees the film and still thinks Johnny held the ball: Eileen and I will take him and a date out to a steak dinner. But if he sees the film and admits that Pesky didn't hold the ball, then he takes us out to dinner. No one has ever taken us up on the bet.

But the Pesky incident remains one of the biggest myths in baseball history, along with the myth that DiMaggio hit in 56 straight games and that Branch Rickey "freed the slaves." Rickey didn't free the slaves; Happy Chandler did and never got credit for it. And the next nickel Rickey pays a black club owner for a black player will be the first. Rickey didn't get black players into the major leagues; they'd been playing major league ball for decades. What he did was to get the black owners and the black fans out. Before 1947 black players played mostly for black owners and black fans. Now they are paid entertainers, and well-paid ones, for white owners and white fans.

Incidentally, I served in Korea about the same time Ted Williams did. I was in the hospital in Japan recovering from a shrapnel wound when I read in *Stars and Stripes* about Ted's last game in Boston just before he was called up to active duty early in 1952. I finished the war in Tokyo, a great town to finish a war in, and used to go to the Japanese major league games all the time. In fact, my first book, *Japan is Big League in Thrills* was published there. It was the first book ever published in English on the subject.

A few years later, in 1957, I called Ted up at his hotel in Washington to ask him what the two wars had cost him. He had just been in the papers for chewing out some writer for something or other, and I expected him to take my head off. But he said, "Okay, come on up." We had a wonderful talk for about two hours. He said he thought he would hit .375 for the year with about 35 homers. I thought, "No 38-year-old geezer is going to hit .375 with 35 homers." I was right, of course. He hit .388 with 38 homers.

Finally, in September 1960 I saw him hit home run 520 in Griffith Stadium. I even took a home movie of him crossing the plate. As he trotted past me into the dugout, he cocked his head as if to say, "Boy, that felt good." It would be the last game I would ever see him play. He was 42, and I was 30. I felt as if my boyhood, and his, had come to an end at last.

BASEBALL BOOKS BY JOHN B. HOLWAY

Voices From the Great Black Baseball Leagues. New York: Dodd, Mead, 1975.

Blackball Stars: Negro League Pioneers. Westport, CT: Meckler Books,
  1988.
Black Diamonds: Life in the Negro Leagues from the Men Who Lived It.
  Westport, CT: Meckler Books, 1989.
The Sluggers (contributing editor). Alexandria, VA: Redefinition,
  1989.
Josh and Satch: A Dual Biography of Josh Gibson and Satchel Paige.
  Westport, CT: Meckler Books, 1991.
The Last .400 Hitter: The Anatomy of a .400 Season. Dubuque, IA: Wm.
  C. Brown, 1991.
The Baseball Astrologer: And Other Weird Tales. Kingston, NY: Total/
  Sports Illustrated, 2000.

7

DONALD HONIG

A year without at least one new Donald Honig baseball book would be like a baseball season without the World Series. The author of nearly 40 baseball books, many of which are illustrated histories, Donald Honig began his career as a baseball author in 1975 when he published a sequel to his friend Larry Ritter's pioneering baseball oral history, The Glory of Their Times. *The book of interviews with players from the 1920s to the 1940s called* Baseball When the Grass Was Real *(Coward, McCann, & Goehegan, 1975) was such a smash hit that Honig followed it with three more oral history collections:* Baseball Between the Lines *(Coward, McCann, & Goehegan, 1976),* The Man in the Dugout *(Follett, 1977) and* The October Heroes*(Simon & Schuster, 1979). The importance of the four books was recognized in 1988 when Simon & Schuster combined them into* A Donald Honig Reader *as part of their "Fireside Sports Classic" series; that same year Honig was given* The Jim Harrison Award *for his "lifetime contributions to baseball literature" by* SPITBALL *magazine. A resident of Cromwell, Connecticut, Honig has also published 12 novels, 19 books for young readers, and over 200 short stories.*

WHEN I WAS DOING the oral history books, somebody would ask me where I was off to next, and I'd say, "Out to Cleveland to interview Bob Feller," or "down to Philadelphia to see Robin Roberts," or something like that. I would get this long, calculating stare and perhaps just the slightest elevating of an eyebrow, followed by another question in a decidedly chilly tone of voice: "And you're getting paid for this, aren't you?" Well, I'm afraid I was, and at times handsomely.

It sounds like one of those "Only In America" stories, doesn't it? A guy traveling to different parts of the country to sit and talk baseball all day and all night and sometimes all the next day and all the next night, too, with his boyhood heroes and then writing a book about it, which in itself is a joy, and then being paid for it.

I didn't start writing baseball books until I was past 40 years old, but I've done more than three dozen of them now. I blush to say it because such productivity implies that you haven't been *truly* successful or that you have nothing better to do with your time. But in my case, one of the reasons I write so many books is that I have the soul of an amateur. I love to be published, to see my name in print, and I don't mind admitting it. I never get jaded, and I've never had writer's block. To me, the greatest thing in the world is a blank piece of paper rolled into a typewriter. I can't wait to attack it.

I've been writing since I was five years old. I was fortunate in that my family always encouraged and supported my writing. They never threw up any blocks. My mother was always very proud of it, and my father, who was not a bookish man, understood and respected what I was trying to do. My brother too. In the early days when I didn't have much money, he always seemed to show up with a ream of paper when I needed it.

I started publishing short stories when I was about 20 and then novels a few years later. I'm very proud of most of the novels even though they never got the critical attention I thought they deserved. Sometimes people ask me if I'm bitter because my novels have been neglected. But being bitter because some critic didn't like my work would be the height of ingratitude. You see, my entire adult life has been my own possession. I have no boss; I'm at nobody's beck and call. I've been able to spend my hours and days doing exactly what I love to do, which is writing. I've never short-changed myself, and to me that's the paramount thing.

But you wanted to know how the baseball thing started. Well, it started because of one of my novels called *Illusions.* My editor thought so highly of it, even though it didn't sell all that many copies, that he wanted another one. He said, "We've got to make you some money so you can take your time and do the next novel without any distractions. You know a lot about baseball. Why don't you write a baseball book? It'll make some quick money for you, and then you can get back to novel-writing."

I immediately thought of a successor to Larry Ritter's *The Glory of Their Times* because I'd been after Larry to do one. I'd recently met him through the Bobo Newsom Memorial Society, an informal group in New York that got together a couple of times a year. Membership was strictly limited. Red Smith, who was a member, once said that membership was limited "to those who thought about Doc Cramer at least once a week." There were only two rules in the club: you had to talk baseball and you had to get drunk. But don't get the wrong idea; we had some very distinguished people in our group. In addition to Larry and Red, we had Jim Bouton, Eliot Asinof, Wilred Sheed, Ed Linn, the novelist David Markson, and the journalist Joe Flaherty. Even Philip Roth showed up a few times.

Anyway, I'd been bugging Ritter to do a follow-up to *The Glory of Their Times*, but he didn't want to do it. Finally, during one of the meetings of the Bobo Newsom Memorial Society, he said, "You do it." This was about the same time that my editor had asked me to do a baseball book. I said, "I can't do that, Larry. I'd be poaching on your territory." "That's nonsense," he said. "There are people out there to be seen, stories waiting to be told. Do it."

Well, not only did Ritter give me his blessings, but he also told me how to go about getting the job done, the logistics of it all: that is, how to find the players I wanted to see, how to approach them, down to how to run an interview. There's an art to interviewing, you know. It was a very unselfish, generous thing for him to do, but that's typical Ritter. If I had been a stranger walking through the door, he'd have been the same way.

On the subject of how to run an interview, I remember Larry saying, "You're going to be asking guys about things they might not have thought about for 50 years. So don't be afraid of long silences. They're taking their time, rummaging through their memories. You can tell when a man is thinking and when he's just sitting there waiting for the next question." That was one thing. Another tip was, never interrupt, and another, never correct them. Inevitably, they're going to get a date or a situation wrong; you've got plenty of time to correct it when you're transcribing. And, of course, you have to be prepared; before you even start the interview you have to have done your homework. Ritter never went with a list of questions, but I always did. Felt more comfortable that way.

So off I went, armed with Ritter's Rules for Interviewing Former Ballplayers, my knowledge of baseball history, and a tape recorder. And that's how *Baseball When the Grass Was Real* got started. The book was not only a commercial success but a tremendous critical success too. The reviews were most gratifying, so that encouraged the publisher to keep after me for more baseball books. As a freelance writer you have to follow the siren call, so baseball books were the direction

I took. I did four oral history books altogether, and then I started doing the illustrated histories on a variety of baseball subjects, and they have been successful too.

How did I choose the players for the books? Well, some of them, like Pete Reiser, had been my favorites as a kid. I would have been crazy not to take advantage of this opportunity to meet them, right? Some like Bob Feller, Lefty Grove, and Charlie Gehringer were icons of the game, while others were sturdy, longtime regulars, such as Elbie Fletcher and Doc Cramer, who are the backbone of any club. Still others I sought out because they had some particular historical interest. For instance, Dick Wakefield, in my second book, *Baseball Between the Lines*. He was the first big bonus player and quite a character . . . outspoken, irreverent, a natural for an interview.

Of course, I didn't want all the players to be from the same three or four teams, and I also wanted a mix of leagues and a mix of pitchers and hitters. Geography played a certain part in the selection process too. I didn't want to go out to the West Coast, so I missed some guys out there. I tried to keep it east of the Mississippi and, if possible, limited to anybody who was within a day's drive. Even so, there were plenty of guys to see, like Bucky Walters, Frank McCormick, Bobby Shantz, Gene Conley, and so on. I also went down to Florida because a lot of the older retired players lived there.

A great place for running interviews was Cooperstown over the Hall of Fame induction weekend. Boy, you'd have them all gathered under one roof at the Otesaga Hotel. That's where I spoke to Fred Lindstrom, Lloyd Wagner, Joe Sewell, and a few others. That's where I saw Lefty Grove, at Cooperstown. Lefty was quite a likable guy, but he could be temperamental, even volcanic at times.

We were sitting on the back porch of the hotel overlooking Otsego Lake. He was grumpy because autograph seekers had been pestering him all day. He'd just signed the last autograph, and we were finally alone. He turned to me and said irritably, "What the hell do people want autographs for? They just throw them away. It's nonsense." I agreed. I wasn't about to argue with Lefty Grove.

I got my interview and got away from him to let him have a little peace and quiet. I walked into the hotel lobby and then remembered: my brother wanted Lefty's autograph. Nobody else's, just Lefty Grove's. Grove had been his favorite player. I thought, "What am I going to do now?" after agreeing with him that autographs are "bullshit."

While I was standing there pondering my dilemma, with all these people milling about the lobby, I got an idea. A beautiful little girl with blue eyes and braided hair, who was about 10 years old, came by. I said, "Sweetheart, would you please do me a favor?" Pointing toward Lefty, I said, "You see that old man sitting out there? Ask him for his autograph." I gave her my pen and a piece of paper from my notebook, and off she went and got the autograph. Later on I saw Lefty again. We were sitting, talking with Ted Lyons, and suddenly Grove looked at me, narrowed his eyes, and said, "You didn't have the balls to ask me yourself, did you?" How did he know?

Clyde Sukeforth was a man I really wanted to interview. Sukeforth's playing career had been mediocre, but I knew he had a story to tell. He was the man who brought Jackie Robinson to Brooklyn to meet Rickey and who sat in the room when Rickey told Robinson that the color line was to be broken and that Jackie would do it. The story, of course, transcends baseball.

I tracked Sukeforth down in a motel in Nashua, New Hampshire. He was over 70 years old but still on the road as a scout, for the Braves, I think. He was a delightful gentleman, from Maine, who spoke carefully, to the point, and with dry wit. He was interesting enough, talking about his playing days, but then, when I asked him about Robinson, he really came alive.

It was as though he knew that Jackie Robinson had embossed the name of Clyde Sukeforth on baseball history. He spoke quite movingly of the whole experience, with a sharp memory for details and dialogue, and with obvious pride in his part in the episode. I was absolutely transfixed, for here I was, listening to the only living witness to what is a very important moment in American history and perhaps the most dramatic moment in baseball history.

For a long-cloistered writer like myself all the traveling I did for the oral history books was refreshing, but things didn't always go according to plan. Take my rendezvous with Pete Reiser, for example. I contacted Reiser at his home in California, and he said he'd be delighted to see me. At the time he was a roving batting instructor for the Cubs. I asked him how far east he came. Salt Lake City, Utah, he said. So we arranged to meet there, and out I flew. Well, while I was somewhere over Ohio, Pete's plans changed. Whitey Lockman had been canned as manager of the Cubs, and his replacement, Jim Marshall, wanted Pete as his third base coach. So Pete had to go straight to Chicago, with no way to reach me in Salt Lake City.

I arrived in Salt Lake City and no Reiser. After a day or so, I called his home, and there was a message for me: Come to Chicago. I backtracked to Chicago to meet him at the Executive House Hotel. The Executive House is a very large hotel, and would you believe when I finally got settled in there it turned out that I had the room right next door to his. We sat and talked baseball for two nights and one day and had such a good time doing it that we developed a friendship. Whenever he'd come to New York after that, for a banquet or Old-Timer's Day, we'd get together; and when we parted he'd always say, "See you in Salt Lake City."

The only time I was ever intimidated before an interview was when I was waiting to see Bob Feller. Let me explain why. When I was five or six years old, Bob Feller hit the big leagues like a cyclone. At 17 he was setting strikeout records. This was not a legend in the making but an instant legend. To my simple little pure-as-a-snowflake mind he had godlike proportions. Something like that gets in your head, you see, and stays there.

Well, it stayed there for 40 years, and it was there while I spoke to him on the telephone to set up the interview. He was working for some hotel chain in Cleveland, and now I was sitting outside of his office, shaking like a leaf. His secretary opened his door, announced my arrival, and the moment I heard him tell her, "In a minute," that old long-buried image of the godlike fastballer resurfaced in my mind; and I was thinking, "My god, I'm going in there to see *Bob Feller*!"

When I finally went into Feller's office, I was tongue-tied, and it took me a couple of minutes to shake off my stage fright. I asked a dumb question, and Feller, who is very candid, said, "That's a dumb question." But I recovered myself, started asking intelligent questions, and won him over because he saw that I knew baseball. Feller gave me a hell of a good interview, and, again, we became friends. Now whenever I see him, he gives me a big handshake and I don't mind admitting I still get a thrill out of it.

I tried to follow Ritter's rules of interviewing and generally found them to be successful. Really, they're just basic rules of etiquette which extend beyond interviewing and apply to the daily conversations you have with people. One day, however, I broke a rule and found out just how perceptive my mentor had been. Larry had told me never to pass on regards from one player to another unless that player had explicitly asked me to do so. Well, I was out in Wisconsin to see Burleigh Grimes, a tough, loveable, crusty old customer. It was Burleigh, who, autographing a piece of paper for a particularly irritating adulator at Cooperstown, handed the man the paper and told him to "reach behind yourself and stick it into the first opening you find."

I decided to break the ice with Burleigh by giving him regards from one of his old teammates whom I had previously seen. Well, the guy had never said a word about Burleigh, who immediately erupted. "That son of a bitch," he said. "We'd have secret team meetings and as soon as they were over he'd run and tell the reporters everything. When I found out, I was going to break his neck." Thereupon Burleigh sat in brooding silence for about 10 minutes, no doubt reliving all of the heresies of that particular teammate. It took me a while to coax him back to his genial self. After that, there were no gratuitous regards.

Just as there's an art to interviewing, there's a further art to writing them up. People who don't understand say, "Oh, it's easy. You interview 'em, then you go home and write down what they say." Well, there's more to it than that. As Ritter told me, you don't transcribe literally. Putting people on the page verbatim is a mistake. Using the craft you've developed as a writer, you have to put what's on the tapes through a creative distillation. And there's no harm in paraphrasing as long as you stay strictly in context, as long as you don't distort.

You also have to boil the interview down, get rid of the stuff that's repetitious or uninteresting. Sometimes I'd have 40 or 50 pages of conversation after I transcribed it because some of the interviews were pretty long. For instance, I was with Burleigh Grimes for eight hours.

After you boil it down, you have to structure the interview. The best thing to do is think of it as a story, and you ask yourself, "What's the best way to tell this story?" I always liked to open on a high note, but sometimes to vary it I used a chronological approach. With the Reiser piece I started with his anecdote about his getting invited to speak at the school for the blind in St. Louis. They kept inviting him year after year. Reiser said, "I don't mind coming, but why *me?*" The principal said, "Well, the kids are blind, and they relate to your problem of running into walls." That was an absolutely perfect start for the Reiser story.

I learned a lot from talking to the 75 or so players I spent time with. Some of the players I saw came to the big leagues in the early years of the century. They came from all different parts of the country, from cities, towns, farms. We didn't exclusively talk baseball either; they would sometimes talk about their parents, about growing up, about what life was like for them. It was insightful about people and places and different times.

I found that all the players had a tremendous sense of pride at having been in the big leagues. It was unspoken, but it was really in the air. They had a sense that they were special. Let me emphasize that this was my reading. Nobody ever said anything to this effect; there was no ego or pretense in these guys. But when you stop and think about it, you realize that ballplayers are special in this country.

And another interesting thing. The people I interviewed ran the gamut, from the highly intelligent and articulate, guys like Paul Richards and Freddie Lindstrom who provided tremendous insights, to the uneducated, less articulate. The one common denominator that united them all was that none of them ever said anything foolish about baseball. It was fascinating how perceptive they were about their game, every one of them. On their subject, their IQs were comparable to Einstein's on physics. You might disagree here or there on their interpretation, but everything they said about baseball was worth listening to.

Money was a factor seldom mentioned. For the players of 50 or 60 years ago the paramount thing was the joy of playing. I never detected any envy over the high salaries that today's players receive; wistfulness, maybe, but no envy. The old ballplayers seemed to feel that today's players deserved whatever they could get. None of them said today's players are overpaid; however, a lot of them said, "They're not as good as we were." There was also among some of them a grim satisfaction—I guess they were remembering how they were exploited and manipulated in the days when ownership was all-powerful. It reminds me of something Jimmy Dykes told me.

"In my day," Jimmy said, "if a player didn't behave himself"— which could mean almost anything—"we sent him to Shreveport, just to straighten him out. Teach him a lesson. The front office would call all the other front offices and say, 'We're asking waivers on this guy for disciplinary reasons. Don't claim him. You do us this favor, we'll do you a favor.' It was rough back then."

You know, I could have done several more oral history books, but after a while I began to tire of the travel. As far as I'm concerned, the best thing about travel is getting back home. Even so, after I'd finished with those books, I found myself still wanting to write about the game. Once baseball gets into your blood, it never stops foaming. So I came up with this somewhat mad, somewhat grandiose scheme to write the entire history of big league baseball in the twentieth century, doing it in words and pictures. I projected some 40 volumes. My friends told me I was crazy. I agreed, but maintained that while that was reason enough to do it, it was not reason enough to not do it.

I plunged right in, doing histories of each league, of the greatest teams, the greatest players, the greatest players by position; histories of decades, of the World Series, of the All-Star Game, of the MVPs, of the Rookies of the Year; big panoramic histories, a social history. I got caught up in the personalities, the folklore, the myths, the legends. It's bottomless, really. I once even thought about doing a book on every season since 1901 but then said, as I once did upon being handed the tab in an expensive restaurant, "I'm outnumbered here." But now I think I'm nearing the end of the project; there are at the moment 38 books finished, and it's getting time to explore new fields. And I don't mean ones where there are nine men in spiked shoes standing.

It's also true that I'm still as stuck on baseball as I've ever been. Even today, if I see some kids playing on the sandlots, I'll stop and watch for a while. One time I was driving somewhere, zipping along at a good clip, and out of the corner of my eye I saw a pitcher winding up and throwing. Just kids on a sandlot, but I had to see what happened next. Kept my eyes off the road until the pitch got to the plate. So there's a magic to baseball, and the less you try to explain it and analyze it the better off you are. It's a basic thing: you get a ball in your hand, you either want to throw it or hit it. What's so profound about that? Somebody throws a ball into the air, your eye is going to stay on it until the ball comes down. Baseball excites the instincts of the Noble Savage; refine them a few million times and you have a big league baseball, all deriving from something that at its core is childishly simple. Try to dissect baseball, perform an act of deconstruction on it, and you're going to come up with nothing. It's like cutting open a football to see what makes it take those funny bounces.

The old ballgame is enjoyable to write about because it's a storyteller's delight. By now it's created its own unique universe with its own mythology and folklore, its own deity (Babe Ruth), its own Lucifers (The Black Sox), and so on. It's an insulated universe, seemingly immune to what goes on around it . . . world wars, a depression. The goddamned game just goes on and on, popping up again every spring, maddeningly irresistible. It's like some good old reassurance from childhood, a talisman we carry with us. It was the most natural thing in the world for me to write about. So I did.

BASEBALL BOOKS BY DONALD HONIG

Baseball When the Grass Was Real. New York: Coward, McCann & Goehegan, 1975.

Baseball Between the Lines. New York: Coward, McCann & Goehegan, 1976.

The Man in the Dugout. Chicago: Follett, 1977.

The Image of Their Greatness (co-author). New York: Crown Publishers, 1979.

The Last Great Season (fiction). New York: Simon & Schuster, 1979.

The October Heroes. New York: Simon & Schuster, 1979.

The 100 Greatest Baseball Players of All Time (co-author). New York: Crown Publishers, 1981.

The Brooklyn Dodgers: An Illustrated Tribute. New York: St. Martin's Press, 1981.

The New York Yankees: An Illustrated History. New York: Crown Publishers, 1981.

Baseball's Greatest Teams. New York: Macmillan, 1982.

The American League: An Illustrated History. New York: Crown Publishers, 1983.

The Los Angeles Dodgers: The First Quarter Century. New York: St. Martin's Press, 1983.

The National League: An Illustrated History. New York: Crown Publishers, 1983.

The Boston Red Sox: An Illustrated Tribute. New York: St. Martin's Press, 1984.

Baseball America. New York: Macmillan, 1985.

The New York Mets: The First Quarter Century. New York: Crown Publishers, 1986.

The World Series: An Illustrated History. New York: Crown Publishers, 1986.

The All-Star Game. St. Louis: Sporting News, 1987.

Baseball in the '50s. New York: Crown Publishers, 1987.

Mays, Mantle, Snider: A Celebration. New York: Macmillan, 1987.

The Donald Honig Reader. New York: Simon & Schuster, 1988.

The Greatest First Basemen of All Time. New York: Crown Publishers, 1988.

The Greatest Pitchers of All Time. New York: Crown Publishers, 1988.

Baseball in the '30s. New York: Crown Publishers, 1989.

The Power Hitters. St. Louis: Sporting News, 1989.

Baseball: The Illustrated History of America's Game. New York: Crown Publishers, 1990.

The Boston Red Sox: An Illustrated History. New York: Prentice-Hall, 1990.

The Chicago Cubs: An Illustrated History. New York: Prentice Hall, 1991.

The Greatest Catchers of All Time. Dubuque, IA: Wm. C. Brown, 1991.

The St. Louis Cardinals: An Illustrated History. New York: Prentice Hall, 1991.

The Cincinnati Reds: An Illustrated History. New York: Simon & Schuster, 1992.

The Greatest Shortstops of All Time. Dubuque, IA: Brown and Benchmark, 1992.

The Philadelphia Phillies: An Illustrated History. New York: Simon & Schuster, 1992.

The Plot to Kill Jackie Robinson (fiction). New York: Dutton, 1992.

Last Man Out (fiction). New York: Dutton, 1993.

Shadows of Summer: Classic Baseball Photographs 1869–1947. New York: Viking Studio Books, 1994.

8

BILL JAMES

For the last decade Bill James has been the most influential person in baseball, as he has challenged the saws of conventional baseball wisdom and led the search for objective baseball knowledge. James first displayed his genius for "the mathematical and statistical analysis of baseball records" in self-published books which appeared annually from 1977 to 1981. For the next seven years The Bill James Baseball Abstract *was published commercially (by Ballantine Books) and revolutionized the way fans, the media, and baseball insiders think about the game. Not merely or even primarily a statistician, James is a graceful, witty writer who abandoned the* Abstracts *to produce a new annual (*The Baseball Book 1990 *was the first in the series) that employs an expository-historical, rather than statistical, approach. James has worked as a consultant on arbitration cases involving major league players, won the 1986 CASEY Award for* The Bill James Historical Baseball Abstract, *and co-hosts a nationally-syndicated radio program called "Baseball Sunday." A native Kansan and a graduate of the University of Kansas, he lives with his wife, the artist Susan McCarthy, and their two children in Winchester, Kansas.*

I ALWAYS FELT there was something special about today, December the 2nd. I got my first pair of glasses on December the 2nd, and I've worn them every day of my life since and I will until I die. One year my father, who was a carpenter, lost part of a finger in an accident at work, and that happened on December the 2nd. Growing up I got interested in Napoleon for a while and was amazed to find out that he also felt there was something special about December the 2nd. He seized power for the first time on December the 2nd, arranged his subsequent coronations on December the 2nd, and he was married, I think on December the 2nd. So it's quite a coincidence that you're here to interview me today on December the 2nd.

Of course, I've always been more interested in baseball players than Napoleon. As a kid I liked Mickey Mantle and Minnie Minoso. Since I grew up in Mayeta, Kansas, my favorite team was the Kansas City A's, but they changed players every two months so it was hard to get attached to any particular A's players. I guess Ed Charles was my favorite A's player. However, my heroes were actually writers rather than ballplayers. I wanted to be Jim Murray and to write funny columns about sports like he did.

I didn't talk about this with anybody. I don't talk about what I'm going to do, and I never have, not even when I was 10 years old. If you talk about what you're going to do and it doesn't work out, then you look stupid. Even now, it's very hard for me to talk with people I work with about what we have to do.

I read a lot when I was a kid . . . Perry Mason mysteries, *Reader's Digest* condensed books, whatever older people would bring into the house. Around 1961 or 1962 I read everything Ed McBain, the mystery writer, had written. Incidentally, after that I didn't read anything by McBain for 25 years or so until I picked up one of his books a couple of years ago when I was on a promotional tour. Since then I've been trying to read all his books I've never read, but it's a real challenge. In the last three years I've probably read 60 Ed McBain books, and I'm still eight or nine books behind. By the time I read them, he'll have written two or three more, so I'll never catch up. The funny thing is I don't like mystery stories in general.

I've always felt that if I had grown up in a larger town it's equally likely that I would have become a movie critic, a writer about movies, because I love movies for the exact same reasons I love baseball games. But Mayeta was such a small town that it had no movie theater, and my family had no TV. But we did have a radio so that's what I fastened on. It was inevitable that I got hooked on baseball because it transmits very, very well over radio.

As I said, I always wanted to be a baseball writer, but as to the kind of baseball writer I became, two things happened in September 1967 which influenced that. One, the team for which I had always rooted, the Kansas City A's, picked up and left town, leaving me emotionally separated from the game. And, two, I went to college to begin my education. I was too much of a baseball fan just to stop thinking about the game, but I no longer had the emotional attachment to it that I had had before. In college I majored in both English and economics, so I started taking what they taught me in economics classes and applying it to baseball. That's more or less how I became what I became.

While I was in college, by the way, I read all of Faulkner's novels. I love Faulkner because he's so liberating. He doesn't follow anybody's rules but his own. When I write, however, I try to follow Hemingway and write simple declarative sentences rather than long complex sentences full of convoluted clauses.

The first article I ever submitted for publication was "Baseball Fielding Statistics Do Make Sense," which *Baseball Digest* bought and published in their March issue for 1976. I sold *Baseball Digest* a couple of more articles, and then I thought, "What do I do now?" I contacted a small publication called *Baseball Bulletin* and started doing a column for them. So I succeeded in getting several things published before I got any rejection slips, which was a very fortuitous thing. An awful lot of people who start out as writers begin by trying to sell a book idea to a publisher like Harper & Row, and, of course, they've got a 99.999 percent chance of being rejected. After dealing with a certain amount of rejection they give up and do something else. I started out at the very bottom of the market and had some success, which is why I'm still writing today.

The idea of doing the first *Baseball Abstract* didn't occur to me until January 1977. By that time I had reached the point at which I wanted to do things that *Baseball Digest* and *Baseball Bulletin* weren't an appropriate market for. I decided that I'd write enough articles to make a book, have the books printed and staple-bound at a quick printer, and sell them myself. If I had had any idea how difficult self-publishing would turn out to be, I would never have undertaken it. And since I didn't start the first *Baseball Abstract* until January, I didn't get it out until after the season had started. It wasn't worth a shit either.

At that time I was working as a night watchman at the Stokley–Van Camp plant in Lawrence, Kansas. It wasn't a very demanding job. Once an hour I had to go around to check all the doors in the plant, and that would only take about 20 minutes. Otherwise, I was supposed to just sit there and watch the front door and answer the phone if it rang, which it never did. So I carried the little research materials I had at the time to the plant and worked through the night on them.

I'm sure that people thought I was underachieving at a tremendous rate. I was 25, and my friends were getting out of law school, still wondering what the hell I was doing. But I knew what I was doing, so I didn't worry too much about what my friends thought. I'm kind of immune to peer pressure. On the other hand, my mother, who died when I was a small child, might have successfully discouraged my writing ambitions. If she had lived, I'm sure she would have been enthusiastically suggesting that I get some kind of "career" job. My father, who was not an ambitious man, wanted me to succeed, but he always understood that it was my life, and he didn't have any inclination to tell me how to run it. My family is like anybody else's family. There are high achievers in my family, but there are an awful lot of people in my family who aren't high achievers. I think everyone just assumed that I was one of the latter.

My wife Susie has always been very supportive. Whenever I would talk about maybe getting a regular 9-to-5 career job, she'd say, "You don't want to do that." It's another interesting coincidence, by the way, that we went on our first date the day I mailed off that first article I ever published to *Baseball Digest*. Susie denies it, but when we first met she didn't know who Willie Mays was. Now, she's a big baseball fan and more knowledgeable than the average fan. In fact, she often remembers to apply ideas of mine to specific situations when I forget to.

Anyway, I had no idea in the world how many copies of the first self-published *Abstract*, if any, I would sell. I had 150 copies printed and sold about 70. In an attempt to sell them I took out a little ad in the *Sporting News*, which strained my budget considerably; however, most of the sales were probably due to my column in *Baseball*, which contained a credit line explaining what the book was and how people could order a copy.

In the next few years I began writing articles for some pretty good publications. I wrote an annual piece for *Esquire* for several years, and one year they wrote a blurb about me and the book for their editorial column called "The Inside Page." That sold several hundred copies of that year's book. And then there was an article about my work in *Sports Illustrated* in May 1981, which pumped up sales of the book quite a bit, to the point that that last self-published *Abstract* sold about 2,600 copies.

Nobody but fans bought the first edition of the book, but, with the second edition in 1978, some baseball insiders started buying it. People in baseball are always looking for information, and at that time I was publishing information which wasn't really available anywhere else, although in retrospect the information is so primitive it seem ridiculous. I won't identify the front office people who bought the book because it's not my place to use somebody else's name to promote myself, but I will admit that I got a big kick out of their reading the book. Out of the 300 copies of the second edition that sold there were actually about 20 that were bought by people who had national reputations in fields other than baseball. There was a nationally known author, a well-known movie director, and a star of a TV sit-com. It was amazing how many people among that small group of 300 were recognizable people in the culture. This probably says something about them more than it does about me: that for whatever reasons these celebrities were active in seeking out information about baseball.

The biggest factor in the *Abstract* being picked up by a commerical publisher was the *Sports Illustrated* article. It was written by Dan Okrent, a reader of the early, self-published *Abstracts*. I didn't know Dan at all before he contacted me in 1979 about doing the article. It took almost two years after Dan wrote the article for it to materialize because of the way things work at *Sports Illustrated*. To be blunt about it, *Sports Illustrated* is the most political publishing institution in the world. Everything at *Sports Illustrated* is a political battle before it gets done. The article about me is a perfect example of what I'm talking about. It got scheduled to be run and then pulled; scheduled to be run, then pulled . . . god knows how many times, before it actually ran. Camps lined up in favor of the article and against the article, and battles were fought over it. Of course, it was far more important to me than anybody else in the world whether the damn thing ran or not. *Sports Illustrated* is a wonderful publication, and I'm always glad to do things for them and to work with them on projects, but I could never work for them full time because the politics would drive me up the wall.

After the article finally came out, Dan Okrent recommended me to a literary agent who read the article, realized that my work had some credibility, and agreed to represent me. Three of four publishers were interested in publishing the next *Abstract*, so we weighed the offers and took the best one. We went with Random House because they were willing to sign a three-year contract on the book. The three-year commitment was important because I didn't want to be in a position where we might put one out and, if it didn't sell, I'd be right back where I was before.

The first *Abstract* that Random House published sold pretty well. In fact, it was on the bottom of a few bestsellers lists. The second one sold better. It leveled off after that because the market fractured. I don't think it ever actually went down, but once there were 17 competitors for it, then it leveled off. I think it was impossible for it to grow at that point. Random House printed around 140,000 copies of the last *Abstract* and sold about 90,000.

The Historical Baseball Abstract was such a natural idea that it would be impossible to say who generated it. I mean, how could you do an annual book like I did and not have the idea of doing a historical book using the same methods? All I did was take the same sort of questions I had been dealing with in the annual books in talking about Reggie Jackson and other contemporary players and apply them to historical figures. Also, since you can't build a good book out of one idea, I came up with the other ideas, such as "The Decade in a Box" and the reference section, and combined them with the main idea to make the *Historical Abstract* a unique book. Still, I wasn't entirely satisfied with the *Historical Abstract.* And that's because the idea of a book as it exists in my head is so much better than the actual book; I always feel very disappointed with the actual book. That's true of every book I've ever written.

This is not just the difference between the ideal world and the real world. I can always look at one of my books and see things I could have done to make it a better book. For example, I might wish that I had done some of the research better, or I might wish that I hadn't said something I said.

This is related to one of the ways I'm like my father. We were quite poor when I was growing up, and one of the reasons we were is that my father was completely unrealistic in evaluating what he could do. When he bid on a carpentry job, he's look at it and say, "Oh, yeah. I can do that for $300." And then it'd take him four weeks to do the job, with three of us working. I'm very much the same way. I don't know why, but I absolutely cannot learn to be realistic about what I can get done in a certain time frame. I always think that I can get much more done between now and Christmas than I can get done between now and Valentine's Day. It perpetually interferes with my ability to plan out what I'm going to do. So I always wind up feeling that if I had more time to spend on them my books would be better than they are.

There's an on-going discussion about baseball, and when you're young, when you're 24, you just want to make a contribution to that discussion. By the time you reach 40, you begin to worry about the quality of your contribution as well as the quantity. One of the main reasons I stopped doing the *Abstract* after the 1988 edition is that

I was no longer pleased with the quality of my contribution to the discussion. I had unmistakably changed the way that baseball was being reported, and it probably wasn't an entirely positive change. If I'd persisted in doing the *Abstract* much longer, it certainly wouldn't have been a positive change.

For example, I'd be watching a game on TV, and there'd be a graphic on the screen: "83 percent of his RBIs have come in the first seven innings of the game." I thought, "Good lord, am I responsible for this crap?" I wasn't directly responsible for that graphic, but at some point it had been my idea to stop and check to see what percentage of somebody's RBIs came in the late innings of a game. Then other people started doing things like that. I'm not taking full responsibility for all the statistical trash that comes out of TV sets during ballgames because I'm not fully responsible for it, but I was contributing to it. And I decided that I didn't want to contribute to it any longer.

I was always shocked at how little other people understood the fundamental ideas of what I was doing in the *Abstracts*. I guess it sounds arrogant for me to say this, but I always wanted to be imitated. I always wanted other people to pick up the things I was doing and say, "I can do this too," and, "I can do this better," because it's fundamental to the approach to knowledge. The reason that systematic knowledge is ultimately more powerful than subjective knowledge is that one person can pick up what another person has done and improve it. I mean, Tony LaRussa certainly knows vastly more about baseball than I do, but when Tony LaRussa dies everything he knows will more or less die with him. When I die everything I know will more or less remain behind me because my knowledge is systematic. And other people will be able to take things that I know and add to them and improve them.

For this process to work other people had to have also tried the types of things I was doing. And they have tried to do them. My work's been imitated all to hell. But what I didn't anticipate was that it would be imitated so badly. I thought that other people who would try the statistical analysis of baseball would be as good at it as I was. They ain't! They by and large fall in love with methodology and forget to work through the logic carefully. In general, they want to start with the numbers, shake them real hard, and see if something interesting falls out. And it doesn't work like that. You have to start with the game and listen very carefully to it, and then find a way to trace what people are saying through the numbers relating to the game to emerge with an end product.

The basic misconception people have about my work is that they think it's about numbers. And it isn't. When I was doing the *Abstracts*, I simply used numbers in an attempt to find the answers to basic, fundamental questions which intrigued me: At what age does a player peak? Do lefthanders really hit better against righthanders, or is that just something we talk about? Do the players today really change teams more than they used to? It seems to me that many people doing statistical analysis of baseball concentrate too much on the numbers and wind up tracing a very short path in their work. The path goes from a page of numbers through the writer to you, the reader. It doesn't start in a question or subject that somebody is genuinely interested in, and it doesn't make a course through a logical evaluation of what the question or subject means. It's simply, "Here's a number that's interesting; let's go with it." I still hope that the situation will change, and, in fact, I'm sure that people will come along who will be very good at the statistical analysis of baseball. But I'm very amazed at how long it's taken for these people to emerge.

There was another reason I stopped doing the *Abstract* after 1988. What I tried to do in the player comments section of each year's *Abstract*, rather than evaluate the players fundamentally, was tell the reader something he didn't know about each player. This was in keeping with my general philosophy that I always want the reader to learn something he didn't know previously. In the early days it was easier to do this. In 1981 the average baseball fan didn't know that 72 percent of Bob Horner's home runs came at home. The average fan didn't know that Bob Horner didn't really have a lot of power if you took him out of Atlanta–Fulton County Stadium. The average fan didn't know that Dave Parker was one of the rare left-handed hitters who had more power against left-handed pitchers than against right-handed pitchers. As the years went by, the public was more and more and more aware of such things, and I was driven to find smaller and smaller and smaller pieces of information to pass on. By the end of the *Abstracts*, I was passing on really small and trivial information in a desperate attempt to stay ahead of the discussion. The discussion was drifting more and more in that direction, not entirely because of me, of course, but partly because of me; and I felt it was time to stop and to find out some other kinds of information to tell people. And that's what I did with my latest book, *The Baseball Book 1990*. Basically, what I did was take out the statistical picture as the resource to draw on and replace it with a historical picture. People think I still do statistical analysis, but I don't. That's not my job anymore. I've changed the type of research that I do.

The Baseball Book has sold well, better than the first *Abstract.* The most popular part of the book seems to be the biographical section. It's my favorite part of the book too. There's a slight problem with the biographical section though. As you know, we only got halfway through the letter *A.* To finish it, all the way through *Z*, I'll have to live to be 150. That reminds me of the old story about the Roman engineer who insisted that he not be paid for designing a bridge until 20 years after the bridge had been built to make sure that the bridge wasn't going to collapse. Well, we're not like that in America. It would be nice to produce the biographical encyclopedia by itself, in one big tome or as a series of volumes, but if I were to start doing the biographical encyclopedia by itself, doing nothing else at all, it would take at least 10 years to finish it. And that's with help from my assistant Rob Neyer and other people as well. I would have to be self-disciplined enough to keep churning out three entries a day for 10 years, and I'm not that self-disciplined, let's be honest. Moreover, a publisher would have to make a 10-year commitment to the project, and that's not going to happen. So, we'll have to take it year by year, a chunk at a time. It will eventually be finished. If I live to be 60, 20 years from now, the whole thing will be out, either from me or from somebody else.

By far, the most important discovery I've ever made is the fact that you can predict a player's major league batting performance based on his minor league record. If you were with a major league team and you were reading Bill James, trying to find out "What is there in here that is useful to me?", by far, the most important thing would be that minor league batting stats do predict major league batting stats.

The second most important thing is that the stability of performance for power pitchers is vastly greater than the stability of performance for finesse pitchers. Take two 25-year-old pitchers with the same won/loss record and the same ERA. Let's say they're both 18-8 with ERAs of 3.00, but one of them is Roger Clemens, and the other one is Jeff Ballard. It's not only more likely that the power pitcher, Roger Clemens, will still be pitching 10 years later than the finesse pitcher, Jeff Ballard; it's probably 100 times more likely. It's an entirely different world.

I have very good evidence that some major league organizations realize these things. There are people in major league organizations who call and ask, "Do you have this year's Major League Equivalencies done?" I won't tell you which major league organizations these people are with, but it does happen. So I know these people are paying attention.

In general, the reaction of organized baseball to me and my work is a lot different now than it was five years ago. I wouldn't say that I'm an insider, but I'm no longer an outsider in the way that I was even five years ago. A lot of it is just the changing of generations. A lot of current major league ballplayers read the *Abstract* when they were in high school, and they accept implicitly my right to do what I do. At first, ballplayers were quite irritated that I was presumptuous enough to say, "This guy's a good ballplayer . . . this guy isn't," never having played the game myself well enough to talk about it. This is no longer an issue. I've done it long enough now that no one questions my right to do it.

Despite my discoveries, there are many questions about which I've never been able to come to a satisfactory conclusion. Lineup selection is a good example. Does it really make any difference? Should Ryne Sandberg bat second for the Cubs? It seems very curious to me that a guy who's maybe as good a hitter as there is in the National League hits second. I don't have any real evidence that it's wrong; it just seems curious to me. Probably the best way to study the question of lineup selection is through simulations: plug the Cubs lineup into a computer model and let them play about a thousand seasons with each lineup and see which is most effective. But there are a lot of problems with that method too.

I haven't really been able to decide whether or not clutch hitting exists either. My attitude toward the notion of clutch hitting is almost precisely the same as Earl Weaver's as expressed in *It's What You Learn After You Know It All That Counts*; which is that some players do hit a little better in some situations than other players but that way, way too much is made of it.

Look at Mickey Tettleton of the Orioles. He doesn't drive in any runs with runners in scoring position for three or four years in a row; he walks an exorbitant amount of times; and he hits .160. I don't believe it's coincidence. I believe it's part of his game. It's not that Tettleton doesn't hit in the clutch but that the pitching pattern to him changes with runners on base. With a runner on second and first base open, pitchers are going to pitch carefully to a good hitter. If you pitch carefully to Mickey Tettleton, you're going to walk him because he won't swing at bad pitches.

I was never able to do a proper study of clutch hitting because the information needed to study clutch hitting first started to be collected as recently as 1983 or 1984. And it takes several years of that kind of data before you can really do anything with it. We've reached the point now at which the information to do a good study of clutch hitting exists, but to my knowledge nobody has done it yet.

And then there are the strategic questions. I've looked at all of them and come to no conclusions; primarily because the number of variables that enter into each situation makes it almost impossible to evaluate that situation with the degree of accuracy you need in order to know for sure what you're talking about.

For example, let's say the Cardinals are playing in Atlanta–Fulton County Stadium. Vince Coleman is on first base with Terry Pendleton at the plate, facing a right-handed pitcher with the wind blowing in. Should Coleman run? If you really measure the percentages, you'll find that the Cardinals's chance of winning the game if Coleman doesn't run will be .3833. Their chance of winning the game if he does run will be something like .3835. If he's successful, the team's chance of winning goes clearly up, and if he's unsuccessful, then their chance of winning goes clearly down; but if the outcome is unknown, it's virtually dead even. So the decision to run or to not run is nearly a dead-even proposition in nearly every case you'd want to consider. In order to evaluate which would be the better thing to do, have Coleman run or not run, you'd have to know how Pendleton would hit, how he'd be affected if he took the pitch; you'd have to know how he hits this particular pitcher; you'd have to know how he hits in this particular park; and you'd have to know how all these things would be changed by the fact that the wind is blowing in. The number of trials to establish these things precisely just doesn't exist. A major league players' career isn't long enough to have the number of trials that you would need in order to know for sure what the percentages are. Strategic decisions like this are nearly impossible to evaluate, so I never really spent that much time on them. We'll always be able to second-guess the manager because we will never know enough that we know for sure what the right decision in any situation would be.

There are exceptions to this. Should Red Sox manager John

McNamara have lifted Bill Buckner during the 1986 World Series and gone with a healthier player at first base? There's no argument that he shouldn't have. He wouldn't have lost anything significant by doing so. So obviously, as things turned out, he should have lifted Buckner. So there are cases where there are clear blunders, but they're damn rare. Most of the strategic decisions made by managers that we argue about are petty little things.

This is one reason I'm not crazy about evaluating managers. I don't really expect anybody to believe I'm qualified to evaluate them in the first place. In the second place, as I said before, I feel that when you read one of my articles you should know something specific at the end of it that you didn't know before you read the article. Whether I think Lou Piniella is a good manager or not is not real knowledge. It's just b.s., so I try to stay away from it.

It's very frustrating for me to read books in which people chew on air. I don't like books in which people take nothing and try to stylize it into something interesting. It doesn't work. You have to work with information.

I certainly don't have a strong enough self-image to write without constantly presenting new information. If I weren't giving the reader anything but myself, I would feel extremely exposed and very vulnerable. I try to make my writings as lively as possible, but I hope that people will read my work for the information that it contains. That's what my work is all about.

BASEBALL BOOKS BY BILL JAMES

The Bill James Baseball Abstract. New York: Ballantine Books, 1982–1988.

The Bill James Historical Baseball Abstract. New York: Villard Books, 1986.

Bill James Presents the Great American Stat Book (co-author). New York: Villard Books, 1987, 1988

This Time Let's Not Eat the Bones. New York: Villard, 1989.

The Baseball Book 1990 (co-author). New York: Villard Books, 1990.

Bill James Presents Stats 1991 Major League Handbook (co-author). Morton Grove, IL: STATS, Inc., 1990.

The Bill James Player Ratings Book. New York: Collier Books, 1993, 1994.

The Politics of Glory: How Baseball's Hall of Fame Really Works. New York: Macmillan, 1994.

The Bill James Guide to Baseball Managers. New York: Simon & Schuster, 1997.
The New Bill James Historical Baseball Abstract. New York: Free Press, 2001.
Win Shares. Morton Grove, IL: STATS, Inc., 2002.

9

PAT JORDAN

*Though gifted with a blazing fastball, Connecticut schoolboy pitching sensa-
tion Pat Jordan did not last long in the minor league organization of the
Milwaukee Braves, and his perplexing failure was a shattering blow to him
and to his family. However, with time, maturity, and the discovery of another, unsuspected gift within himself, Jordan transformed his athletic failure
into the remarkable literary achievement of* A False Spring *(Dodd, Mead,
1975), one of the most beautifully-written baseball books ever published. As
a freelance magazine writer, he has demonstrated an unusual ability to produce strikingly honest and perceptive profiles of notable persons from a wide
spectrum of occupations; especially controversial were his profiles of Steve and
Cyndy Garvey (for* Inside Sports*) and of Pete Rose Jr., (for* Gentlemen's
Quarterly*). In addition to* The Cheat *(a baseball novel) and* The Suitors
of Spring *(a book about pitchers), Jordan has published a book about a black
high school football coach, one collection of profiles of female athletes, and
another of retired professional athletes. He lives and works in Ft. Lauderdale,
Florida, where he and his wife are body-building enthusiasts.*

I WAS IN BASEBALL for three years. When I got released, I went back
home to Connecticut, and I didn't leave the house for six months. I
was shell-shocked because I was the golden boy who had to come
back home a failure. I was embarrassed, and my pride was hurt.

The hardest part was that my failure was so indefinable until I
wrote *A False Spring* that I couldn't explain it to people. If you get a
sore arm, you tell people, "I hurt my arm," and that's the end of it.
But how do you tell them that you got all mentally screwed up, that
you forgot how to pitch. You can't do that. So I didn't want to see
anybody.

For a while I worked construction, digging ditches; then I worked for a mason. Finally, I pulled myself together and started taking some college courses. Before that college was just a way of pleasing my parents, but now I got into it. It took me seven years to get through Fairfield University, and by the time I graduated I had three kids, more than any of the professors had. I supported myself during this time with all the usual odd jobs: soda jerk, clothing salesman, gas station attendant, more construction.

I also played semi-pro basketball for $50 a game, and the coach of the team was the sports editor of the local newspaper. One night I complained to him, "I need a night job. I want to go to school during the day, and all these part-time jobs during the day are killing me. I need one job at night." He said, "I'll put you on the sports staff." And he did even though I knew nothing about the business. I couldn't even type. And never in the furthest reaches of my imagination did I think of writing.

I was 23 then, and my job was to write the little headlines for the high school basketball games: "Harding Beats Central 59-58; Smith Scores 20." Pretty soon I was taking the little stories about the games over the phone, but this was still beginning at the absolute bottom. I was no Truman Capote who had wanted to be a writer since he was 12 years old. My writing career began by complete accident.

One day I wrote a story for the newspaper about a kid who got killed in an auto accident. I had met him one time when he was hitchhiking, and I wrote about that. It was a nice little piece. People called up the newspaper to say how much they liked it, and they stopped me on the street to congratulate me. It was ego gratification and the first ego gratification I'd gotten since I left baseball. I loved it. That got me thinking about writing as a career.

I mentioned this to an old sportswriter at the paper who was an alcoholic and a big smoker. He was hunched over his typewriter with a bottle of bourbon on his desk, a cigarette dangling from his mouth, and ashes spilling down his shirt. I said to him, "You know, John, I think I'd like to be a writer too." He said, "Well, Pat, I owe everything I am in life to this business." So I looked at him and thought, "Holy shit . . . this is my future?!"

After I graduated from college in 1956 I got a job teaching English at an all-girls high school, and I kept the newspaper job too. I did both. Eventually, it got to be too much, and I quit the newspaper job; however, another newspaper gave me a weekly column for $50 a week. And again, I started getting positive feedback.

One week I had nothing to write about, so I did the column on

Ron Hunt who'd just made the major leagues with the Mets. I wrote about when we were kids in the minor leagues, and everybody around town loved it. Naturally, I wrote three or four more columns on the same subject. Then I collected them and sent them to Al Silverman at *Sport* magazine. Silverman bought them, and that was the beginning of *A False Spring*. That was when I really began to think about writing a book about my minor league baseball experiences.

I sold that piece to *Sport*, and I thought, "Great! I'm on my way." Then Silverman didn't give me an assignment for a year, and altogether I only did four pieces for *Sport* between 1970 and 1976.

In 1970 I did a story for Norm Smith at *True* on Phil Niekro, who'd just won 20 games for the first time the year before in 1969. *True* gave me $1,500 for the story, and I was only making $6,000 a year as a teacher. Norm Smith said, "I'm going to give you four stories a year, guaranteed." I thought, "Four stories a year at $1,500 a story. . . I'm going to quit teaching." And I did. I turned in my resignation at the end of the year.

Two months later, in June, I went to Norm Smith's office, and there's another guy sitting in his chair. I said, "Where's Norm Smith?" The guy says, "He got fired."

"Well, I'm Pat Jordan. I'm supposed to do four stories a year." He says, "I don't know anything about that."

So I had no job, no connections, five kids by that time, and $3,000 in the bank. It was too late to go back to teaching because they'd replaced me by then. I told my wife, "Alright. I'm going to write all summer, and when the money runs out, I'll have to get a job digging ditches again."

I started writing stories, and I sent the first one I wrote, which turned out to be part of *A False Spring*, to *Sports Illustrated*. Ray Cave, who was the editor then, called me in, and I thought he was going to buy the story. Instead he said, "The reason I called you in is that you might become a writer, but this thing doesn't work. It's too self-pitying." At the time I was into blaming the Braves for my failure without realizing that it was me. You know, I was going to get even with everybody. Cave said, "Here's $400. Go home, and whenever you do write this book," meaning *A False Spring*, "just let us see it." They wanted first crack at running an excerpt. That's what the $400 was for.

A couple of weeks later I called Ray up and told him that there was a kid in my area being heavily scouted and that I wanted to do a piece on what these old scouts were like. He gave me an assignment to do a little 1,000-word piece for the back of the magazine. I went to this high school ballgame, and all the scouts who'd scouted me were there. We ended up sitting there for hours, telling all kinds of stories. I called Ray back and told him that I was on to a big story, that I needed 5,000 words. He gave me the go-ahead, I did the piece, and they bought it for $1,500. Since then, June 1970, I've been writing from story to story. I write a story, sell it, then scramble around and write another one.

Ray Cave was the best editor I ever worked with. He's the one who helped me re-focus *A False Spring*. The first draft was really embarrassing. I started one chapter that was about me on the way down: "There's nothing more depressing than when your life is like an empty pie plate containing nothing but the last crumbs of success." I was really working at the self-pitying angle. But it was good because I got it out of my system. I still have the first draft somewhere back in Connecticut. Someday I'll drag it out and read it again.

The original title was "The Days of Wine and Bonuses," not *A False Spring*, and I found the eventual title at the movies, indirectly. A lot of writers read when they have trouble writing. When I have trouble writing, I go to movies. When I was writing *A False Spring*, I saw *American Graffiti* and *The Last Picture Show* about 20 times because they both put me in that 1959 mood frame. I'd go but I wouldn't really watch the movie. I'd just immerse myself in the images. The whole tone, the whole mood of that McCook chapter in *A False Spring* came out of *The Last Picture Show* . . . the small town in the middle of nowhere, the girl looking for a way out, all that stuff. The movie would put me in the right mood, and then I'd go home and write.

Anyway, I went and saw a lousy movie called *The Alice B. Toklas Cookbook*, and while I was watching Alice and Gertrude Stein and Hemingway in the movie, I remembered *A Moveable Feast*. I left in the middle of the movie, ran home, dragged out *A Moveable Feast*, and saw the quote about "a false spring," and immediately knew that that would be the title of my book. I'd been a Hemingway buff for years and had read *A Moveable Feast* five or six times, but it wasn't until I saw that Alice B. Toklas movie that it all clicked.

The first question everybody always asks me about *A False Spring* is whether or not I really got the girl in McCook, Nebraska, pregnant. In the book I call her 14 years later, and she tells me that we have a child. But I've always felt that when I got off the phone I was never sure whether or not I edited the conversation to coincide with the guilt I had had over the fact that I hadn't treated her well. So to this day I don't know whether that was a distortion of reality or precisely the conversation that we had. I've never tried to find out for sure because I think it's better this way. I wrote it in the book as if it were a fact, but I don't know.

My first wife was pissed at me, but she got over it, mainly because I told her the same thing: I'm not sure that the conversation as I wrote it in the book really happened.

I think what happened was that I was so terrified I was going to burn in hell after having sex with this girl that I didn't want to see her again and I treated her badly. Then I transferred that guilt onto this conversation and made myself look worse than I was, which is something I did in a lot of places in the book. I did that mainly to free me up when I talked about other people. In other words, if I'm that hard on myself and make a couple of negative comments about somebody else . . . Ron Hunt, say . . . then nobody's ever going to be able to say I made myself come off as this golden hero and dumped on everybody around me. Whenever there was a question of balance, I always weighted it against myself. I never gave myself the benefit of the doubt.

For instance, I wasn't that stupid, even when I was a green rookie in McCook, to come up to two guys on the team who were talking to girls and say, "Who are the cunts?" I didn't do that. I might have said, "Who are the 'broads'?" or something. I wasn't *that* stupid but I made myself look that way because it's very difficult and dangerous to write a first-person book that people sympathize with. Even when you do something noble, if you write it, people don't like it. It sticks in their craw.

Tennessee Williams said that whenever you use the first person you should always be perceived by others. Let other people or characters look at you, rather than you look at yourself because when you look at yourself people will find it difficult to accept your writing about yourself in a positive way. So *A False Spring* is a lot of me looking at other people, and when I do look at myself it's always in a negative way: my failure, my betrayal, my cowardice, my misdeeds. Very rarely in the entire book is there anything positive about me. You'd have a hard time finding places where you could say, "Oh, there's where Pat was a good guy."

One of the few times I was a good guy was when I didn't screw that girl who borrowed $10 from me and wanted to repay me the only way she could. I didn't screw her because I knew it was wrong.

But in the book it becomes something different that, again, makes me look worse than I was. I made it look like a perception that had been imposed on me that I didn't want but that, once it had been imposed on me, I was bound to it; so that even though I didn't screw her I wanted to. And I made it look like an unwanted perception. It wasn't. I knew I shouldn't do it. I knew it wasn't right, and I didn't have to have an epiphany.

Those were the distortions in *A False Spring*: to always give myself a little negative twist to allow me the freedom to say exactly what I thought about a lot of other people.

In retrospect, the simple explanation for my failure was fear of failure. I was afraid of failure. When I didn't have the instant success in the minor leagues that I'd had in high school, I started to panic. When I panicked, I started to press; and when I pressed I got wilder and wilder and tried to throw harder and harder. It was stupid. Finally, I got so panicky that I started to listen to the wrong people who told me to change my motion and just throw strikes. After I changed my motion I lost my rhythm altogether and I never could get my original motion back.

I throw all right now. Last fall I tried out for the Miami team in the Senior Professional League. I only had two weeks to get ready though, and I rushed and hurt my hip. But I was throwing all right, and I might do it again. I might take this whole summer to get in shape to pitch this September when they start practice again. The problem is that I've been lifting weights so much, I've become somewhat muscle bound. I used to have long, thin arms and a whip-like motion, but now I can almost see my arm going over my head in slow motion.

I still get letters and calls from people who've read *A False Spring* and were moved by it. More and more I hear from women who tell me that their husbands hounded them to read *A False Spring*, but they resisted because they didn't want to read a baseball book. A lot of the letters say something like: "The husband and I got divorced, and I was throwing his stuff out and saw *A False Spring*. I was going to throw it out, but I figured, 'What the hell, I'll read it.' . . . Now I know why he wanted me to read it, and maybe if I would have read it sooner I would have understood him more." That kind of stuff. It's always some kind of emotional response; it's never simply: "I liked the book."

I knew *A False Spring* was a great book. I know when I'm doing something good and when I'm not. It was so easy to write that book it was just like filling in the blanks. It took me two years, but it was absolute pleasure. It took me six months to get going, to write the first chapter, but once I wrote the first sentence it was all over. I knew the whole book. Hemingway said, "All you have to do to write a book is write one simple declarative sentence." Write one *true* simple declarative sentence, and you've got a whole novel. And to this day that's how I work. I don't write a story until I get the first sentence. Once I get the first sentence, the story's done.

Everybody who loved *A False Spring* hated my novel *The Cheat*. It's Holden Cauldfield without the innocence. I've got a friend, Eddie Kaplan, a sports deejay, who reads everything I write and loves everything. The only thing he hates is *The Cheat*, but then again he doesn't think Ellen Barkin is sexy. I told him, "You've got a screw loose, Eddie. If you don't think Ellen Barkin is sexy, then I don't worry that you hated *The Cheat*."

The Cheat is supposed to be a baseball novel. That's the assignment I got. The publisher gave me one sentence: "The Elmer Gantry of baseball." They gave me one sentence . . . and $70,000 . . . "Do the Elmer Gantry of baseball." And that's what I wrote. The publisher loved it, but it didn't sell because my readers didn't associate it with me. With *A False Spring* I'd built up about 20,000 readers, but I don't think even 1,000 of them associated *The Cheat* with *A False Spring*, and so they didn't buy it. And a lot of people who did buy it were put off, not so much by the sex, but by the hardness of the main character, Bobby.

Everybody thinks the main character is me, but I patterned him after me and Bo Belinsky. A lot of the things that happened to the character happened to me, but a lot of the character's style was Bo. I kept thinking, "What would Bo do in this situation; what would Bo say?"

There are other characters in the book that everybody swears are real, and people think they know the models for these characters. For example, the villain wasn't Steve Garvey as everybody assumes. It was another guy, and I won't mention his name. And then there are characters I didn't model after anybody. The old baseball writer living in the mobile home . . . everybody thinks he was a real person, but he was completely fictitious.

Every novel is autobiographical, and I always worried whether I'd be able to fill in those gaps between the autobiographical events and people and those I'd have to totally invent. And I think I did it with

ing engagements. I don't speak. I don't go anywhere. I basically do nothing but sit here and write everyday until two o'clock in the afternoon.

I have a list of things to write about on the wall, and when I don't have an assignment, I'll pick something off the list and write a story. And I'll just send it around myself. I don't have an agent.

I write a certain number of pieces for *Gentlemen's Quarterly*, and they pay me a certain amount of money, but that's only year to year, and they can cancel the agreement any year they want to. I also have an arrangement with Whittle Communications of Knoxville, Tennessee. Whittle publishes a large format magazine like *Life* that they give to doctors for their waiting rooms on the condition that there are no other magazines in the doctor's office. That way they cut out magazines like *Time* and *People*. They have six different sections, like Personality, Family, Sports, Health, etc., etc. They pay very well, and Mario Puzo, John Updike, all the big names have written for it. But you never see it unless you're in a doctor's office. Everytime somebody says they saw my story in *Whittle*, I say, "What was wrong with you?" They think I've been spying on them, but I know they had to be sick.

When Ray Cave gave me magazine assignments for *Sports Illustrated*, he used to say, "Go there and tell me what you see." That's all. For a while I thought everybody worked like that, but then I realized that wasn't the case. Finally, I asked Ray, "Why do you always tell me that? You never give me any other directions besides 'Go tell me what you see.'"

He said, "Pat, I do that because you see things in such a screwy way." At first I was hurt; I thought he meant I was a little crazy. But he said, "You're not really crazy, but as a writer you see something the way everybody else would except it's just four degrees off, and that changes it all. You're not like Hunter Thompson who goes and sees something in *Fear and Loathing in Las Vegas* and then turns it around 180 degrees to create his own fantasy. You see what everybody else sees except it's off just enough to make it a different story. That's why I send you out there."

I've never forgotten what he said. I never thought I saw things off base. I thought I saw them the way everybody else did.

People think I sit down and think about my subjects and analyze them. I don't. They can't believe that I don't work at it, but I never worked at throwing a fastball. Why was I able to throw a ball so fast? It was a gift. And the second thing that was given to me, I think, was the ability to perceive certain truths about human nature. It's not a moral thing. It's just like being six feet tall instead of five nine. And it's what you do with it that counts.

When I get an assignment from a magazine I usually don't know much about the subject. When the stories are my ideas, they're almost always positive. I don't present a negative idea. I don't say, "Oh, I hate that asshole. I want to call my editor and do a story on him." For example, I told *Gentlemen's Quarterly* I wanted to do a story on the actress in *Pretty Woman*, Julia Roberts, and it wasn't just because I liked the movie or the fact that she's pretty and sexy. There was something about her that made me think she was a nice girl. So generally I begin with some kind of positive feeling. But sometimes my impressions are 180 degrees off.

The Pete Rose story for *Gentlemen's Quarterly* began with the idea that Pete Rose Jr. was probably a carbon copy of his famous father. I figured that his father had made him into a clone, "Pete Rose II." It turned out that the kid was so far removed from his father it was night and day. He was nothing like his father. He was a sweet, sensitive kid.

I liked Karolyn Rose a lot. I don't understand her fixation on her ex-husband. I liked Pete's daughter Fawn a lot too. Nobody knows about her. She hides because she's overweight. But she's pretty and very bright. She was the most objective of all of them. When the story came out, Karolyn denied everything, and Pete Jr. denied everything, so my editor at *GQ* called me up all worried. I told him, "Look, the day Fawn Rose denies what she said will be the day I'll write a retraction"—because I know that girl won't lie. Afterwards Pete Jr. would say, "Oh, my father's a good guy," and Karolyn would say, "I didn't say all those things." But nobody could ever get Fawn to say a word about the story being untrue.

The original idea for the Garvey story in *Inside Sports* had nothing to do with the Garveys at all. I saw Bucky Dent and his first wife Stormy on the *Stanley Siegal Show*. She was complaining bitterly about how she hated being the wife of a star: it wasn't all it was cracked up to be. So I thought about that and decided it would make a great story to do two wives: one who hated being the wife of a baseball star and one who loved it. And I knew that Nancy Seaver loved it. So I called *Inside Sports* and gave them the idea. They loved it but said, "We can't do a Yankee and a Met; it's too New York. We've got to get somebody from another team, another city." They suggested Cyndy Garvey. They said Garvey's wife loved it.

So I go out to California to see Garvey, and by the end of the first day I find out that although she used to love it *now* she hates it. I call up *Inside Sports* and say, "There's no sense in doing Stormy now because I've got somebody who both loved it at one time and now hates it, so I've got both stories in one girl." And that's how that story came about.

The story ran as I wrote it except for one thing, and I've never forgiven them for this. They were so stunned by the story that they couldn't believe it. *Inside Sports* knew it was going to be a big story, but they just couldn't believe it was so good. They gave it to Pete Axthelm, who was *Newsweek's* jock writer, so that he could tell them it was good. And right away he said, "Well, you gotta rewrite the lead, you gotta do this, you gotta do that . . ." And Axthelm fucked it up royally. When they gave it back to me and said, "Here's what Axthelm did," I said, "Good. Let him write the whole fuckin' story. You're not running it." I eventually took it back and rewrote the lead myself, but I've never forgiven *Inside Sports* for that. That's why I quit doing stories for them. They wanted to sign me to a contract, but I was too pissed.

I'd rather be a writer than a pitcher. Pitching was an innocent thing I did. It was absolutely innocent and physical in the sense that it was a boyhood thing. You don't grow up wanting to be a writer; you grow up wanting to be a baseball player. I loved to throw a ball. I still do. I love to watch a ball spin when I release it. I love to make it do things, and I love to throw it over the plate. But I wouldn't want to be a baseball player anymore. Have somebody tell me I have to cut my beard? Or tell me what kind of clothes I have to wear? Or tell me I can't have a drink tonight, or that I have to be in bed by a certain time? Or live with 25 other guys, 23 of whom I can't stand? I couldn't live with all that.

And I do love writing more now. Throwing a ball was satisfying but on a very elemental level. Writing is so much more complex. If I only played baseball, I probably wouldn't be very nice. I'm not one of those guys who's naturally nice, you know what I mean? It's not my nature to be a nice, easy-going guy. I'm competitive and egocentric, and baseball would have given me every opportunity to let these things go wild and people would still kiss my ass because I was a big-deal baseball player.

As a writer it's different. In *A False Spring*, for instance, I learned what was wrong with me as a 20-year-old kid. So everytime I write something, I think it makes me better. Once I write about my stupidity in a certain way, I can't be like that anymore because it's too engrained in my consciousness. If I write about what an asshole I was over this particular thing, now I'm trapped. Once you admit it and write about it, how can you be an asshole in that way again? You can't. So writing forces me against my nature, step-by-step, to be better. That's one reason I love writing.

I'm such a writer now that I focus only on what I'm doing in the present. As far as I'm concerned, *A False Spring* is out there sort of like my Little League no-hitters. It's no longer part of me. It exists by itself. I find no identification with it. When I write something, it's over with. Then it's not mine anymore. Obviously, I'm glad my name is on it instead of somebody else's, but that's not my first perception of it . . . the fact that it's "my book." I mean I can talk about it in the abstract or in the third person in the same way as I'd talk about a building without thinking in terms of the architect. The building exists by itself.

Just like stamps, which I've been collecting since I was 10 years old. I don't know who engraves the stamps, but I collect them because they're little miniature works of art. They exist all by themselves. They're not mine except when it comes time to sell them. But I like them because of the way they look. I appreciate *A False Spring*, but it's mine only in a very tenuous way.

Put it this way. If somebody said, "Okay, Pat, you can't write anymore and we'll give you $150,000 a year and you'll have written *A False Spring* and *The Cheat* and a couple of other books and that'll be your legacy or whatever, but you can't write anymore. Or you can keep writing; you can keep writing whatever you want until you die, but we're going to erase *A False Spring* and *The Cheat*," I'd erase *A False Spring* and *The Cheat*. I'm a writer. All I have to do is write.

BASEBALL BOOKS BY PAT JORDAN

The Suitors of Spring. New York: Dodd, Mead, 1973.
A False Spring. New York: Dodd, Mead, 1975.
Sports Illustrated Pitching. New York: Harper & Row, 1977.
The Cheat (fiction). New York: Villard Books, 1984.
A Nice Tuesday: A Memoir. New York: Golden Books, 1999.

10

ROGER KAHN

Roger Kahn was a struggling freelance writer in 1972 when he published The Boys of Summer *(Harper & Row), a poignant memoir based on his two-year tenure as the* New York Herald Tribune*'s Brooklyn Dodgers beat man. The book quickly became a huge popular and commercial success, immortalized the Dodgers of the early 1950s, and today reigns as the most famous and most literate sustained piece of writing on baseball in existence. Kahn later produced five other baseball books, including the 1985 CASEY Award–winning* Good Enough to Dream *(Doubleday, 1985), a warm and thrilling account of Kahn's season as the president and principal owner of the Utica Blue Sox, who won the 1984 NY–Penn League championship;* Joe & Marilyn: A Memory of Love *(Morrow, 1986), a fascinating analysis of baseball's most notorious romance between Joe DiMaggio and Marilyn Monroe; and the ill-fated biography of baseball's fallen favorite son,* Pete Rose: My Story *(Macmillan, 1989). In 1987 Kahn was inducted into the Brooklyn Dodgers Hall of Fame, and in 1988 he was the guest of President Ronald Reagan at a private White House showing of* The Winning Team, *the film biography of Grover Cleveland Alexander starring a young Ron Reagan. Forthcoming from Kahn is a memoir of his son Roger Laurence Kahn and a book about New York baseball in the 1950s.*

YOU'D LIKE TO KNOW how the *Boys of Summer* got started? Well, sometime in the 1950s I went from the *New York Herald Tribune* to *Newsweek,* which was memorable only because I got to know John Lardner, Ring Lardner's son. Later the *Saturday Evening Post* asked me to become an editor-at-large, which meant that I'd write a certain number of stories a year. Some were sports stories but not many. Around 1967 Al Silverman, who has become chairman of the board of the Book-of-the-Month Club, had *Sport* magazine and said, "It's our 20th anniversary. Would you do a retrospective on 20 years of baseball?"

Well, I'd gotten away from baseball a little bit, and I told Silverman that I really wasn't the person to write the piece. Silverman kept after me anyway.

Now, Billy Cox had always fascinated me because he, rather than Brooks Robinson, was the best glove at third I've ever seen. And he'd been in the first wave at Guadalcanal or Anzio which had done terrible things to him . . . being under mortar fire for five days, hearing all those screams of death. Cox never spoke about that, but we'd have little talks about things that interested me, and he had a kind of wit. He drank and would disappear from the team for a few days and then come back. And there was, of course, still in my head after I had switched my allegiance as a kid from playing first base to third base the idea that if Cookie Lavagetto, my childhood Dodger hero, was a good third baseman, then Cox was a matchless third baseman. I also remember this little black glove Cox had used that Vin Scully used to say he got at Whalen's Drugstore for $3.95. Billy simply fascinated me. He was very hard to write though; I only wrote once or twice about him because he didn't say much. So finally I told Silverman—lord knows why—"Look, I'll do a 20-year baseball retrospective for you if you let me find out where Billy Cox is so I can just go say hello to him."

I don't know where that came from, but it was something I wanted to do passionately. And Silverman said, "Sure." I then found out where Billy was and phoned him down in Newport, Pennsylvania.

I said, "What are you doing?"

He said, "I'm the substitute bartender at the American Legion hall." Substitute bartender? Billy Cox?!

He said, "The hall's not hard to find. You come to Newport, make a left at the Gulf station, and go up the hill."

Who the hell knew where Newport, Pennsylvania, was let alone the Gulf station. But I made my way, found the American Legion hall on top of one of those severe hills you find in western Pennsylvania. And there was Billy, now with Falstaff's belly, but the face was the same.

Newport was an old railroad town through which the railroad had stopped going. Three or four old and hostile-looking people, hostile to an outsider, were sitting at barstools, wearing the striped caps that railroad engineers wore.

I was excited to see Billy, and Billy was excited to see me. He ran out from behind the bar, and then he said, "You seen me. Could I play ball?"

I said, "Billy, you were the best damn glove I ever saw."

He turned to these guys drinking beer, guys who'd been drinking beer since the trains stopped running, and he said, "You hear that? A New York writer said that."

And I got a stab. I felt the same way Pete Rose felt about being cut from the Western Hills High School football team. "When I got cut from the team," he said to me, "it was a pitchfork in my heart."

It was a pitchfork in my heart when Billy said, "A New York writer said that." Why do I have to tell these solemn bastards that Billy Cox was a great player? Why don't they know that? Why don't they know what the glove was?

I wrote the piece for *Sport,* but the meeting with Billy stayed with me as I was finishing a book about the Columbia University student uprisings called *The Battle for Morningside Heights.* I wanted to do more with Cox, but I was practical enough to know that I had to finish the book I was supposed to finish before I could go to work on another one. So I finished *The Battle for Morningside Heights,* and I began to find out where the Dodgers were.

I knew that Roy Campanella was in a wheelchair in Tarrytown, New York. I knew Clem Labine's son had lost his leg in Vietnam. And Jackie Robinson I always saw. I knew Robinson was a great man, and I wasn't going to let that get away. If there was any kind of excuse, I'd say to Jack, "Let's have lunch." And he'd say, "Why?"

"Well, we can talk about Goldwater and Nixon and Rockefeller." Robinson was very interested in Republican politics.

And I knew that Jack had gone through an ordeal with his child. Jack and his wife, Rachel, didn't know what to do with Jackie Robinson Jr. He was a good athlete and a fine student, but he was always in trouble. The Robinsons sent him to a private school for kids with problems, but that didn't help much. Finally, they suggested to young Jack that he join the army, a European way of dealing with a difficult child. "The army will make a man out of you," you know.

And Jack Jr. joined the army. He had some of his father's hand-eye coordination, so he became a great rifle shot. He starred in Vietnam, was a terrific rifleman in Vietnam. But he also learned about heroin there and came back and dealt, didn't just use, but dealt heroin in the Stamford, Connecticut, railroad station.

In a hotel near there he was picked up, and he actually drew a gun on a detective. Somehow he wasn't shot. He was disarmed.

After that terribly painful scene, a young journalist who'd never seen Jackie Robinson play baseball said, trying to get him to talk,

"Mr. Robinson, it must comfort you to know that you have helped so many children with your career."

And Jack said fighting back tears, "I couldn't have helped many children. I haven't helped my own son." The boy had just been arrested.

I just had this powerful feeling that "I want to get this down. I don't care how broke I am when it's over, or if I have to go to work for *Time* magazine writing dreary stories for dreary editors, I am going to get this book finished. This is the book I am going to write."

I got a relatively small advance, $25,000, small because I would have to travel the whole country and at least half the advance would go for traveling expenses; but I was doing this as a book of moral purpose. I thought it was a book that should be done, and I wanted to do it.

In order to survive, I had to agree to do a medical book, the story of "the training of 10 surgeons in a hospital." Once in a while I went to work in this hospital, but finally the chief surgeon wrote a letter saying, "I don't think we are going to continue to cooperate with you. You're more interested in these boys from Brooklyn. You admire Jackie Robinson more than you admire me." That was true.

I took some money on the medical book because at that time I had three children, an ex-wife, and a current wife who didn't work. I felt I was supporting a large part of the United States of America. I was making no progress on the medical book, and now this surgeon pulled out, for some good reasons and for some crazy doctor-type reasons. I remember wondering what would happen if Harper & Row found out. I wasn't going to lie, but I didn't have to volunteer anything either.

As I began talking to these extraordinary ballplayers, they became less Olympian, less god-like, and more human, and I started gathering these wonderful human stories. Doing the book was encountering the people; it wasn't interviewing. As I saw them as older, they saw me as older. All of them were too polite to say that. But it was emotional for all of us. *The Boys of Summer* was a very emotional book to write.

When I finished, I had no thought of a number one bestseller. But I thought I had done good work. And I also thought that the children continuing to eat meant that I had to do something fairly lucrative, but I didn't know what. I figured that this was probably the last book I would ever write and that, as I said, I'd probably be doing dreary stories for a news magazine.

The lady I was married to then was Alice Russell. One of Alice's comments during the course of the book, about a year and half into it was, "I'm becoming the world's outstanding expert on Pee Wee Reese under the age of 35." At the end I had $380 left in the bank. I probably owed back alimony and probably owed back taxes. So I said to Alice, "This is something pretty good. Work that I'm proud of. Maybe the children will be proud of it and you will be too. We have $380; we might as well have nothing. Let's throw a party and invite everybody in New York we care about."

Alice went to a gourmet food store, Zabar's, and bought a Norwegian salmon which she poached. And everybody that we cared about in New York City who was free came.

Jackie Robinson had never visited my home. I don't know if it was some subtle black-white thing or not, but he'd never come over. I said, "I've finished the book." Jack was not the kind of guy who'd say, "Congratulations!" He'd say, "Well, that's what you get paid to do, right?" That was Jack, hardnosed conversationally. So I said, "I'm having a party, and I'd like you to come. And I'd like to thank you for helping me."

He said okay and asked what time, how many people, and all that. He came without Rachel. I had a sense he was checking out the party, to see if this was some kind of red-neck party transposed to New York. Jack didn't know my friends. We were close, but maybe I was a secret racist. There were no racists at the party.

Two things happened that night which I remember very clearly. One of my guests was Howard Fast, who was either a Communist or a fellow traveler. In either case, Fast, who wrote *Spartacus* and *Citizen Tom Paine* among other books, was far left. And it was then public that Jackie had diabetes. There was a couple at the party who had a diabetic child, and Jack was talking to them about living with diabetes and how you could live a rich and full life with the disease. Jackie was in no way aggressive. He was actually quite shy. He just found this couple with trouble where he could help them.

And suddenly Howard Fast said, "Why did you testify against Paul Robeson?" Right here is Arthur Ashe's book, *Hard Road to Glory*, about black sports in America, and in it Ashe talks about Paul Robeson's leftist "siren song in bass," which is from Jack's testimony. Robeson said, "If the United States went to war with the Soviet Union, no black person would fight for America because he has nothing for which to fight." That was public statement. Congress asked Robinson to come, and Robinson said, "I'm not an expert on Communism, Fascism, or any other 'ism'. I'm only an expert on being a Negro in the United States because I've had 30 years of experience at it." Great forgotten speech. And somewhere in that speech he says, "We must not listen to this siren song in bass." Well, this offended the extreme left, and Fast said to Jackie, "How could you possibly testify against Paul Robeson?"

Jack was startled and not ready for that because he was comforting these people about their daughter. And he said, "If Branch Rickey had asked me to jump off the Brooklyn Bridge I would have done that." Fast began to lecture Robinson on politics. At that point I stepped between them, and I can laugh today when I say if Fast had said one more word I was going to hit him.

If Robinson had hit him, he would have knocked him 10 blocks! But I was not going to have anybody be that rude to Jack. And Jack was upset. Who wants to have his politics challenged at a party? I don't think there's anything in Robinson's statement to Congress that he ever had to apologize for.

So the evening went on, and more drinks were served, and Zero Mostel was there. Suddenly, Zero shouted in the booming voice of Tevya, the "Fiddler on the Roof": "MISTER JACKIE ROBINSON!" Robinson, who had his back to Zero, cringed. His shoulders went up, and his head went into his shoulders. He turned as if to say, "What now?"

Then Zero said, "You . . . are . . . my . . . hero!" And he walked up and hugged him.

So the party winds down, it's Monday morning, and now we have $80. We've blown the $300 on the salmon and the booze. And I just had no thought of where I would go; I didn't want to go work for *Time*. Well, the phone rang, and it was somebody from Harper & Row saying, "Have you heard? Have you heard?"

My editor was cruising the Aegean Islands, so this was the editor's assistant. And she said, "*The Boys of Summer* is the main selection of the Book-of-the-Month Club." That was about $100,000. I went from $80 to $100,000 that quickly, and I thought, "If there is a God, I wish he'd stop playing these games with me."

The book did well, though it was sharply attacked in the beginning by numbers of people. It got a terrible review in *Life* by Wilfrid Sheed. He said, "This is about eight ballplayers" . . . it's about 13; he said my parents were "immigrant culture-vultures" . . . my great grandmother was born in New York, and both my parents were born in New York. And he said that I "romanticized" the players; "they're really oafs." A cocktail waitress told Sheed that the players were poor tippers, and that was the basis for the *Life* magazine comment on the book. Some years later Wilfrid Sheed wrote a novel that didn't do anything called *The Boys of Winter.* So I'd like to give him not a CASEY Award (for best baseball book of the year) but a chutzpah award. He couldn't stand *The Boys of Summer* and then wrote a book he called *The Boys of Winter!*

The *New York Times* gave it to a woman to review, in what was a parody of women's liberation. She said that any sports book which begins with a line of poetry can't be all good. That's from W. C. Fields: "Anybody who hates dogs and small children can't be all bad." Then she said that the book had much too much about the *Herald Tribune* and much too much about growing up in Brooklyn. Finally, she said I was all wrong. The 1952 Dodgers were not so great. The 1955 Dodgers were great. Well, she was full of it. Because the 1955 Dodgers were the 1952 Dodgers older and slower. Robinson didn't get better from 1952 to 1955; Pee Wee Reese didn't get better. Cox was gone, Gil Hodges didn't get better, Campanella didn't get better. They got older. And now, instead of being 30-ish, they were 33-ish, 34-ish. The Yankees also got older. The Dodgers finally won the World Series in 1955 because Johnny Podres pitched a good game and Sandy Amoros made a fine catch in the seventh game.

So I was thinking, "Geez, what do I have to do?" They were pummelling me. And there was another slap in the face. Roger Angell had a collection of *New Yorker* pieces called *The Summer Game* come out in the same spring. The *Times* carried a front-page review which said I was Vinegar Bend Mizell and Roger Angell was Warren Spahn. How terribly cute. The reviewer called *The Boys of Summer* a pastiche of New Journalism and obscenity. The word "fuck" appears once in 550 pages.

Ed Fitzgerald was running the Book-of-the-Month Club, and as *The Boys of Summer* got to be number one, he took me to lunch at a place I had never been before, the Banker's Club. After a few martinis he asked, "I bet you think you beat the bad reviews in the Sunday *Times.*"

And I said, "I think I did. Mostly because I'm number one."

He said, "Think of how many more books you would have sold if you had gotten the reviews you deserve."

Newsweek's review was great. Most reviews were great, but you

remember the ridiculous shots people take at you. Jonathan Yardley
said, "It's two books. It's a book about his growing up, and it's a
book about these players." Well, no, it's not two books; it's one
book. I was pleased after the documentary of *The Boys of Summer*
came out, and the *Times* movie critic said it left out the sense of what
Brooklyn was like and of what growing up in Brooklyn was like.
Good call. I believe you need an Aristotelian sense of place. *The Boys
of Summer* begins with my father and me in Brooklyn. It begins with
Sam Leslie and Pete Coscarart and Lonnie Frey, who made 55 errors
in a good year—they're not Boys of Summer. It ends at the tomb of
Ebbets Field. It's all one; it has the Aristotelian unity of place. And I
get somebody saying, "It's two different books."

Later there was a love feast between many people and the book,
and as it went on and on, one day the editor at Harper & Row called
me and said, "I have a bottle of Chivas Regal. Come over, and you'll
be pleased when you see why I have the bottle of Chivas Regal." He
had the Sunday *Times* book review which showed that the book was
number one, and he asked, "How does that make you feel?"

Well, I didn't feel anything. I just felt dazed. I'd written the book
I'd wanted to write. It was certainly nice to get a little money and pay
off the medical book I didn't have to write anymore. But I felt dazed,
and after a while I said, "Gosh, I hope it doesn't fall to number two
next week." It stayed up there an honest eight weeks. Some writers
will say, "My book was number one for 41 weeks," and people don't
look it up and they get away with it. But there's no reason for me to
do that. *The Boys of Summer* was on the list for 25 weeks, number one
for eight.

Two weeks after the book came out Gil Hodges died. I was in Philadelphia then, and the *Philadelphia Inquirer* ran a headline, "It's Winter for the Boys of Summer." I was doing a TV show, *Live at Five* or
whatever the hell it was, and the interviewer asked me, "Do you
think Gil Hodges' death is helping the sales of your book?" That
remains the worst question I have ever been asked.

Dick Cavett brought in some of the players, and we did his show.
Everybody was excellent: Reese, Clem Labine, Joe Black, and Carl
Erskine. I told a few Bums stories. For instance, Frenchy Bordagaray
seems to be out at the plate but may have a chance if he slides. He
doesn't slide, and he's tagged out standing up. Casey Stengel says,
"For Chrissakes, why didn't you slide?" Bordagaray says, "I was
gonna, Case, but I was afraid I'd crush my cigars." That was 50 . . .
50 Depression dollars.

In another one, Bordagaray was standing on second base tapping the bag with his foot, and ZIP, "Yer out!" They picked him off. "Case, he musta caught me between taps."

Erskine talked with great beauty about raising a Downs Syndrome child. Black talked about growing up black, also with great beauty. Labine talked about visiting his son in a hospital where there were 32 people like Clem Labine Jr., who had lost a leg in Vietnam, and in the ward there were two wheelchairs. He said, "This war is costing this country more than a million dollars a day. I think for a million dollars a day we ought to be able to afford a wheelchair for every kid who's lost a leg in Vietnam." The audience stood up and cheered. So the book goes into, I think, the America of the time and is not just about curveballs and sliders.

Reese talked about Robinson, and I guess we all talked about Robinson. And there was no Robinson on the show. After a while, Joe Black or Pee Wee or somebody called me and said, "Gee, why wasn't Jack on the show?"

I said, "I don't know. I don't produce the Dick Cavett show."

But I called the producer about it, and he said, "Oh, god! We just forgot."

So then they had a special segment for Jack. And, in truth, Jack wasn't very good. He was embarrassed by all the praise that we had given him. Right after that Jack called me and said, "You son of a bitch, the fan mail has started again."

There was some talk that because he was a Republican and an executive in capitalist industries that Jack was an Uncle Tom. The book showed some of the fire in Jack. Long after that sad October day when Jack died, I was pleased that my book had made him current again in the last summer that he would know.

The Boys of Summer was quite a long book, more than 700 pages on my typewriter. Some of the stories were quite searing. There was a New York City B'nai B'rith dinner giving Gil Hodges the Baseball Sportsman of the Year Award. I went there and Erskine had come in. I congratulated Gil and went off to Toots Shor's restaurant with Erskine.

I said, "I can't finish this. It never ends. These stories are so searing to my soul. I can't get this finished."

Erskine gave me a Knute Rockne pep talk. He said, "Roger, the story should be written, and everybody is counting on you. Pee Wee is and Jackie is and I am, and you're the only person who can do this. If you don't do this, we'll all be forgotten."

The next day I shook the cobwebs out of my head, and I started to finish the book. That was Carl Erskine's gift to me.

You saw that poem at the house, hanging on my living room wall, called "My Masterpiece" by Robert W. Service. It ends:

A somber way I go tonight,
With all my thoughts and dreams remote,
Too late a better man must write
The little book I never wrote.

Carl Erskine transcribed that poem in his own hand for me in 1987, saying that this was for me from my friend Carl Erskine for "having the courage to finish this book that no better man had to write."

I framed that on paper which will last for a long time, and I wrote Carl how moved I was by it. And then I wrote, "Ps. You owe me $40.00 for a frame." We can joke around like that.

When Furillo died, Erskine did a eulogy—how hard that must have been to do. He said, "This man was velvet and steel." The little part of the eulogy printed in the *New York Times* read to me like Carl Sandburg. Erskine told me, "Isn't this amazing? You always wanted to be a major league ballplayer. And I have always wanted to know literature and music, and we're so close."

So when he did the Furillo eulogy, I didn't make any joke at all. I just said that describing Furillo as velvet and steel sounded like Carl Sandburg. I told Carl, "You are a poet." I thought that was the nicest thing I could tell him. So you joke, and you don't joke.

Shoot, the three strongest guys on the team are dead: Robinson, Hodges, and Furillo. What do you make of that? I don't know what to make of it. We're getting to an age where we're all going to go.

Four different newspapers, including the *Los Angeles Times,* asked me to do a Carl Furillo obituary. I decided the piece should go in a New York paper because Furillo played in New York; he wasn't a Los Angeles Dodger. He had a couple of burnt-out years there. It was 10 o'clock at night, and I had some of the piece done. I was upset because Furillo was such a good fellow, and life was so cruel to him, even giving him leukemia while he was working four nights a week as a watchman because he had no money. He'd say, "Everybody's got to work, even writers, ha, ha." And as I was lying here in bed, resting, I found tears on my face. I thought, "What are you crying for?" Then I thought, "Carl Furillo is worth tears."

The Boys of Summer brought us all closer together. After my son died, I was touched that Pee Wee called to comfort me. I know how hard it was for Reese to have made that call . . . because when Jackie Robinson's son died, I called. When Jack answered the phone, I wanted to say something, but I choked up for a second. I finally said, "Jack, I'm trying to tell you you have my love."

Jack said, "You don't have to tell me that. By making this phone call you already have."

So when Reese called me, he said, "You remember, I was the captain. I just wanted to say for all the fellas . . . we are very, very sorry." As Erskine said, "A family is more than blood."

Yes, I suppose that I'll always be known as the author of *The Boys of Summer,* no matter what else I write. Certainly it was my reputation as the author of *The Boys of Summer* that got me invited to the White House in 1988.

Contrary to your assumption, I was personally predisposed to like Ronald Reagan. I remember him saying, "No, no, not Ronald Reagan for president. Jimmy Stewart for president; Ronald Reagan for best friend." I'd seen a lot of Reagan movies, and there'd been a few glimmerings of a poetic soul in his speeches.

Politically, no, I wasn't predisposed to like Reagan. My father was a New Deal Democrat, and I wasn't very happy with the war in Vietnam, and I was close to Eugene McCarthy. I covered him, he liked my story, and he wrote me a "thank you" letter. And then when I wrote the book about the Columbia uprising, *The Battle for Morningside Heights,* Gene wrote the foreword, for a hundred dollars. He typed it himself. Seven pages. He wrote me a letter saying, "Here is a foreword for your book. If it's too long feel free to cut it. If you don't like it, feel free to use none of it. Regards, Gene." So McCarthy and I became pretty good friends, and that kept me in the ranks of the Democratic party along with my anti-Vietnam sense.

So here comes Reagan: "Oh, god, now the country's in the hands of the extreme right wing." Of course, it didn't work out that way. I liked from the beginning that Reagan would quote from *Pilgrim's Progress* and talk about the "shining city on the hill." I liked his eloquence, his respect for beautiful language.

Then the Challenger tragedy happened. There's a poem I read in high school during World War II written by an Army Air Corp pilot that begins, "Oh, I have slipped the surly bonds of earth . . ." It's a sonnet and a very beautiful sonnet. Unfortunately, I don't remember more than the first line, but the young pilot died over Germany. The beginning of the poem stuck in my head, and now Challenger goes down, probably the most horrible live thing ever on television. And there was President Reagan saying to the families of these seven brave people that he had read a poem once and it began, "Oh, I have slipped the surly bonds of earth." I think if you like my kind of poetry, I'll forgive a lot.

And finally, he did this amazing thing with Gorbachev. It was the first time the United States and the Soviet Union both said, "we're going to unscrew these warheads, take them apart, and blow them up in front of each other." A tremendous achievement for President Reagan.

The left-liberal press then said, "Well, Gorbachev did it all." No, he did not. Takes two people to do that. I don't go with the line that Mikhail Gorbachev did it by himself.

I thought, "Tremendous President Reagan. There are still homeless people in New York City, no national health insurance, and lots of other problems, but you did this one thing which may end the cold war."

So, on a July night in the summer of 1988 I found this message on my machine, "Please call the White House." I thought, "What could they want but that I go there to appear at some function." It turned out not to be a function. It turned out to be a private party given by the president of the United States.

When you get invited to the White House, you're on your own on travel arrangements. This is not the Cincinnati Reds when you climb on a charter. There was no written invitation, but I was told: "Sports jacket and tie. Dessert, soft drinks, and coffee. It will be a private party in the family screening room."

I drove down from Croton-on-Hudson, New York, to Washington, D.C., and it was the greenhouse summer and frightfully hot. I got to the hotel, and I was in no way nervous, but I discovered that I had brought a couple of sports jackets, several pairs of pants, a bunch of shirts, and no tie. I had to walk out in this oppressive heat to go shopping, and it turned out that the cheapest tie at the store nearby was $50.

I put my pin from the Brooklyn Dodgers Hall of Fame in my lapel, and I thought, "If I don't know what to say to the president of the United States, I can say, 'This is the pin from the Brooklyn Dodgers Hall of Fame,' and maybe he'll say something." That was my escape method.

When you went into Reagan's White House, bearing in mind that he'd been shot, they checked you carefully and through two different X-ray machines. They also asked for a photo ID, but all this was reasonable in view of what happened to Reagan.

I finally was ushered into a room where there were a series of small tables covered with white table cloths with the rose garden beyond. I was a little bit early, but then a few more people started to come in: Connie Mack, the Republican congressman; Wilmer Vinegar Bend Mizell; Joe Garagiola; Terry Smith, Red's son; and Shirley Povich, the distinguished columnist for the *Washington Post* these many years. Not many people and no Nancy. This was for a screening of *The Winning Team.* Then I realized that even the president of the United States would like to have a couple of friends around on Friday night to watch a movie and talk a little baseball.

After a while the president appeared. About eight of us were standing in a row, and he said his hellos, pausing very graciously for a moment with each of us. I think Lynn Faulkner, the White House social secretary, said my name, and he paused for a minute. Right away I said, "This is a button from the Brooklyn Dodgers Hall of Fame." He said, "I used to broadcast the Cubs games," and that was as far as I could go with that moment of conversation. He went to a table, sat, and had some coffee.

I didn't think I was going to sit next to the president of the United States until Miss Faulkner said, "Oh, Mr. Kahn, don't let the president sit alone. Please join him." So I did, and he asked me if I had known Charlie Grimm. Of course, I had known Charlie Grimm. He was a pretty good manager and good left-handed banjo player. So Reagan began to tell a few Charlie Grimm stories.

And I noticed that when you tell a story he looks at you very hard, and when he tells a story he also looks at you very hard. His eyes are never away from you, and there is a kind of presence. Maybe he's a descendent of Irish feudal kings, but there's a presence. You're not just talking to one more politician.

After a while I mentioned that I had covered Jackie Robinson, and he seemed to know that. I never said "Mr. President," but I said a lot of "sirs." You'd be surprised how many "sirs" you say when you're one on one with the president of the United States. I said, "You know, sir, he became a Republican, and perhaps you'd want to know why."

Well, Reagan did know that Robinson became a Republican, but he didn't know why, so I said what Robinson had told me, that he didn't want all the blacks to be in one party and all the whites to be in the other party.

Reagan took that in and then said, "Roger, it's the darnedest thing—he didn't say "damnedest thing"; he said, "It's the darnedest thing"—"I don't know if it's the media or what where people get the idea that I am a racist." And he went on to tell me how he grew up in Illinois from a mixed Protestant and Catholic family, and how the Klan gave him a very bad time when he was a kid. He played football for Eureka College, and he was a guard and the center was a black fellow. He told me the name, but I've forgotten it. Anyway, the black fellow went through a lot, and because there were no face masks then he got his lip bloodied a lot. Well, one game somebody on the other team was giving it to him pretty good. Reagan said between halves, "We're going to take this fellow on for you." The black guy said, "No, Dutch, this is my fight. Just let me fight it." And Reagan said, "I respected that, but I'll tell you this: I am the least racist man in the United States."

There was a pain in his eye and a pain in his visage as he said that. I had meant to say something about the treaty with Gorbachev. So I was able to say, "Sir, anybody who knows where you began with the Soviet Union and where you have taken us with the Soviet Union knows that that is an expression of a great largeness of spirit. Surely, sir, nobody with the largeness of spirit to do the ANF treaty could possibly be a racist. And I thank you for the nuclear treaty for my children." Reagan's eyes misted. You know what happened next? My eyes misted.

We had 40 minutes to an hour during which we were just talking. He told me some Gorbachev jokes. He said, "Gorbachev has a sense of humor. I have to be tactful, but I can tell him some jokes. Would you like to hear a joke which made Gorbachev laugh?" Obviously I did. So Reagan says, "An American and a Russian are arguing about who has the better system. The American says, 'We have the better system. I can go into the White House, and if I pass security I can go into the Oval Office and I can pound my fist on the table (and Reagan pounded his fist gently on the table) and I can say, "President Reagan is doing a terrible job."'"

"And the Russian said, 'Our system is just as good as yours. I can go into the Kremlin. If I pass security I can see the Secretary General of the Communist Party, and I can also pound my fist on the table, provided I too say, "President Reagan is doing a terrible job."'"

So thinking of these two men with the fate of the world in their hands . . . that story broke me up!

Then he said, "People say I'm getting old. There are three difficulties with getting old. The first is your memory goes . . . I can't remember the other two." I don't mean to diminish the presidency, but Reagan did a few minutes of Johnny Carson. You're not going to fall off a chair in the White House . . . you're constrained, and I did have my $50 tie on, but he was just wonderful.

Then there was the movie in which Reagan plays Grover Cleveland Alexander and plays him very well, I think. Doris Day plays Mrs. Alexander and is very beautiful. I thought it was a pretty good movie, much better than I had remembered it being. There is a scene in the movie that had a startling effect on me. My father had admired Grover Cleveland Alexander, "Old Pete," as he was called. When I was a kid, Old Pete was going to be in Coney Island describing how he struck out Lazzeri in the World Series, and my father took me to that show. I remember this vividly because Alexander didn't appear. There was a dog act there instead.

I told that to Mr. Reagan, and Mr. Reagan just nodded, said nothing. Now in the movie Alexander is pitching to Rogers Hornsby (Reagan assures me that this is so), and he has two strikes on Hornsby. He's the great Alexander, and Hornsby is just a rookie. The catcher calls time, comes out, and says, "If this kid doesn't get a hit, he goes down in the minors." So Alexander grooves one, and Hornsby singles. Early in the film.

Late in the film, Alexander is drinking too much, he's down and out, and now he's making appearances in Coney Island, right where my father took me. It was the most amazing and hair-raising thing. Reagan is playing a disheveled and drunken Alexander; can you imagine Ronald Reagan disheveled and drunk?

Suddenly there's a knock at Alexander's dressing room door. He's looking into a dirty mirror. He doesn't do the show, maybe the very show at five I went to see which he failed to appear at. There's a knock at the door, and Reagan-Alexander says, "Who is it?"

"Landlady. I have a telegram."

He goes to the door, and it is a telegram. But it's not the landlady; it's Doris Day. And its a telegram from Rogers Hornsby inviting Grover Cleveland Alexander to come back with the St. Louis Cardinals.

Reagan is a mess, and Doris Day is very beautiful. They hug and kiss, and Reagan says, "With the drinking and the other stuff, people could say I've had a terrible life. But God must have loved me to have sent me somebody like you." And that's how the movie ends.

Reagan then got up and said he had a few comments to make. "Before I was a politician," he said, "acting was my craft, and the most beautiful line I was ever asked to say was the line about 'God must have loved me . . .'"

"People ask me, because Doris Day was so beautiful, 'Did you become emotionally involved with Doris Day while you were making this movie?' Well, first of all, I had just gotten engaged to Nancy. And second, we were professional actors, and when we kissed we barely brushed lips because if you kissed hard it distorted one side of your face." Reagan distorted one side of his face to show us.

Then he said, "Of course, that was then. In the movies today they kiss *through* each other. My only regret with this movie is that Jack Warner would not let me say that Alexander was an epileptic. He said, 'Ronnie, nobody will go to see a baseball movie anyway. If it's a baseball movie about an epileptic, absolutely nobody will see it.' I wanted to say it, but they wouldn't let me." I found this interesting because Reagan didn't like to be censored any more than any other artist.

He went on and showed his pitching motion, wound up, and threw a balled-up paper napkin against the curtain. He said, "I threw some of those balls." His pitching motion was the way it was in the movie: okay. For some of the heavy scenes when they needed a tremendous pitch, they used Bob Lemon.

Because they wouldn't portray Alexander as an epileptic, there's a scene when they have him shell-shocked in World War I, and he sees two moons. A little later in the movie Reagan-Alexander sees this single moon. The script calls for him to go out and throw a ball at a glove that is nailed to the barn wall. He's going to make one pitch under the full moon, he's going to hit the pocket of the glove, and then you know Alexander will be okay.

Reagan said, "Lemon threw a lot of pitches, but he couldn't hit the pocket of the glove. I hit the pocket of the glove."

Then at 10 after 11 he said, "They tell me I have to go first," and off he went.

Kenneth Duberstein, chief of staff of the White House, came over and said, "The president hasn't read *The Boys of Summer,* but he's going on vacation in August, and he'd appreciate a copy."

Well, I'm a little spacey at this point, and I said, "I don't know if I have a hardcover copy, but I have a paperback copy in the cellar. Wait a minute . . . ones does not send a paperback book to the president of the United States."

And Duberstein said kind of kindly, "No, one does not."

So I said, "Ken, I'll find a book."

And I put in the book, "To President Ronald Reagan, With my personal thanks for a fine evening at your abode and with thanks from all my family for leading the world towards nuclear peace."

I got a letter back, not form 26B, but the loveliest letter that brought back the moment when we were talking about nuclear catastrophe and both our eyes misted, and he said along the bottom of the first page of the letter which goes on for two pages, "By the way, I put five sticks of gum in my mouth before I started to pitch. Alexander, whatever his faults, thought chewing tobacco was an ugly habit. And so that he wouldn't do it, he put five sticks of gum in his mouth when he started a game. Not a great historical fact, but something I thought you should know. Best regards, Ronald Reagan." He knows a lot of baseball, and he was so proud of the historical accuracy of the movie.

After I got the letter, I had him made an honorary member of the Brooklyn Dodgers Hall of Fame, and I got a thank you note for that, also not a form letter. And I thought, "If I can do one thing for my daughter, I could introduce her to a president of the United States."

So I called Duberstein and told him, "Before you leave office, I would like to do this." Duberstein said, "Okay. He's going to be in New York, addressing the United Nations." He gave me the date, and I called my daughter Alissa and said, "If you'll come down from the Rhode Island School of Design, we'll have a few moments with the president of the United States."

The president was staying on the top floor of the Waldorf Towers. The Secret Service called to get a physical description of Alissa. I had to drive through horrible Manhattan traffic, but I finally got there and I was a little late because Alissa was blow drying her hair for a few extra minutes.

We took the elevator from one to the top with two Secret Service guys escorting us. We got off the elevator and walked up the back stairs. There were two more Secret Service guys wearing bullet proof stuff and holding machine guns. Alissa was wearing high heels—I didn't know she could do that—and a semi-mini skirt, a pearl choker, and a white blouse with long sleeves. She looked like the daughter everyone wants to have. And when she saw the two Secret Service men she said, "Scare-ree!" And one smiled; and those fellows don't smile. They aren't supposed to.

When we got upstairs Duberstein was there, and he said, "If you'll wait a minute in the foyer . . ." You wouldn't believe the presidential suite at the Waldorf, the real presidential suite, not the one people from Des Moines rent. The foyer had a chandelier that was just beyond belief. It was not in bad taste. That would be like saying Versailles is in bad taste, but it was opulent.

We stood there for a few minutes, and I later learned that he had been doing NATO work from 9:30 to 10:30, dealing with what the Germans wanted, what the Italians wanted, what the English wanted.

He came into the room, and he looked at me, and his face sort of lit. He came over and clapped me by the shoulder. Everybody else receeded so it was my daughter, myself, and the president of the United States. And I'm thinking, "Long after I'm gone, she's going to know she was with the president of the United States."

I wanted to help her talk to him. She's very poised, but this is a bit much for a kid. I said, "Sir, when Alissa is not studying art, in the summers she works. And didn't you work when you were in college?"

And Ronald Reagan, 77 or 78, took a step back and looked at this red-headed kid with good knees with a twinkle which I had never gotten. He said, "Yes, Alissa, when I was at Eureka College I did work, and I was a dishwasher."

I could see Alissa's face kind of react: "The president of the United States was a dishwasher!"

He said, "It was the best job I ever had because I was the dishwasher in the girls dormitory." So he won a couple of votes there, didn't he?

When it was about over—someone leaned in and said, "You have another appointment, Mr. President"—he said, "Roger, don't you have another baseball story for me?"

I did have one prepared just for this eventuality: "Sammy Snead is in a Washington Senators uniform taking batting practice against Yankee pitchers. Bob Grim is pitching, and he's throwing hard sliders. Grim could throw hard sliders all day and all night, and Sammy Snead wouldn't hit them. I was sitting next to Casey Stengel in the dugout, and Stengel goes, 'Bob! Bob! Throw it up around his eyes.' Grim got Snead out 10 to 12 times in a row, but after a while he threw a fastball up around his eyes. Snead tomahawked it, hitting the ball a long way to left-center. Stengel elbowed me in the ribs and said, 'Imagine that. A golfer who's a high ball hitter!'"

Reagan laughed and laughed and said he had to go now. He started towards these incredible doors.

I said, "I'm going to miss you."

He said, "You don't have to miss me. I will speak out on important issues."

I said, "Peace."

He looked at me and winked and said, "Trying."

And that's the last I've seen of President Reagan.

BASEBALL BOOKS BY ROGER KAHN

Inside Big League Baseball. New York: Macmillan, 1962.

The Boys of Summer. New York: Harper & Row, 1972.

A Season in the Sun. New York: Harper & Row, 1977.

The Seventh Game (fiction). New York: The New American Library, 1982.

Good Enough to Dream. Garden City, NY: Doubleday, 1985.

Joe & Marilyn: A Memory of Love. New York: William Morrow, 1986.

Pete Rose: My Story. New York: Macmillan, 1989.

Games We Used to Play. New York: Ticknor & Fields, 1992.

The Era 1947–1957: When the Yankees, the Giants, and the Dodgers Ruled the World. New York: Ticknor & Fields, 1993.

Memories of Summer: When Baseball Was an Art, and Writing about It a Game. New York: Hyperion, 1997.

The Head Game: Baseball Seen from the Pitcher's Mound. New York: Harcourt, 2000.

11

W. P. KINSELLA

A native Canadian and a graduate of the University of Iowa Writer's Work-
shop, W. P. (Bill) Kinsella was well known north of the border as the author
of three collections of contemporary Indian short stories before he became an
overnight sensation in the United States as the author of Shoeless Joe
(Houghton Mifflin, 1982). This highly imaginative novel about the ghosts
of the infamous 1919 Chicago Black Sox magically appearing to play ball
on a homemade diamond carved out of an Iowa cornfield marked Kinsella as
a true original; won him numerous awards, including a Houghton Mifflin
Literary Fellowship; created a cult following for his fiction; and was eventual-
ly turned into the hit movie Field of Dreams, *starring Kevin Costner and*
James Earl Jones. Involving time travel and a 2,614-inning ballgame,
Kinsella's second baseball novel, The Iowa Baseball Confederacy
(Houghton Mifflin, 1986), was even more fantastic than Shoeless Joe;
while The Thrill of the Grass *(Penguin, 1984) and* The Further
Adventures of Slugger McBatt *(Houghton Mifflin, 1988) are clearly the*
best collections of baseball short stories since Ring Lardner's. Kinsella, who
declined tenure at the University of Calgary to devote himself to his fiction,
writes a monthly column on American literature for the Vancouver Sun
Book Page *and frequently tours to give readings from his works. He has a*
third collection of baseball short stories, Searching for January, *scheduled*
for publication and is currently completing a trilogy of novels on his upbring-
ing in rural Alberta, Canada.

BASEBALL WASN'T A BIG PART of my childhood. I never saw a game
until I was about 11 years old, I guess. My dad had played some
minor league ball when he was young, but he settled down late in
life, and there was no baseball played where we were, in rural Alberta, Canada, in the 1940s. On the rare occasions when my dad would
get into the city, he would come back with a copy of the St. Louis
Sporting News. He talked a good game and liked to talk about when

he played ball. He taught me how to read a boxscore and all that sort of thing, but the only real baseball I had contact with in my early life was the World Series on radio.

I had a couple of friends who played a type of miniature baseball in their backyard. We made baseballs out of papier mache and had a little bat made out of plywood. If you hit the ball into my friend's mother's garden, you got a home run and generally lost the ball also. I also played, a lot by myself and a lot with friends, dice baseball games like J. Henry Waugh of The Universal Baseball Association. I used to invent whole leagues and keep track of them. I picked out of the *Sporting News* names of teams I thought were exotic, and I would give them players and keep their batting averages and pitching statistics. So baseball for me back then was more a game of the imagination than the actual thing.

I don't think I saw a major league game until 1965 or 1966. I was in San Francisco, and I saw Juan Marichal pitching against Don Drysdale. I froze my ass off, but Drysdale won which pleased me because I preferred L.A.

I never had any dream of playing major league baseball, not even a fantasy. I was not a good ballplayer. I have serious depth perception problems, and there was no place on the field that was safe for me to be. As a matter of fact, if *Shoeless Joe* hadn't been successful, I probably wouldn't have written any more baseball fiction. But I discovered that there was a market for baseball fiction, that there were lots of people out there willing to read it, and that it was an area of fiction that hadn't been well explored. There'd been very little good baseball fiction written.

Of course, when *Shoeless Joe* came out, I became an instant expert on the game. The next year I was doing the pre-season picks for *TV Guide,* and now everytime something unusual happens in baseball the phone starts ringing and they want my opinion on it. I enjoy the absurdity of that because I don't know any more about baseball than your average knowledgeable fan. And I'm certainly not a stats person. I can't even think of the uniform number of a single player in baseball history. I always figure you can look statistics up. I don't see any reason I need to keep any of that stuff in my head.

When I was a kid, my dad talked to me about Joe Jackson: about what a raw deal he'd gotten and about some of the things that had happened to him after the Black Sox Scandal, like his ending up playing for a dollar a game in the commercial leagues back in South Carolina. The stories about Jackson's hardships weren't necessarily true because Jackson never did suffer financially. He owned a couple of liquor stores in Greenville, and he had a wife who was a good financial manager. But it was good material for fiction. I was living in Iowa in 1978, trying to think of something to write about, and I thought of those stories my father had told me. And I wondered what would happen if Joe Jackson came back to life in this time and place. That was the beginning of *Shoeless Joe*. I went to the library, checked out *Eight Men Out,* and reread it because it's the definitive book on the Black Sox Scandal. And then I sat down and wrote "Shoeless Joe Jackson Comes to Iowa," the short story that would become the first chapter of *Shoeless Joe*.

The first chapter of *Shoeless Joe* is 99.9 percent the same as the short story. The only change I can think of is that we put Ray's name in the novel; the narrator was nameless in the original short story. Interestingly, the father-son business was an afterthought. Right after I finished the story I moved to Calgary. My wife Ann had not moved to Calgary yet, but she came up for a visit. She was typing the final draft of the story for me, and I said to her, "How far along are you? I've got another paragraph I want to add." She said, "I'm on page eight" or something. I said, "Oh, good." And I took the end of the story and added the paragraph where Ray says, "I know a catcher," and Shoeless Joe says, "You build the rest of the field, and we'll take a look at your catcher." That business, of course, becomes the absolute main point of the movie, if not the book. But it was an afterthought. I created the whole story without thinking of that. I didn't see the importance of the father-son connection in the beginning, and the opening lines of the story were somewhere on page 9 or 10. But as I was revising, I said, "No, this stuff has got to go at the front." So I took the paragraph that says, "My father said he saw him years later playing in a tenth-rate commercial league in a textile town in Carolina, wearing shoes and an assumed name" and made it the opening. And the second paragraph was buried on page 12 or something, and I pulled it up to the front too.

I wrote "Shoeless Joe Jackson Comes to Iowa" for the *New Yorker,* but they rejected it as being too sentimental. What happened, of course, is that the story was eventually published in an anthology called *Aurora: New Canadian Writing,* and the anthology was reviewed in *Publisher's Weekly.* I've never seen the review, but apparently it contained a two-line mention of my story. A young editor at Houghton Mifflin in Boston named Larry Kessenich read the review of the anthology in *Publisher's Weekly* and wrote to me on the strength of it.

He was right out of editor's school and didn't know that editors can't be bothered finding new writers, that they wait for them to come through the door. And he wrote to me saying, "We're all baseball fans here, and this idea of this man building a baseball diamond in his cornfield sounds so wonderful that if it's a novel, we'd like to see it, and if it isn't it should be." So I wrote to Larry and said, "Well, I'm a well-established short fiction writer, but I've never written anything successful longer than 25 pages. If I were going to write a novel, I'd have to have a good editor work with me." And at that point I started thinking novel. Larry wrote back and said he would be willing to work with me, again not knowing that editors don't want to work with writers; they want the finished product to come over the transom.

And I knew I had all the things stacked up that I wanted to write about. I wanted to write about J. D. Salinger because he makes himself conspicuous by hiding. If he didn't want to be in the limelight he could give one interview a year to some second-rate magazine, and he would have been forgotten about years ago. Instead he gives no interviews, and everytime someone mentions his name he threatens a law suit, which has kept him in the public eye. I mean, how many living writers who haven't published since 1962 manage to keep their names in front of the public for almost 30 years and continue to do it? So I knew that was an interesting phenomenon I wanted to investigate.

I knew I wanted to write something about Moonlight Graham because of his one line in *The Baseball Encyclopedia*. I wanted to know how playing one instant of major league baseball and never coming to bat had affected his life.

And I knew I wanted to write something about Eddie Scissons, the character based on an old fellow I met on the streets of Iowa City who turned out to be a sports imposter, the first of several that I've encountered.

The problem was "How am I going to tie all these people together?" I found the key to the problem when I went back and reread all of Salinger's collected and uncollected work and discovered that he had used two characters named Kinsella in his work. There's a Richard Kinsella that Holden Cauldfield talks about in *Catcher in the Rye* . . . the kid who rambled on and everyone in the class yelled "Digression" at. Then there's an uncollected story called "A Young Girl in 1941 With No Waist At All," and the boy telling the story is named Ray Kinsella. So I said, "Okay, now this'll be the connection, the tie-in. I'll name my character Ray Kinsella after the character in the uncollected story, and he can go off and turn up on Salinger's doorstep and say, 'Hi. I'm a character out of your fiction come to visit you'; and surely something interesting will happen if that goes down." So that was how I tied it together. Everything just rolled after that, and we only had one false start. *Shoeless Joe* was just like a baby. I wrote it in nine months, and it was virtually unedited.

By the way, a man named Jack Kinsella recently wrote to tell me he had been Salinger's college roommate, which is why, I guess, Salinger used the name twice. He hadn't seen Salinger in 40 years, but he saw *Field of Dreams* and thought I'd be interested to know about his connection to Salinger.

Overall, I suppose it's the believability of my work that draws people to it. For some reason fiction readers want to believe that what they're reading is based on truth of some kind. They want to be able to say, "Yes, I believe that's the way it is." And I think that pretty much all my work falls into that category. What I know doesn't matter; being believable is what counts. Even with my fantasy material people see the possibility that it could happen.

The most challenging thing about writing fantasy is that you have to make your reader believe in the transition from realism to something outside of or on the edge of the realms of possibility, which is what I've been able to do in a number of cases. I think it's because I do it in a straightforward manner; I don't beat around the bush with it at all. I just go right ahead, like when Gideon and Stan go across the line in *The Iowa Baseball Confederacy* and find themselves back in 1908, and when Ray meets Doc Graham on the streets of Chisholm, Minnesota, in *Shoeless Joe* and discovers it's himself who's been thrust back 15 years in time. I don't waste a lot of time with preliminaries. I just let it happen, and for that reason I think it's easy to follow and easy for the reader to suspend his disbelief and go along with it.

Also, people seem to feel good when they read my fiction, particularly *Shoeless Joe*. My fiction leaves people laughing or with a little twinge of sadness that makes them feel good. I've always felt that fiction is meant to be entertainment, and so much fiction is not entertainment. Too much of the fiction being published today is hard work to read, and I have no patience with it. My feeling is that fiction goes back to the days of the caveman when Ugh would stand up around the campfire and beat his chest and say, "Listen to me. I want to tell you about the brontosaurus I killed this afternoon." And if he wasn't a good storyteller, everyone would yawn and slink off to their caves. So those who wanted to tell stories learned to be enter-taining, and that has always been my goal. I don't want to educate anyone, and I don't have any particular axes to grind. If I do have axes to grind, I certainly don't want to grind them in my fiction. That's what essays are for.

I think baseball is conducive to fiction writing because of its open-endedness. The other sports, football, basketball, hockey, are twice-enclosed: first by time limits and then by rigid playing boundaries. In contrast, there's no time limit on a baseball game, and the true baseball field has foul lines which diverge forever, eventually taking in a good part of the universe; and that makes for myth and larger-than-life characters, and that's what a fiction writer is looking for. That's my canned answer that I give whenever somebody asks me why so many writers write about baseball. I don't think I ever do an interview that I don't get to make that little spiel.

But I really do believe that it's the open-endedness of the game that makes it so conducive to fiction writing. I mean, Wayne Gretzky may be the greatest hockey player who ever lived, but he's trapped in that little space. Michael Jordan's faced with the same thing. He is quite a magician on the basketball court, but he's trapped too. What can you write about? You don't have to think watching a bas-ketball game because there's no subtlety involved. One team gets the ball and scores, then the other team gets the ball and scores.

With baseball, it's all subtlety. Baseball fans have to be more intel-ligent than other sports fans because they have to have imaginations. There are no baseball fans without imaginations, except for the ones who are drunk and falling asleep in their seats. Baseball's all a game of anticipation because the ball is in play for what . . . five minutes out of three hours? And the thrill of the game is in outguessing the managers and players and in anticipating what is going to happen.

The amazing thing about *Shoeless Joe* is that I've made an interest-ing story about a guy who's happily married to a wife he really loves and who loves him. You virtually never see that in fiction because it's hard to write a story about nice people in normal relationships. It was a real breakthrough that I was able to do it. Stories about nice people who are happy usually are not very interesting, and people like it when you can make them work. *The Iowa Baseball Confederacy*, a much darker book than *Shoeless Joe*, is back to the more normal side of fiction writing in that Gideon is very much in love with Sunny who either doesn't love him or can't bring herself to stay around or whatever it is. Gideon also loves and loses Sarah, so it's not a happy ending, although as I see it, it is certainly a hopeful ending.

I never conceive of a theme for anything I write, and I hope that anything I write doesn't have one. Again, I try to tell a story that will entertain people and have strange and magical things happen to my characters. That's all I set out to do. Critics will find whatever they want to find in a work, and I like to plant things that will give these pasty-faced little guys, wherever they are, an erection for a minute or two while they find something they think is symbolic. As far as I see it, it's all gamesmanship. I'm generally very conscious of the things that I plant in my work because I do like to give the critics a cheap thrill now and then.

If pressed, I'd say the theme of both *Shoeless Joe* and *The Iowa Baseball Confederacy* would be "Follow your dreams . . . Do what you have to do to get what you want, regardless of what other people think." Both main characters are in the same situation. People think Ray is crazy for building a baseball field and spending the last of his money to buy a tractor to trim the outfield grass when the farm is going bankrupt. People thought Matthew Clark was crazy, and they think his son Gideon is merely eccentric because he lives in this big house, doesn't spend any of the money he has, and wastes all his time trying to prove that this non-existent baseball league existed. So, it's "Go ahead and do what you have to do regardless of what other people think."

Fiction writers are essentially writing for people who don't have a whole lot of imagination. And most of the people don't realize that they don't have a whole lot of imagination. Reading fiction is sort of like vicarious living, and I would think that most people have some sort of dream like Ray and Gideon, but, unlike Ray and Gid, they never do anything toward realizing it.

Once in a while, especially with *Shoeless Joe*, people get shaken up into actually doing things that they hadn't planned on doing. I've been told of a number of people who have quit jobs and gone to do things they really wanted to do. Like the fellow in Vermont who was inspired to start the Brautigan Library by seeing *Field of Dreams*. Richard Brautigan, of course, is one of my favorite writers, and his book *The Abortion* is about a library for unpublishable manuscripts that no one wants. This fellow named Todd Lockwood, a successful entrepreneur in Burlington, Vermont, came out of *Field of Dreams* and said, "You know, I've always wanted to do something to commemorate Richard Brautigan's memory, and I'm going to do it." He got a bunch of people together, they rented a little building, and they now have the Brautigan Library. So for $25 or so you can send your manuscript to the library, and it'll be bound in hardcovers and put in the library. They've had all kinds of inquiries, and last I heard manuscripts have been pouring in. And that came directly from Todd Lockwood seeing *Field of Dreams.*

It's not easy to follow your dreams because when you do you usually look eccentric and irresponsible to other people. I've been through that myself. I'd given up several good careers because I wanted to write, and I don't think my mom, who's had a bad stroke and is not really with us any longer, ever really understood what it was that I was doing. I think she still wished that I would get a "real job."

Shoeless Joe sort of opened the doors of North American literature to me. It sold well enough that I was able to quit teaching and write full time, and it made me well enough known that I can go out on tour to do readings and entertain people. But *Field of Dreams* hasn't really changed my life very much. I suppose it's made me somewhat better known but not that much. The author is never all that important to a movie.

Originally, *Shoeless Joe* was optioned by a small company which had two years to get a script together and sell it. They didn't get it done though, so it was next optioned by Twentieth-Century Fox, which had three years, I believe, to get it together. A fellow named Phil Robinson, who had fallen in love with the book, spent at least two years of his life writing the screenplay. He really wanted to do something good with it. But when it came time for Twentieth-Century Fox to decide, they said, "No, we're not going to make the movie. We're not going to make any movie which isn't going to gross at least $50 million at the box office."

At one point one of the executives at Twentieth-Century Fox got together with Phil Robinson, went to Twentieth-Century Fox, and said, "Look, I'm going to leave the company. The only thing I want is your permission to take this 'Shoeless Joe' script with me. Since you're not going to make the movie, you shouldn't care." They said, "Well, if you have to leave, you have to leave, and you have our blessing to take the 'Shoeless Joe' script with you."

So this executive and Phil Robinson took the screenplay to Paramount and Universal, the other two major companies. Both companies decided they wanted to make the movie, so the executive and Phil played one against the other to get the most favorable financing and to ensure that Phil would get to direct the movie. That was a big point because Phil only had one movie to his credit, a little cult movie called *In The Mood.* I went out and rented it and thought, "Oh, god. This guy's going to direct my movie when the script is so good they could get Robert Altman or some other well known director to do it!" I think they took a little less money in order for Phil to direct the movie, which turned out to be the right move because the screenplay was so good and it didn't get changed. Ordinarily, if they had brought in a famous director to do it, he probably would have looked at it and said, "Well, this isn't the way I see it. Let's change this and this and this." I knew the movie was going to be successful because I had tears in my eyes when I finished reading the screenplay. I said, "Wow! This is my own work, and it's done this to me. If this can get to the screen in this form, it's going to be great." And when I got on the set and saw what they were doing, I knew the movie was going to be great.

While he was doing the screenplay, Phil kept in touch with me because he wanted me to like what he was going to do. He'd phone and say, "I'm a third of the way through, and you realize that turning a book into a movie is kind of like changing an apple into an orange. You're going to have a different finished product when you get through. There's no way you can get a 300-page novel into an hour and 40 minute movie, so I'm going to have to cut things— Eddie Scissons has to go; Ray Kinsella's twin brother has to go—and I have to telescope time to move the story along."

The only thing I really argued for was the inclusion of the little scene where Ray and Salinger and young Archie Graham break into Metropolitan Stadium on the way back to Iowa from Chisholm, Minnesota. I said, "Couldn't you find 90 seconds, couldn't you find even a minute for this scene because it's so visual and so wonderful, these guys playing ball on the wet, shimmering grass in the moonlight?" He said, "There are so many things I would like to have in here that I can't and I don't see any way we can find space for that scene either."

Obviously, the main change in the movie is the substitution of Terrence Mann for J. D. Salinger. This was done for a couple of reasons. One, although demographics have changed recently, at the time when the project was first going in 1985, the age of the movie-going audience was 12-23, so most of the audience wouldn't have known who J. D. Salinger was anyway. Now a lot of older people are going to the movies; hence the success of movies like *Field of Dreams* and *Driving Miss Daisy*. But back then it was a young crowd, and that was a consideration. And, two, they were afraid that Salinger could wait until the movie was about to be released and then file a nuisance law suit that would tie up the release of the movie for a few months and cost them several million dollars in advertising. They didn't want to take a chance of that happening, so they moved the time sequence ahead 10 years and made Terrence Mann to the 1960s what Salinger had been to the 1950s. And I think they did it very successfully. The part was written specifically for James Earl Jones, and I think he did real well with it.

I think the father-son material is much more prominent in the movie than it is in the novel, and I think it works wonderfully well which is the magic of screenwriting. They created the PTA scene to develop Annie's character and to give us information about the reclusive author before we go off in search of him. So those are the main changes between the novel and the movie.

I'm totally pleased with the movie. Most writers are not pleased with what Hollywood does with their work, and generally with good reason, but Phil captured the essence of the novel. He got the tone perfectly, and because the script was so good they were able to get actors like Kevin Costner, Burt Lancaster, and James Earl Jones to work in it. I don't see how they could have done a better job with it. And I'm pretty sure Twentieth-Century Fox is sorry they didn't do it because I imagine *Field of Dreams* grossed somewhere around $80 million before it went into video.

We'll never see any more money from the movie. You get your money up front with Hollywood; however, there is a case pending, the Art Buchwald case, which may change things. Art Buchwald sued Eddie Murphy and the people who did *Coming to America* for ripping off an idea he had several years before. The courts have already decided that Murphy and the movie people did rip off the idea. And now Buchwald is entitled to 3 or 4 percent of the net profits of the film, but . . . there is never any net profit in Hollywood. *Rain Man* has grossed over a billion dollars worldwide, and they still claim it hasn't made any money. *Coming to America* grossed $200 million or $300 million, and they claim there is no profit. What Hollywood does is, let's say, spend $30 million making a movie of *Jack and the Beanstalk* starring Sylvester Stallone. It stays in the theaters one day and grosses $200,000. They then write off the $29 million loss against the profits from their successful movies. It's one thing to do that for tax purposes, but they shouldn't be allowed to do it for profit purposes, to bilk people who have a percentage of the profits. I don't see how this can be legal, but obviously Hollywood has enough money that they've owned the lawmakers for years. So this Buchwald case may have wide-ranging implications.

The title of the movie didn't bother me because we didn't know what to call the novel in the first place. The logical title was *Shoeless Joe Jackson Comes to Iowa,* but we'd already used that as the title of a short story collection so we couldn't use it as the title of the novel. I wrote the novel under the title *The Oldest Living Chicago Cub,* and the publishers considered a number of alternatives; one, coincidentally enough, being *Dream Field.* Universal didn't know that when they came up with the title *Field of Dreams.* The director wasn't terribly happy with it, and Kevin Costner was incensed. He flew back from Mexico where he was filming *Revenge* and went three rounds with the people at Universal Studios about renaming it because he wanted it left as *Shoeless Joe.* But their survey indicated that *Shoeless Joe* had no appeal whatever to women. It wasn't only that *Shoeless Joe* connoted sports; women just wouldn't want to see a movie called *Shoeless Joe.* Whereas *Field of Dreams* had much more appeal to them. It's interesting that the term "Field of Dreams" has almost become generic now. It turns up on the sports page every day, and that's fun to see. One day *USA Today* had three references to "Field of Dreams" in their sports section. One was a headline, and two others were major references used as metaphors to equate "Field of Dreams" with somebody doing something out of the ordinary.

I spent about four days on the set with Ann and my daughter Shannon. I was there when they did the feed store scene and the PTA scene and one interior scene I don't think made it into the movie. The interior scenes were done in a house about 20 miles outside Dubuque, and the farm was in Dyersville, Iowa. The field was laid out when I was there, but it wasn't finished. The lights weren't up, and the corn was only about ankle high and looking wretched. They were seriously thinking of trucking full grown corn in from Georgia, but then they discovered a spring on the back of the property, so they hired a tank truck and did a lot of watering and fertilizing and finally got a nice field of corn.

I think moviemaking is one of the most boring things in the whole world. The first take is interesting, and the second take is interesting, but after that it gets boring. Kevin came up to that counter in the feed store with that bag under his arm 31 times, I think. It's the scene when somebody says, "Ray's hearing voices." And Kevin says,

"No, not voices. Noises, noises. A little 3-in-1 oil will fix that up."
And he turns and walks out. They did that over and over and over.

I enjoyed seeing the rushes, the film from maybe three days previously. They'll fly all the takes out to L.A., and the people out there
will pick the best six or seven and send them back. And every evening they show the rushes. So I enjoyed seeing the rushes, but I
didn't really enjoy hanging around the set. When they were doing
the PTA scene, it was 120 degrees in the gymnasium. You had to
stop fanning yourself whenever they called "Action!" and get the
paper fans out of sight. We were there most of the day, and about
3:30 I said to Ann, "The next time they open the back doors, I'm
leaving. You can come with me or not." She left but would have
been happy to stay. She and Shannon went back when they were
filming the baseball stuff, and they got to meet everyone but Burt
Lancaster. I got to meet Kevin, Amy Madigan, and the little girl. Ann
and James Earl Jones got along well, and they ended up watching
the Democratic National Convention together. And my daughter,
who's 32, had a little romance with Ray Liotta, who played Shoeless
Joe. So Ann and Shannon had a real nice time.

Phil Robinson didn't know we were coming out to the set when
they were shooting the PTA scene, otherwise he'd have sat us next
to Kevin Costner and Amy Madigan or next to one of the people
who stands up and shouts out something in support of Lee Garling-
ton who was the book burner. And thank goodness he didn't. They
couldn't have changed the composition of the audience between
takes, so we would have had to sit there all that day and half of the
next day while they filmed the rest of the PTA scene.

Because Phil didn't realize we were there, we stood at the back of
the hall, and if they'd used some of the early takes of Amy's little
speech out in the aisle, you would have seen me standing behind
her in a candy-striped shirt at the back of the hall. But they obviously
used one of the later takes after we had left. It didn't really matter
to me though. I have a little ham in me, but I'm a writer, not an
actor.

BASEBALL BOOKS BY W. P. KINSELLA

Shoeless Joe (fiction). Boston: Houghton Mifflin, 1982.
The Thrill of the Grass (short stories). New York: Penguin Books,
    1984.

The Iowa Baseball Confederacy (fiction). Boston: Houghton Mifflin, 1986.

The Further Adventures of Slugger McBatt (short stories). Boston: Houghton Mifflin, 1988.

Box Socials (fiction). New York: Ballantine Books, 1991.

The Dixon Cornbelt League: And Other Baseball Stories (short stories). New York: Harper Collins, 1993.

Shoeless Joe Comes to Iowa (short stories). Dallas: Southern Methodist University Press, 1993.

Go the Distance (short stories). Dallas: Southern Methodist University Press, 1995.

12

DANIEL OKRENT

After a decade as a book editor in the New York publishing industry, Daniel Okrent entered a book packaging partnership which enabled him to produce and edit his conception of what would be the greatest pictorial baseball history ever published. Despite his lofty goal and the book's audacious title, Okrent (and a lineup of hand-picked contributors) succeeded brilliantly with The Ultimate Baseball Book, *called "The Rolls Royce of baseball books!" by the* Baltimore News American. *In 1989 he co-authored* Baseball Anecdotes *(Oxford University Press), but his masterpiece is* Nine Innings *(Ticknor & Fields, 1985), a wonderfully microscopic, penetrating, and digressive book about a single game between the Milwaukee Brewers and the Baltimore Orioles in mid-season 1982. A recognized baseball pundit who nevertheless has the self-control and humility to limit his pronouncements about "the meaning of baseball," Okrent lives in western Massachusetts where he watches a lot of minor league baseball, a game he prefers to the major league variety. The former editor and part-owner of* New England Monthly, *he now works as a consultant to* Time *and other magazines.*

I ALWAYS SAY that if between now and the time I die I find a cure for cancer and bring lasting peace to the Middle East, my obituary will still say, "Okrent Dies, Invented Rotisserie League Baseball." That's what I'm doomed to be known for, no matter what else I do in life. People have actually stopped me on the street to say, "You're Dan Okrent, aren't you? Thank you for changing my life" . . . or "Damn you for changing my life." And more than one woman has blamed the breakup of her marriage on Rotisserie League.

When I had the idea for the game in the winter of 1979-80, I certainly never dreamed Rotisserie League would become what it's become, or I would have found a way to retire on it. I just thought I had to come up with something to amuse myself and my friends who love baseball. However, Rotisserie League got a lot of exposure, almost immediately, because nearly all of the original players were involved in the New York media, were well connected in the media. Within a month of the time we first started playing the game in 1980 there was a big article about is in the *New York Times.* A month later we were on *The Today Show* and a week after that on the *CBS Morning News.* Then I wrote an article about the game for *Inside Sports,* which included an abbreviated version of the rules, and it just took off.

As soon as I cooked up the first version of the rules, I explained them to a group of Philadelphia Phillies fans whom I had been bringing together for lunch once a month at a place called La Rotisserie Francaise on East 52nd Street in New York. That's why the game got named Rotisserie League Baseball, because of the restaurant our group had been meeting at. Only two people in that group were interested in playing the game though, so the three of us found some others outside the group who joined us to make the first league. The real meeting of the people who actually played the game for the first time was held at a restaurant on 3rd Avenue called P. J. Moriarity's, so the game should be called Moriarity League Baseball rather than Rotisserie League. People think that Rotisserie League is a clever twist on "Hot Stove League," but it wasn't that at all. It's incredible, though, how widespread Rotisserie has become. It's even entered the language. The *New York Times* uses the word in lower case without explaining it, and it's going to be in the next edition of *Webster's International.*

Even though I might be chagrined at being known primarily for the invention of Rotisserie League Baseball, baseball has always been important to me, except for the four years I spent in college, which is a subject I'll get back to later. I grew up in Detroit, and my dad took me to my first Tigers game in 1954 when I was six years old. It was the classic father-takes-son-to-the-ballgame experience, but my dad never took me to another game. He had once been a great Tigers fan—as a high school student in the 1920s he had ushered at Navin Field—but he turned against them in the late 1940s because they wouldn't sign any black players. Except for the Red Sox, the Tigers were the last team to field a black major leaguer. My father was very concerned about civil rights, and he really came to hate the Tigers because of their stance toward blacks. Consequently, my father took me to that game in April 1954 out of a sense of duty, and then he basically said, "Now it's your thing."

Well, I didn't get to many Tigers games without my dad until my last two years of high school, when I must have seen 30-35 games a year. The high school I attended, Cass Technical, was located in downtown Detroit about half a mile from Briggs Stadium, called Navin Field in my dad's day and Tiger Stadium now. There were a lot of day games back then, and my friends and I would walk down to the stadium after school and get there by the second or third inning. And, of course, we never paid because we knew how to sneak in.

Throughout my boyhood and adolescence the Tigers were a classically mediocre team, except in 1961 when Norman Cash had his unreasonable year and the Yankees had a far more unreasonable year, so that even though the Tigers won over 100 games, they didn't win the pennant. They were a fourth, fifth-place team every year. The thing we used to boast about, the Tigers' only distinction, was that up through my adolescence they had finished last only once, in 1952. That was fewer times than any other team.

I grew up a Yankee-hater, like every other kid who grew up in the 1950s in any American League city other than New York. I hated the Yankees for so long before George Steinbrenner showed up that when George came along it was almost a pleasure that I could hate them more and know that everybody else finally agreed with me.

I graduated from high school in 1965 and went off to college at the University of Michigan in Ann Arbor. And, as I said, for four years baseball didn't matter to me. I think this is characteristic of people my age. For some reason I thought that serious matters like the Vietnam War and social inequities were so important that they sort of invalidated baseball. So even in 1967, with its incredible four-team race, and in 1968, when the Tigers won the World Championship, I was only vaguely aware of what was going on in baseball. I do remember watching a couple of World Series games on TV, but I didn't care who won the games. It was too trivial to get emotionally involved in. Of course, now I look back longingly at 1968 and ache for some connection, which I don't have, to that great World Series which the Tigers won.

A related aspect of this phenomenon is that I still have a blank spot for the teams and players of the late 1960s. There are players of that era who I intuitively know were prominent, but I couldn't tell you if they were .220 or .290 hitters. To this day I'm more fluent with the lineups of National League teams of 1933 than I am with the lineup of the 1967 Tigers. I've even tried to study those four years in *The Baseball Encyclopedia* to find out, for instance, whether Leon Wagner was a good player or a bad player. Because I don't know. Players like Wagner who reached their peaks during those years are lost to me, and I don't think I'll ever be able to retrieve them, no matter how much studying I do.

After graduating from college in 1969, I moved to New York to take a job with Alfred A. Knopf. Then came Vida Blue, who brought me back to baseball. I vividly remember cutting Blue's picture out of the newspaper and taping it to the door of my office. People at Knopf thought I was some kind of nut. But there was something about Vida Blue's name, his style, and that incredible season he had. From that point on I was back into the game as completely as I had been as a child, and I've been following baseball with greater and greater intensity ever since.

I always wanted to be a writer. My father had a friend named Paul Lutzeier, a former journalist, who saw something in me and encouraged my interest in words. Paul knew a lot of people in the newspaper business, and he'd take me with him to the city rooms of the *Detroit News* and the *Detroit Free Press* to watch the teletype machines clatter away; he'd take me to political events; and he got me started writing letters-to-the-editor. He made sure I started out the letters, "I'm only nine years old, but . . ." And it worked. The first thing I ever published was a letter-to-the-editor in one of the Detroit newspapers when I was nine. Because of Paul's influence and my own lack of imagination, I thought that anybody who wrote for a living wrote for a newspaper. So I grew up thinking I'd one day be a newspaper reporter.

I was the editor of my junior high school newspaper; I was the sports editor of my high school paper; and when I got to Michigan I dropped my bags off at my dormitory room and went straight to the offices of the *Michigan Daily,* the student newspaper, where I spent the next four years virtually without leaving the building. I hardly went to class. I majored in the school paper.

The summers between my senior year in high school and my first year in college, and between my freshman and sophomore years, I worked as a copy boy at the *Detroit Free Press.* Between my sophomore and junior years I worked as an intern reporter for a chain of suburban newspapers. And my junior year I became the *New York Times* stringer in Ann Arbor, a position which got passed on from one student to another. It was a real plum. You could make 50-60 bucks a month, and since my rent was only 50 bucks a month that was meaningful money. And, gosh, you could say, "I work for the *New York Times.*" Well, I didn't really work for the *New York Times,* but I sort of did.

Unfortunately, I learned along the way that I was a lousy reporter, at least in the newspaper sense. I was fast, but I wasn't accurate when I was fast. I was also curiously timid as a reporter. I was uncomfortable imposing on the time and privacy of the people I needed to question. Normally I'm not timid at all; in fact, people who know me well would probably say that I'm hideously extroverted.

Anyway, by the time I was a junior in college I realized I'd have to be something other than a newspaper reporter. In the spring of 1968 I read an article in the *New York Times Book Review* about Bob Gottlieb, now the editor of the *New Yorker,* who was then the editor-in-chief of Alfred A. Knopf. The article fascinated me because, as I implied earlier, it never occurred to me that there were people who made their livings as book editors. I didn't know that book editors existed. I think it was just the nature of my Midwest boyhood. Book publishing is an industry that simply doesn't exist in a town like Detroit.

So I wrote this man a very ingenuous, open, kind of nutty letter. Gottlieb's secretary happened to be on vacation, and he was opening his own mail. The day after the article appeared he got 50 letters, but 49 of them said, "Dear Mr. Gottlieb: I'm an English major graduating with high honors. I've always wanted to be in the book business. Here's my resumé." My letter went on for two pages and was kind of strange, so he was struck by it.

He wrote back and said, "I don't know why you want to be in the book business. It's a job like any other job. And we don't have an opening for you, but if you ever find yourself in New York, let me know and I'll be happy to talk with you."

Now this runs counter to the timidity I just claimed for myself, but out of a combination of nerve and naiveté I got on a plane *that* day, flew to New York, and called his office from the airport.

Well, by then Gottlieb's secretary was back. I told her, "This is Daniel Okrent. I'm a student at the University of Michigan. Mr. Gottlieb told me to come and see him."

"Do you have an appointment with him?"

"No, but Mr. Gottlieb said for me to come see him."

"I'm sorry, but that's impossible."

I said, "Miss, you have to understand. I'm just a student. I don't know anybody in New York, and I'll have to sleep here in the airport waiting for my return flight if I can't see Mr. Gottlieb."

She put me on hold for a few minutes, then came back on with instructions on how to get to the Knopf offices in Manhattan. I showed up around 3:30 in the afternoon and wound up talking to Gottlieb for about four hours. And, as incredible as it sounds, he offered me a job upon my graduation a year later.

My last final exam at Michigan was over at 11 on the morning of April 23, 1969. As I finished taking it, a friend, who was from New York, sat outside the classroom in her VW van with the motor running and with everything I owned and everything she owned in the back of the bus. We drove all day to get to New York, she dropped me off at the YMCA on 34th Street, and I went to work at Knopf the next morning.

I worked as a book editor at Knopf for several years, moved over to Viking Press for a while, and then was made editor-in-chief at Harcourt Brace Jovanovich, at a very early age. I was only 27, and I wasn't ready for the position. It was their mistake. They should have known better. Within a year and a half I washed out of the job; however, while I was there, I had the idea for a series of books that would cater to the passion of enthusiasts. We'd do baseball and boxing and skiing and stamp collecting and on and on, and each book would be called *The Ultimate _____ Book.* The basic idea was lavish pictorial representation combined with superb writing.

I was very excited about the concept, but it never got off the ground at Harcourt Brace Jovanovich. The marketing director there, a very supercilious guy who was my equal in the chain of command, shot it down. He was absolutely dismissive and acted as if I were wasting his time. "You mean, *this* is the great idea you had to talk to me about?" That sort of thing.

When I left Harcourt Brace Jovanovich, I got offered other publishing jobs as an editor or senior editor, but I decided I wanted to be self-employed—partly because I had been singed by the experience of failure, but more because I simply felt temperamentally more suited to working for myself. One of the things I then did, taking advantage of the experience and contacts I had, was to become a book packager. As you may know, a book packager does everything necessary to produce a book, and the publisher finances it and distributes it. I became a book packager in partnership with Lee Eisenberg and Bruce McCall. Lee later became the editor-in-chief of *Esquire,* and Bruce is a major figure in the advertising industry. In the course of the two-year partnership, we packaged 10-12 books. One of our projects was going to be this "Ultimate" series, but then I decided I wanted to do the baseball book myself rather than farm it out to somebody else.

You might find this hard to believe, but it wasn't easy finding a publisher for *The Ultimate Baseball Book*. The climate for publishing baseball books back in the 1970s was a lot different from what it is today. Baseball literature could boast about *The Boys of Summer, Babe,* and *Ball Four;* earlier there had been Brosnan's books and *The Glory of Their Times;* and going way back there had been Ring Lardner. But the books between Lardner and the books I just mentioned were pretty limited in ambition and literary appeal, with a very few exceptions. There certainly weren't 75 or 80 new baseball books coming out every spring, as there are these days. So seven or eight publishers rejected the book before Houghton Mifflin agreed to do it.

I made two primary contributions to *The Ultimate Baseball Book*. I wrote all the captions, and I commissioned all the writing. Harris Lewine found all the pictures and designed the book. And David Nemec wrote the decade-by-decade historical text, combining tremendous prose skill with an encyclopedic and *interesting* knowledge of baseball history.

Writing the captions was a bigger job than it may sound, because there are 850 photos in the book—almost enough captions to make a separate book. I spent the winter of 1979 on the captions and just had a ball doing them.

Only two writers declined to write an essay for the book. One said no politely, and one said no impolitely, but everyone else I asked really wanted to do it. Except for Red Smith and Bob Creamer, the nine writers who did the essays were not baseball writers. They were writers who happened to love baseball. Tom Wicker, Wilfrid Sheed, John Leonard, Mardecai Richler, and the others had never had the opportunity to write about this thing they loved until I came along saying, "Here's a check. Pick out somebody or something in baseball history that you really love and write about it."

I was particularly gratified to have Red Smith involved because he was my hero among baseball writers. In my opinion he wrote the best prose of anyone who has ever made a living writing about baseball; however, Red had very little, if any, experience at writing magazine articles. He was a newspaper guy. Red had been doing his column for so long that he could write an 800-word column to the very word. And the funny thing is that if you look at his essay about Pepper Martin and the Gas House Gang, you'll see that it's really three 800-word pieces. That's the only way he could do it.

Creamer was terrific to work with; he couldn't have been better. Jon Yardley got a little prickly. I wanted to edit his piece more than he wanted it to be edited. Wilfrid Sheed's piece on Connie Mack was the most beautifully written one, I think. There's an image from it that I'll never forget: in describing how Connie's career went on and on, stretching into the 1950s, Sheed wrote that Mack was like a tree still standing from the Garden of Eden with Adam's and Eve's initials carved into it. What made Sheed's piece even more amazing is that he was able to be so interesting about a person who had already been written about a great deal. Sheed's essay was probably the most stunning, but I really shouldn't single any of them out because all of the essays are terrific in their own ways.

Did the book turn out any differently than I had envisioned? Well, because of Harris' brilliant design work it turned out to be more beautiful than I had imagined. Also, baseball being baseball, I figured on more statistical stuff, but I found that David's text handled statistics so well that the book didn't need any separate statistical treatment.

I certainly didn't expect a chapter on Enos Slaughter. I have a certain lack of fondness for Slaughter because of his involvement in the Cardinals' attempted boycott against Jackie Robinson, a role Slaughter has at times tried to deny. But what I wanted to do was harness each writer's passion, and Slaughter was what Wicker wanted to write about. So I gave him my blessing, and Tom got on a plane and went to see the old guy.

On the other hand, I had to twist Roy Blout's arm to get him to write about Joe DiMaggio because Roy had already written about DiMaggio. Like most good writers, Roy doesn't like to repeat himself, and he had done a terrific article for *Sports Illustrated* about DiMaggio as a coach for the Oakland A's. I understood Roy's reluctance, but I was confident he could do something wonderful on a different aspect of DiMaggio. And he did.

I had to do a certain amount of juggling with the essays to make certain that there was only one manager, and one World Series, and so on. There were some instances when a writer wanted to do a certain topic and I had to say no because of what another writer was already doing. The great thing about Sheed wanting to write about Connie Mack was that I could put him in practically *any* decade; Connie offered that kind of versatility. Even so, there is some obvious shading and overlapping. For example, George Higgins' "Ballpark" piece about Fenway is as much about the Red Sox franchise as Leonard's "Franchise" piece is about the Dodgers.

It sounds presumptuous to say this, and I don't mean to claim for a second that I attained it, but I guess the goal I had going into the book was to publish, as the title implied, the definitive history of baseball. Not the definitive "scholarly" history of baseball—that's Harold Seymour's territory—but the definitive enthusiast's history of baseball. And I think the book holds up pretty damn well. It's not David's text alone, or the photos alone, or the captions alone, or the essays alone; it's the combination of elements which makes the book so dazzling. I really can't say, though, that I achieved anything resembling the "ultimate" baseball book—there have been 7,000 baseball books published since then. But I hope that people who are looking for a one-volume history that is fun as well as informative will turn to this one.

The reviews of *The Ultimate Baseball Book* were simply astounding. There was not a single review that was anything but wildly enthusiastic. I mean, not only were there no bad reviews, there were also no so-so reviews. Once in a while I look back at my file of reviews, and I'm stunned at how much people loved this book. It's been in print now 11 years, and we still get a royalty check for it every six months. It's sold well over a quarter of a million copies. Another decade has passed, so I'm revising the book. George Will is writing the essay about the 1980s, and David Nemec is updating his historical text.

What *The Ultimate Baseball Book* did for me personally was enable me to turn my avocation into a vocation. Since college I had been working as an editor and hadn't written anything more than memos, advertisements, flap copy, and catalog descriptions. Now I found that I could make part of my living as a baseball writer, doing articles for magazines such as *Sports Illustrated, Inside Sports,* and *Esquire.* One of the articles I wrote for *Sports Illustrated,* an article about Bill James, turned out to be pretty significant, too.

If I can be so unhumble as to put it this way, my greatest contribution to baseball literature is not anything I've written—it's that I discovered Bill James. I have the nerve to say this only because Bill has been very generous in giving me that credit. I discovered Bill in the sense that before my story about him for *SI,* nobody knew who he was or what he was doing. But after the story appeared, his career just took off.

As you may know, the story almost didn't run. There was a fact checker assigned to the story who kept nitpicking it to death. This fact checker, who was later fired, had a lot of contacts in the game, and she basically thought she knew more about baseball than Bill. For instance, Bill said that the Cubs had not been producing much talent in their farm system but that they had traded incredibly well to remain somewhat competitive. Bob Kennedy was the Cubs' GM at the time, and this fact checker said, "Everybody knows that Bob Kennedy is a laughingstock as a trader." I said, "But look at the evidence that Bill presents to the contrary." She said, "But everybody knows that Kennedy's not a good trader." I said, "But look at the evidence." We went around and around like that. Larry Keefe, who was the baseball editor at the time, had to back up his fact checker, but then Bob Creamer, who had helped me revise my original draft, said, "This is unfair to Okrent, and it's unfair to James." Despite Creamer's support, the story was killed that spring in 1980; however, I rewrote it, and *Sports Illustrated* ran it in the spring of 1981.

Before the story ran I'd been trying to interest some publishers I knew in publishing Bill's work, which Bill had been self-publishing. These guys were baseball fans, and their typical response was, "Dan, I love this stuff. It's fabulous. But it's just for baseball nuts like you and me. The public wouldn't be interested. If we published it, nobody would buy it." It's difficult now to appreciate how revolutionary Bill's ideas and methods were back then. But the *SI* article validated Bill's work, and suddenly there was a bidding war to publish him. One of the publishers who could have signed Bill for $2,000 before the *Sports Illustrated* article wound up spending something like $50,000 to sign him.

I'm proud that I discovered Bill James; I'm also proud that I gave W. P. Kinsella's *Shoeless Joe* its first rave review in a major publication, the *New York Times Book Review*, and I'm very proud of *The Ultimate Baseball Book,* of course. But as far as my own baseball writing is concerned, there's no doubt that my best work is *Nine Innings,* which was published in 1985 at the end of a labyrinthine course of events.

After I left the publishing world in New York and moved to western Massachusetts, I got a contract from Harper & Row to write a book, peculiarly enough, about Harvard University and its role in American culture. I used my advance from the book to make a down payment on a house, and then I didn't do a damn thing on the book. One night I was having dinner with my friend Walter Lippincott, who was then the director of the Cambridge University Press, and Walter said, "Who the hell are you to write a book about Harvard? . . . What do you know about it? . . . You're not qualified to write such a book . . . What you know about is baseball. Why don't you write a book about baseball, you idiot?" He was extremely blunt, and absolutely correct.

So I talked to my agent, and he went back to Harper & Row and told them, "Okrent wants to do a baseball book instead of the Harvard book. He has this idea about writing a book about a single game." Harper & Row said okay, but they wanted me to do the book about the NY Mets. I wasn't interested in the Mets, and I thought they'd been overexposed as it was. Harper & Row lost interest, so we then shopped the idea around. We got a contract for it from Viking where an old friend of mine was going to be the book's editor. I spent two and a half years doing the book, and right after I turned it in my friend got fired. Viking then decided they didn't want to publish it. Some complicated legal and financial maneuvers ensued, with the result that I was free to take the book elsewhere again.

Eventually, it went to where my editor friend went, to the Ticknor & Fields division of Houghton Mifflin, which actually was perfect for me because Houghton Mifflin had published *The Ultimate Baseball Book*. As I said, Houghton Mifflin had done very well with *The Ultimate Baseball Book,* and to their sales force I was a known quantity. If Viking had published it, their sales people wouldn't have had the same initial enthusiasm. The publishing snafus delayed the appearance of the book, but it all worked out for the best in the long run.

I picked Milwaukee as the team to write about because I wanted a team that would be at or near the top of the standings; but, as I said before, I didn't want a team that had been overexposed, such as the Red Sox, the Dodgers, or either of the New York or Chicago teams. By this time I'd been around major league press boxes and inside major league clubhouses enough to know just how much coverage those teams get. The Red Sox, for example, have 15 reporters following them around, and a Boston player can't belch without it becoming a headline story. In Milwaukee there were two guys, one from the *Journal* and one from the *Sentinel,* and the guy from the *Sentinel* didn't go on road trips all the time. It helped a lot that the Brewers had not been subjected to the media hordes. They were not constantly on their guards, as players from some other teams would have been.

I also had to find a team whose management would be amenable to giving me the access I needed. Though I didn't know the Milwaukee general manager, Harry Dalton, several people told me that he'd be a likely candidate. I wrote Harry a letter about the project sometime in early 1980—I was shooting toward 1981 as the season in which to find my game to write about—and he showed it to the

Brewers' owner, Bud Selig. They invited me out to Milwaukee, we spent a day together talking it over, and they agreed to let me do it.

The way Harry cooperated was simply fabulous. During the time I worked on the book, the Brewers had three managers—George Bamberger, Bob Rodgers, and Harvey Kuenn—and each of them was terrific to me. And Tom Flaherty of the *Milwaukee Journal,* who was the senior man of the press corps, was very generous. At the 1980 winter meetings in Dallas, I was in the room with the Milwaukee brain trust while they were discussing the blockbuster Ted Simmons trade, and Tom didn't object. The New York or Boston press would have gone wild: "Why is this guy getting this access?" Tom understood that the book would be coming out much later, and he didn't feel threatened at all by what I was doing. In fact, I was able, without betraying any confidences, to give him a lead on occasion that he followed up on his own.

I went to spring training with the Brewers in 1981; I started spending time with the team in the regular season; and then the strike happened. The publisher said to put the book on hold for the rest of the season, and they gave me some more money to tide me over. I went to the winter meetings in 1982, then to spring training, and finally found my game on June 10, 1982.

There was a reason that I wanted Baltimore as the Brewers' opponent. At the beginning of the 1978 season I'd gotten an assignment from the *New York Times Magazine* to write a piece about Earl Weaver as the greatest manager in baseball, which I believed he was. I spent three weeks with Earl in spring training and got to know him quite well. He's a marvelous character and just incredible copy. Well, the Orioles began the season something like 3-17, which killed my story about Earl. How could the magazine run a story saying, "This is the greatest manager in baseball," when his team was getting off to such a horrible start? I ran into Earl at Yankee Stadium later that year, and he said, "Hey, Dan. Sorry I fucked up for you." I said, "Earl, I'll get that piece published somewhere." I never got the piece published, but I did use the information in *Nine Innings.* And that's why I wanted the Orioles in the game I wrote about, because I had such good Earl Weaver material. It also worked out well because Harry Dalton had come to Milwaukee from the Orioles, and that connection provided a rich vein of fascinating interrelationships. And then the last game of the 1982 season turned out to be that game in Baltimore between the Brewers and the Orioles, with the divisional title on the line. I was lucky beyond belief throughout the whole project. Nearly every card fell face up, showing an ace.

I wanted the game to be in Milwaukee because I had so much stuff about the Brewers' operation: the grounds crew, the stadium management, the marketing of the team, and so on. I didn't want to wait until the end of the season because, if I did and something went wrong, I might have to wait another six months to find my game. I picked out a four-game series at Milwaukee in the first part of June. Now, I also wanted Milwaukee to win, and preferably they'd win a close game. So wouldn't you know, the first three games were all blowouts and were all won by Baltimore. The players were aware that this was my series and that I had to have a Brewers win for it to work. Ben Oglivie said, "We're trying, Dan. We're trying." It came down to the fourth game of the series, and fortunately Milwaukee won in a fairly close game.

For each of those games I hired five or six people, radio reporters and feature writers from the newspapers, to cover different aspects of the game as they were happening. This enabled me to be in several places at one time, so to speak. I also had a spy in uniform on the Brewers' bench. He'd pretend he was taking a leak or having a cigarette, but he was really taking notes on what people were saying during the game. And several players made a point of trying to remember things that were said during the game. For instance, after Cal Ripken singled down the third baseline and later went to third, Paul Molitor told me that he told Ripken, "If you're going to keep hitting it down the line, let me know, and I'll play over a bit." I didn't put this in the book, but Harvey Kuenn, who knew a lot of this was going on, said, "You know, Okrent, the reason that we lost those three games is that some of my players were thinking more about your fucking book than about what was going on out there on the field." He was joking, of course, because he did a good job himself of remembering dugout conversations.

The Brewers' marketing director, Dick Hackett, got a video tape of the game for me that was obviously very helpful. I was able to study the tape carefully, reformulate questions I needed to ask, and go back to the players about minute details of the game. The incredible thing is that some players, such as catcher Charlie Moore, remembered everything, including the exact sequence of pitches, and were happy to discuss minor details. Other players didn't have as good a recall, especially after a few weeks passed. I'd call a player long distance to ask about a certain pitch, and he'd say, "What the fuck are you talking about?" Click.

My hope had been that the game would take place on "Bloom's Day," June 6, the day on which James Joyce's *Ulysses* is set. If it had, I would have been able to begin *Nine Innings* with an echo of the opening of *Ulysses,* which would have been very pretentious but also very funny. Instead of "Stately, plump Buck Mulligan came from the stairhead, bearing a bowl of lather on which a mirror and a razor lay crossed," it would have been "Stately, plump Buck Martinez came from the dugout carrying the tools of ignorance." But the game wasn't played on June 6, and Buck didn't play anyway. Charlie Moore was the catcher that day.

One thing that gave me credibility with the players was my association with *Inside Sports,* for whom I was writing baseball articles at the time. Having a book contract alone wouldn't have been good enough, but having *Inside Sports* behind me helped a great deal because the players, especially guys like Gorman Thomas, loved that magazine. And having some of my pieces appear in the magazine during the time I spent with the team helped me gain acceptance. Ted Simmons, for instance, was at first a very off-putting guy, but when my piece about the big Cardinals-Brewers trade, in which he was the key figure, appeared in *Inside Sports* he opened up entirely and helped me with other players who didn't really want to talk to me.

It was almost never a personal thing. Some players just weren't interested in the book: some because they were too stupid to be interested, and some because they were too smart. Reggie Cleveland, who was probably the most well-read person on the team, said, "What's to be gained by this? I'm near the end of my career, and I've got better things to do than talk to you." He gave me some time, but it was grudging. Fortunately, he wasn't a critical figure on the team.

Pete Vuckovich was a pain in the ass. The Vuckovich off the field was the same as the Vuckovich on the mound, with the bizarre behavior: the head twitches, the death-ray stare, the five different deliveries. His purpose in life, at least while he was playing, was to keep people off guard. One day he'd be as sweet as could be, and the next day he'd scream at me not to come anywhere near him. Generally, I found that the player off the field was very close to the player on the field, except for Robin Yount. As you know, I wrote about that at some length, the odd disparity between the incredible intelligence he brought to the way he played baseball and his apparent lack of imagination otherwise. I know this being in the book bothered Robin, and I was sorry for that because he's a nice guy, but I thought it was relevant and had to be included.

The hardest thing to do was to repress some of the unpleasant things I witnessed. It's my theory as an editor—that's basically what I am, an editor who writes—that the story you tell your friends over a beer is the story that should be in what you write, because you naturally use your most interesting stuff when you're trying to entertain your friends. However, I knew that some things I'd tell my friends confidentially I just couldn't include in the book, mostly involving sexual behavior on the road or drug use. I saw a lot of drugs, it's sad to say.

Nine Innings got overwhelmingly good reviews and only three bad ones. The trouble was that the worst of the three bad ones appeared in the most important place, the *New York Times Book Review.* The review was written, I'm convinced, as a personal vendetta. It's been written about a lot. Anytime anybody does a piece about the politics of book reviewing, they bring up this story.

It all started when I reviewed the novel of a well-known baseball writer, whose name I won't mention, for the *New York Times Book Review.* I didn't think the novel was any good, so I said, "This is a very fine non-fiction writer. He should stick to non-fiction," along with some rather disparaging things about the fiction he'd written.

When *Nine Innings* came out a few years later, the *Times* gave it to this very same writer to review. The *Times* has a very clear policy prohibiting any two writers from reviewing each other's books, but the staff had changed a lot and there was no institutional memory. This writer didn't tell them that I had reviewed his book a few years earlier. He didn't say, "Okrent panned my book. Do you really want me to review his book?"

After the review of *Nine Innings* came out, I wrote a letter to the editor, Mitchel Levitas, that said, "I thought your readers might like to know that three years ago in this same forum I gave a bad review to a book written by the man who recently said 'X,Y,Z' about my book. I didn't think the *Times* considered itself a vehicle for revenge."

Well, Levitas wouldn't publish my letter. He told me that when he called this writer about the situation, the writer told him that he had never read my review of his book, that he had asked his publishers to send him only good reviews. I wrote Levitas back and said, "I can tell you from my own very recent experience that when you get panned in the *New York Times Book Review* the only way you don't hear about it is if you have no friends who call to commisserate, or no enemies who call to gloat, or you're dead." The review reduced the amount of money I got up front for the paperback sale of the book, but more than anything else it was the humiliation that hurt. I would meet people in the following weeks, and you could see in their expressions what they were thinking: "Oh, you're the poor guy who got such a savage review in the *New York Times Book Review.*" The whole thing is still a bitter memory for me.

The other two non-positive reviews made a very good point about the book. They basically said, "This isn't really a book about one game, as much as it's a framework into which the author has dumped everything he knows about baseball." That was true. And this criticism brings to mind a funny story which I will now admit to in public for the first time. By the time I turned the manuscript in, it had been read by my wife, several friends, and my editor, and everything seemed to be fine. The book was almost in type when somebody pointed out that there was no bottom of the fifth inning. I had just skipped the bottom of the fifth! That really exposed the gimmick. At that point in the book the game had gotten so lost in the digressions and elaborations that 10 readers—and the writer—had not even noticed that I had skipped three outs. That half inning in the middle of the game was the last part of the book to emerge from my typewriter.

Still, although I was using the game as a framework in which to dump everything I knew about baseball, I prefer to view the digressions and elaborations as a virtue rather than a fault. The point of the book was to show that the game you see at the ballpark is only the tip of the iceberg, that everything else is hidden beneath the waterline.

The game itself wasn't the point of the book. That's why the game I chose to write about had to be an unimportant game, unlike the World Series game that Arnold Hano wrote about so skillfully in *A Day in the Bleachers,* the other book concerned with a single baseball game. I wanted a little bit of drama so that I had the element of things unfolding, which you don't have in a 13-1 blowout; but I didn't want the significance of the game, who won and who lost, to take precedence over the digressive matters. And the people who liked the book—thank goodness there were many people who did like it—recognized that the digressions were relevant. They recognized, for instance, that Jim Gantner's upbringing in Eden, Wisconsin, was materially important to that game. And the Ted Simmons trade . . . Nobody else has ever written in that detail about a baseball trade. Not before, not since. That's how a baseball trade works, and it was an incredibly complex trade. If the Simmons trade wasn't important to that game, what was?

Actually, I did *Nine Innings* not because I knew so much about baseball, but because I wanted to know so much about baseball. From my prior reporting I had more than an average fan's knowledge of baseball, but this book was the opportunity for me to get paid to learn what I didn't know. I'd start on a topic I didn't know much about and begin asking questions of coaches and players, including retired players. I went down to Jupiter, Florida, to see Bob Shaw, the former major league pitcher, because I'd been told he could explain pitching as well as anyone alive; and in one afternoon at a pizza place Shaw really opened my eyes. And it was an exhilirating experience to find those players, such as Simmons, Cecil Cooper, and Sal Bando, who were truly articulate about what they did for a living and about how they did it.

I was also fortunate that I was largely dealing with players who didn't bite my head off or shut me out when I asked the incredibly obvious questions, the idiot question, like: what's the effect of ice on a pitcher's arm after a game? I asked a lot of those questions, but the players by and large answered thcm patiently for me. The beat reporters don't dare ask stupid questions. But I could, and I like to think I was functioning as a surrogate for the reader who would like to ask those same questions. And I think the book answers those questions. Why do you do that? What does this mean? How does it work?

I'm not really a "professional" baseball writer anymore. The reason I'm not is that I found that when I professionalized something I loved, it became a job. And when it became a job, it was harder to love it, particularly when I was around the ballplayers. By being around the players as much as I was, I was continually confronted with the fact that these people have feet of clay. Most of the players have feet of clay because they have lived stunted lives. Not all of them, of course, but of 650 major league players, I'd guess 500 of them have led stunted lives.

So I soon discovered that I wasn't being as much of a fan as I had been before, that I couldn't love baseball as I had before. I knew too much. I wanted my heroes to remain heroes, and that was impossible when I saw an MVP trying to score drugs during batting practice off a former batting champion; when I saw nationally admired figures engage in truly repellent behavior with women on the road; when I saw the rudeness, the insensitivity, the profound self-absorption of some of these people. I didn't want to see all that anymore, so I got away from it.

Plus, I'd gotten typecast as a writer who writes baseball pieces for non-baseball audiences. Non-baseball magazines would call me about baseball assignments because they'd figure: "We need a baseball piece, but it shouldn't be done by somebody who's a regular baseball writer, who's a jocksniffer, who uses baseball clichés . . . ah, Okrent!" Well, I love baseball dearly, but there's more to life than that, and I'd like to think there's more to me as a writer than that. Also, everything I know about how baseball is played is in *Nine Innings,* and everything I know about baseball history is in *The Ultimate Baseball Book* or in *Baseball Anecdotes,* a book I co-wrote with Steve Wulf. I may do another baseball book someday; I'd love to do a biography of Branch Rickey, for instance, because he's a figure whose importance extends beyond baseball and into the larger culture. But right now I'm dry; I've got nothing new to say about baseball.

So I'd rather stretch my wings a little bit, not be typecast, and go to the ballpark as a fan. And that's what I do now. When I'm sitting in the stands and a friend asks me what Don Mattingly is really like, I say, "I don't know." A few years ago I had some sense of what most of the major league players of any prominence were like as individuals. Now I have no idea. But I don't care. It's too much fun being a fan again.

BASEBALL BOOKS BY DANIEL OKRENT

The Ultimate Baseball Book. Boston: Houghton Mifflin, 1981.
Nine Innings. New York: Ticknor & Fields, 1985.
Baseball Anecdotes (co-author). New York: Oxford University Press, 1989.

13

GREG RHODES

Called "The Unofficial Historian of the Cincinnati Reds" by Hall-of-Fame Reds broadcaster Marty Brennaman, Greg Rhodes was born August 17, 1946, and raised in Richmond, Indiana. He graduated from Richmond High School, then attended Indiana University (Bloomington) where he obtained a doctorate in education. After teaching history at various levels in schools in Indiana, Kentucky, and Hawaii, and authoring textbooks, teacher guides, and other curriculum materials, Rhodes moved to Cincinnati in 1985 and took a job with the Cincinnati Historical Society. In 1988, he edited Baseball in Cincinnati: From Wooden Fences to Astroturf, *a collection of historical essays published by the society, and in 1993, he wrote and produced an audio biography of broadcaster Red Barber ("Red Barber: From the Catbird Seat," issued on cassette and CD by WVXU). In 1994, Rhodes formed a publishing company called Road West Publishing, primarily for the purpose of publishing books about the Cincinnati Reds. He has authored five books about the Reds.* Crosley Field *and* Big Red Dynasty *were both honored as finalists for* Spitball Magazine*'s CASEY Award;* Big Red Dynasty *was a finalist for the Macmillan Book Award; and* Reds in Black & White *won The Sporting News/SABR Research Award for 1999. Rhodes was a founder and original playing member of Cincinnati's first Vintage Baseball team, the Sharon Woods Village Shamrocks, and in 2000, he founded a vintage team modeled after baseball's first professional team, the 1869 Red Stockings. He lives in Cincinnati and works at home in an office filled with Cincinnati Reds photos, artwork, and memorabilia.*

I PLAYED VINTAGE BASEBALL for three or four years before John Erardi and I wrote our book about the 1869 Red Stockings. The experience definitely helped me in writing the book, but I wish that I had played even more Vintage Baseball before starting the book because now I've got an even better understanding of what the nineteenth-century game was like.

How did I get started in Vintage Baseball? Well, in 1988, I was working at the Cincinnati Historical Society, and I got recruited along with four or five other guys who worked at the society to play against the Muffins, the vintage team sponsored by the Ohio Historical Society in Columbus. The Muffins wanted to get some other teams started so they'd have somebody to play, and they had been seeding teams all over the state—I guess you could call them the Johnny Appleseeds of Vintage Baseball. And they do deserve a tremendous amount of credit for spreading the game. Anyway, the guy who was the director of the village at Sharon Woods here in Cincinnati had been in touch with the Ohio Historical Society in Columbus, and he was the one who recruited us to play against the Muffins. I guess they contacted him because the Sharon Woods Village was the best spot in the Cincinnati area to play Vintage Baseball. They've got this great field out there that is a perfect nineteenth-century venue. And when I say *field,* that's exactly what I mean . . . not a laid-out diamond at all but an open piece of pasture—a field. At this point I didn't know anything about Vintage Baseball, and I'd never heard of the Muffins; but we played the game against the Muffins and enjoyed it so much that we started our own vintage team, which we named the Shamrocks. There are now two of us left still playing. The others lasted a little while, but they eventually dropped out.

To this day I find that it's a real kick playing Vintage Baseball. I guess the attraction is that you're not only playing ball, but you're also performing—you're putting on a show for people. I enjoy the challenge of playing, and it is a real challenge because we play on rough fields, we don't use gloves, we swing heavy bats, and we try to mimic the way the nineteenth-century players stood at bat and the way they swung the bat. All of that's fun, but it's also fun to try to take on the role of a nineteenth-century player.

For instance, we try to keep out of the game as many modern intrusions as possible. All the equipment is replicated, and we try to speak and act in ways we think would be consistent with what they would have done back then, particularly in decorum and the use of language. It still was very much a gentleman's game back in the 1860s. Clearly they were competitive, and clearly there was an elite group of teams, of which the Cincinnati Red Stockings were one, that were definitely out to win. There's no question about that. But it was very typical in that time period that if there was a close play at a base and the umpire couldn't see exactly what was going on, he'd come out and ask the players. And you were expected to give the guy an honest answer. Well, the crowd loves this kind of stuff! And when you do something like this, you get a chance to explain to the spectators that that's the way things were done back then. And the umpire can even ask the crowd to help him make a call. I can show you newspaper clippings from the 1869–70 seasons, when the Red Stockings were playing high-caliber, competitive ball, that indicate the umpire turned around during the game and asked the fans, "Did the catcher catch that ball or not?" And, in cases like that, the umpire would take the word of the fans.

And, of course, the terminology and rules are different too. For example, we know from studying game accounts and player interviews in the papers that they did not use the terms *single, double, triple*. Those terms had not been invented. They said, "Make your base," "Get to your second," "Take your third"—things like that. *Home run* was used; it had been invented. But they often used *hands* instead of *outs*, and so we say things like "Two hands down!" We also try to use current phrases of the day like "Leg it to first (or second)" and "Show a little ginger," with *ginger* meaning hustle or enthusiasm.

There are some things we just don't know for certain, like bunting. Did they or did they not bunt? It wasn't against the rules, but you never see a reference to the term or anyone doing in essence what a bunt is. On the other hand, it's probable, in my opinion, that guys were in fact doing something very comparable to bunting . . . sort of trying to steer the ball to a certain part of the infield. I don't know when they started doing it, but obviously they did start doing it at some point. And I'm certain that the first time somebody did it, the umpire did not say, "Wait a minute . . . you can't do that." He probably just accepted it as something new in the game. We have umpires in our vintage games who say, "Hey, come back. You can't bunt." But I think that's just a misguided artificiality of our efforts to re-create the 1860s game because we just don't know exactly when bunting became common.

As a matter of fact, when the Muffins set up the game they play, they misinterpreted the rules and developed some customs of play and some rituals that were never, ever part of the game, according to the research that I and some other people have done. A good example of this is the tally bell that the Muffins have. When you cross the plate, you're supposed to go over and ring this little bell they have on the scorekeeper's table. It's cute, it's quaint. You go over and ring the bell and everybody knows you've scored. It's really not a bad idea because back then they didn't have PA systems or anybody announcing anything, but I have never, ever seen a reference to a tally bell in any of the newspaper accounts I've gone through, nor have the guys who've done even more research than I have. And there's certainly nothing in the rules about it. The funny thing is, the Muffins themselves, who started back in 1981–82, they don't know why they use the tally bell. They just do. If you ask them to show you any reference to the tally bell in a printed source, they can't do it. When we first started playing Vintage Baseball, we just accepted it; but when I got into doing the Red Stockings research, I found out it's just not there, and other researchers started asking, "Where'd the tally bell come from?" So several teams quit doing it.

As for equipment, we have much better knowledge because by the 1860s there were a lot of photographs and a lot of line art in the newspapers. So it's relatively easy to replicate the bats and the uniforms—there were no gloves, so we don't have to worry about them. Plus, there were certain specifications in the rules about the ball and the bat. There were certain limitations on how long the bat could be and, I believe, on how heavy it could be; and the ball definitely had specifications as to its circumference and weight. The rules also specify the ball's composition. It had to be made of yarn or wool or cloth wrapped around a rubber core and then stitched in hide of some sort. So we have a fair amount of direction when it comes to making the equipment.

All the equipment has to be handmade, though. The bats are easy to make, and most teams make their own, but usually a couple of guys wind up making balls for teams all around the country. There was a guy in Louisville who made balls for a number of years. His last name was Ferguson, so everybody just called his the Ferguson Ball, which was a nice touch because that's what happened in baseball before everything became run on an "official" basis. Back then the balls had odd names because people would often attach the name of a proprietor to his ball, or they would name the ball after one of the ball's real or supposed characteristics. Ferguson quit making vintage balls a few years ago because it got to be too time-consuming. A guy up in Columbus, Ohio, is making balls now, and the baseballs are actually part of a nice little vintage manufacturing business he's got going. He makes all sorts of vintage clothing, furniture, and artifacts, some of it baseball related and some of it not. Actually, he recently hooked up with a guy in Mexico who makes the balls for him. Because of trade policy, "Mexico" has to be stamped on the balls. The stamped "Mexico" is real small, but you can definitely see it on each ball, so we always try to scratch it out. Nobody involved in re-creating the invention of a prime American institution—the game of baseball—that supposedly represents so much about the essence of our nation wants to use key artifacts of the game that are made in Mexico.

By the way, the balls run about $35 to $40 a piece—they're fairly expensive—and we buy three or four new baseballs at the start of each season. It's interesting that in a lot of the photographs of the period the balls appear to be brown, appear to be darker. In some of the other photographs, the balls appear to be a little bit lighter. Maybe the brown balls started out lighter and got dirty, or maybe because of the different kinds of hide that was used some of the balls started out brown and some others started out white. At any rate, we've discovered that the dark balls are hard to see, especially since we play on fields with really high grass and lots of tall trees in the background. Of course, over time they darken up anyway. The other thing is that they get soft, they get mushy. Sometimes the seams even start coming apart because these balls are all handmade. To a certain extent, this is good because when we first get them the balls are very compact and pretty hard. They feel very much like a modern baseball. After you play with them for a game or two, they definitely start to loosen up. But then, after you play with them for too long, they'll get out of round and become dead or the stitching will fall apart. So they don't have a long life.

We don't really know how long a ball typically lasted for them, but I do know that the balls themselves varied, from maker to maker, and even within a group of balls produced by the same maker. Some of the balls were definitely wound or stitched much tighter than others, and some of the balls were definitely harder than others. In fact, one of the balls that was sold was called a "Bounding Rock"! That ought to give you some idea of how hard that ball was. Other balls were more elastic and livelier.

Before each game the captains of the two teams would come out for a meeting to decide various things about the game, and one of the key issues they'd discuss was what ball they were going to use because there was no official ball up until the first league was formed in the 1870s. Prior to that you had a choice of what baseball to use. Sometimes the home team supplied the ball; but oftentimes, as I found out researching the Red Stockings, the game was delayed 15 minutes or longer because the captains couldn't agree on which ball to use. I suspect in some cases that the home team got to use its preferred ball on a home-and-away basis, but the thing is, teams often didn't play each other on a home-and-away basis; they'd only play once a year. The Red Stockings, for instance, would go east and play some teams in Philadelphia, let's say, but there was no guarantee that all those teams would go west later in the same season and play in Cincinnati. They might or might not.

Once the ball was decided on, though, whatever it was, that was the ball they used for the entire game. They never changed balls. They would only change balls if the ball got lost. Or if it came apart. My favorite story about this was a game played up in New England somewhere. They were playing in a city park, and somebody hit a foul ball that bounced through a window of a nearby house. They stopped the game, went over to the house, recovered the ball, and brought it back. They didn't keep playing. Oh, no, they stopped the game, went after the ball, and brought it back. And only then, and after the captains had examined the ball and agreed that it had too many glass shards in it, did they decide to throw the ball out and put a new one in play. So the choice of ball was very critical back then. Today it's something we take for granted.

I suspect that part of the reason they kept the same ball in play was to keep down expenses, but they also did it because there was simply no custom back then of the fans keeping a foul ball. If a ball went into the crowd or the stands, it was always thrown back into play. Cubs fans today at Wrigley Field throw opponents' home-run balls back onto the field as a symbolic rejection. That's a slightly different thing than what we're talking about here, but in a sense, like so many other things about contemporary baseball we think is new, it has a precedent in baseball history.

I think a bigger reason for the custom was the fact, which we referred to earlier, that the balls varied so much, even balls of the same brand, so to speak. They just believed that it was best to stick with the same ball, out of fairness to both teams. And then there was the custom of the winning team keeping the ball as a trophy after the game. If you won the game, you'd write the score and the date and the opponent's name on the ball and stick it in your trophy case. Today, when a guy throws a no-hitter, he keeps the last ball used in the game, but, shoot, 40 or 50 other balls were probably used in the same game. Back then that trophy ball would have meant a lot more because it was the ball that was played with the whole game.

As you know, the name of our original Vintage Baseball team in Cincinnati was the Shamrocks, and that was a fictitious name. I don't know why we didn't name the team the Red Stockings. There was a team called the Shamrocks that played in Cincinnati around the turn of the century, but when we picked the name we didn't know anything about that team. It was just a coincidence. We played in Sharon Woods Village, and the alliteration in the "Sharon Woods Shamrocks" was basically the reason for the name.

The Ohio Historical Society didn't do much better than we did in naming its team, as the Muffins is a made-up name too. There was never a Columbus Muffins. In the nineteenth century, *muffins* was a derogatory term used to designate second-string-caliber players. It would have been ironic for them to unwittingly name a team that, but they knew what muffins meant, and they chose it in a self-mocking sort of way. It is ironic in the sense that the Muffins are a good team; there are 30 or 40 guys on their roster, so it's never the same team, but when they put their best nine on the field they are very good. What is a little unfortunate as far as the naming of their team is concerned is that there were two or three teams in Columbus back in the 1860s whose names they could have picked, and I don't know why they didn't choose one of them. In fact, a group of guys who spun off of the Muffins call themselves the Columbus Capitols, and that was the name of a real nineteenth-century team. They have a description of the old Capitols uniforms, so they have made up uniforms to match those of their ancestors.

Many of the other Vintage Baseball teams in Ohio use made-up names, but not all of them. There's a team up in Cleveland named the Forest Citys after a real team that played the Red Stockings. There's a famous photo of them and the Red Stockings on the wall right behind me. There's also a team that plays out of Detroit at Greenfield Village called the Lah-dee-Das. I thought, "That's ridiculous to name a team that," but I later found out that there was a real nineteenth-century team in the Detroit area called the Lah-dee-Das!

About five or six years ago I started pushing for the name "Red Stockings," but we couldn't just change overnight because vintage uniforms are very expensive to make. Well, a few years later the Shamrock uniforms started wearing out, and we were going to have to get new uniforms. Also, some of the core players on the Shamrocks who'd been playing six or seven years were starting to lose some of their enthusiasm, and our roster had sort of fallen off. So last year we started to reorganize the club with the idea of bringing in new people and starting a new team that would be called the Red Stockings. Since we know a fair amount about the real Red Stockings players, the plan was to have our guys imitate specific Red Stocking players. For example, whoever played third base would be called "Fred Waterman," and ideally that guy would resemble Waterman as much as possible.

The idea of forming a club modeled after the Red Stockings was such a draw that our roster expanded to about 30 guys, enough, in fact, for us to stock not only a Red Stockings team but a second new team as well, the Cincinnati Buckeyes, the Red Stockings's main local rivals in 1867–68.

We were able to get a little financial support for the Red Stockings club from the Cincinnati Reds. I've gotten to know the Reds's CEO John Allen from all the Reds books we've done, and I'd been talking to John for a couple of years about my plans to get the Red Stockings going. At the end of last summer, we had three or four prototype Red Stockings uniforms made. This past January we set up a booth at Reds Fest, the Reds's wintertime promotional event, which is also a big baseball card show, and we had several of our guys dressed in these sample Red Stockings uniforms. They were a huge hit. They walked all around the convention center where Reds Fest was held, and people came up to them all day long to talk to them and get their picture taken with them. John Allen saw them, and he loved them too. I told him that we were looking to get some corporate underwriting because the uniforms were so expensive to make, about $175 apiece, and he said absolutely the Reds would be glad to make a contribution. In the end, I think they gave us around $2,500, which really helped out.

Almost all of the Vintage Baseball being played conforms to the baseball played in the 1860s, primarily because of the game itself. The pitching is underhand from 45 feet, so there's not a lot of skill involved in pitching, or in hitting, for that matter. I mean, it's basically slow-pitch underhand softball, with no big arc, of course. And it's also very clear that the baseball of the 1860s era was still a gentleman's game, and that's very important to almost all the teams playing. The guys don't want it to be too competitive. They want to put on a good show, they want to play well and play hard, but the gentleman's aura that surrounded the game is important to everyone involved in re-creating the vintage game. Once you go past the 1860s, you start getting into a more competitive environment with faster pitching, and in the 1880s you go to overhand pitching.

Most teams play by the rules that governed the game in the early 1860s. The most significant rule change of the time occurred in 1863 and involved catching fly balls. Starting with 1863 you had to catch the ball on the fly. Prior to this you could make a legal catch on one bounce. When the Muffins started playing, they were using 1859–60 rules, and you could catch a fly ball on one bound. Since we've adopted the Red Stockings, we are definitely in a post–Civil War era, and so we play the catch-it-on-the-fly rule. But a lot of teams don't like to play the fly game, so we often play with the catch-it-on-one-bounce rule to keep them happy.

Here, again, the Muffins made a mistake by placing themselves in Ohio playing club baseball in 1859. Well, there was no club baseball in 1859. There could have been little pickup games played here or there in Ohio, but there were no clubs playing; there was no organized baseball until after the Civil War. So, really, the Muffins should have positioned themselves in the years 1866–67, and they should have been a fly club. I believe I know why they made this mistake. I've heard that somewhere in the bowels of the Ohio Historical Society was a set of rules for a team in Hamilton for 1858 or 1859, and those were the rules they decided to follow, figuring, "Well, if they were playing in Hamilton, then surely they were playing in Columbus, the state capital. So we'll be an 1858–59 club." Hamilton, of course, is the city north of Cincinnati where former Reds pitcher and longtime Reds radio broadcaster Joe Nuxhall is from. As it turned out, the rules they modeled themselves after were from Hamilton, New Jersey, not Hamilton, Ohio. So they jumped the gun. The fact is that there was very little organized baseball being played outside of the New York–New Jersey–Philadelphia area up until the Civil War, and after the Civil War it just took off everywhere, especially out in the Midwest. There were three clubs in Cincinnati that started in 1866, including the Red Stockings. Those were probably the first organized teams in Ohio. But by 1867, 1868, only a year or two later, there were definitely teams all over the state. So, clearly, 1867–68 are the years every team in the Midwest should be playing.

There're usually several things that go into the making of a book, and when you're finished you sometimes lose track of how it all started, but I can think of three things that went into the making of *The First Boys of Summer,* the book about the Red Stockings. First of all, when I was working at the historical society back in the 1980s, I was the only baseball fan on the staff. Whenever we got baseball questions or inquiries, they'd say, "Oh, give it to Greg. He'll do it." And that was fine with me. Because all the baseball was funneled to me, I became involved in two or three projects that required me to do research on the Red Stockings. And this was great too because, like all Reds fans, I'd grown up revering the Red Stockings because they had started professional baseball in Cincinnati. So here was a chance for me to go back and look up all the stuff we had on the team. Before this, I'd never read nineteenth-century newspaper accounts of baseball, and they were a revelation to me. I was stunned to find long accounts of games and detailed descriptions of the crowds and the opposing teams, and even box scores. I'd never imagined that I'd find box scores in the Cincinnati papers of 1869!

There was so much rich material that I remember thinking fairly early on, "Gosh, there's probably a good book in all this." So I started piecing the Red Stockings's story together, little by little. Around that time I became aware of Darryl Brock's novel about the 1869 Red Stockings called *If I Never Get Back*. I didn't meet him until after the book had come out—I think we finally met at a book signing he was doing in Cincinnati—but I'd read the book and loved it, and we hit it off right away. I was invigorated by his book, and, in fact, it spurred me on even more. I didn't walk away from his book thinking, "Well, I might as well quit because he's already done the Red Stockings." As meticulously researched as Darryl's book was, I felt we weren't really in competition with each other because (1) his book was a novel; (2) his book concerned only a slice of the 1869 season, about three months' worth; and (3) there were a lot of important issues he didn't deal with. And, of course, as a novelist he wasn't under any obligation to deal with those issues. So I still felt that there was a nonfiction account waiting to be written. Nobody else had ever done it. Oh, sure, there were chapters on general baseball histories such as Seymour and Voigt, but there'd never been a full-length treatment of the team.

Besides the fact that I wasn't going to be writing fiction, my book was going to be very different from Darryl's because I was going to include the 1870 season, which had always been more interesting to me than the 1869 season. The 1869 season gets more attention, and deservedly so—it's such a landmark season since it involved the first professional team—but 1870 was the season that had all the fun stuff. In 1870, the Red Stockings lose for the first time and have to start dealing with that indignity; the club leadership unravels in the middle of the season; they suffer an injury to the star player, shortstop George Wright; Charlie Sweasy and a bunch of the guys get in

a fight on board a steamboat on the way back from a game in Ports-
mouth and get suspended for a couple of games; and then, at the
end of the season, all the financial and organizational problems
come to a head and the club leadership says, "We're getting out of
the professional experiment, we're not going to do it next year,"
and the club completely folds up! That's a lot of great stuff to write
about. I also realized that the team's sudden demise sewed up the
story in a neat package for me as a writer: you have a beginning in
1869 and the issues of why and how they went professional; there's
a middle part, which is the story of the great winning streak they
went on; and then you've got a clean, definitive end. All the elements for a good book were right there.

A final impetus for the book came from my association with the
Cincinnati Enquirer's John Erardi, who became my coauthor of the
book and who now is a good friend of mine. John had come to the
Cincinnati Historical Society on a number of occasions to do some
research, and I was always impressed with the fact that here was a
newspaper sportswriter who was spending the extra time in a library
because he was always looking for a historical angle on things. John
too had always been fascinated with the Red Stockings, and there
were some fundamental questions about them that we both wanted
answers to: Why did they become the first professional team? Why
here and not someplace else? They went undefeated in 1869, but
what did that mean? Who were they playing, in other words? To
make a long story short, John and I decided to team up on the book,
and we had a great time digging up the answers to our questions.

What was it that did make the Red Stockings such a great team?
Well, you would assume that it was the money. As the first and only
professional team, they must have gone out and hired all the very
best players and put together an all-star team. But that's not what
happened. For one thing, guys had already been getting paid, under
the table, for several seasons prior to 1869 in other cities, and so
they didn't have to come to Cincinnati and play for the Red Stockings in order to get paid. And moving to Cincinnati from the East
Coast back in those days was not insignificant. It was a big move, and
a lot of big-time players didn't want to come to Cincinnati. Although
the Red Stockings had a couple of all-stars and some other really
top-quality players, they had to fill in with some guys who would have
been considered good ballplayers but not great ballplayers. So it
wasn't the fact that the Red Stockings had all the best talent; other
teams had great players too. No, the difference was that the other

teams did not have the leverage over their players that the Red Stockings had over theirs. The other teams' players got paid but only out of the gate receipts, and the other teams had no leverage to make their players get in shape or show up for practice or do anything at all. Because the Red Stockings paid their players salaries, they could get away with a no-drinking policy, a rigorous preseason training program, and the requirement that the players show up for practice. In addition, Harry Wright, the team captain who functioned as the field manager, was great at drilling the team in the fundamentals. The Red Stockings were in essence a well-coached team. And then the directors ran the club like a business; they ran it very professionally. It was a combination of all these things, including the all-around ability of the players. The Red Stockings were definitely an outstanding team, and that helped too.

Why would you give up so quickly? Why just walk away after putting together the most successful team in the world? Well, the answer to that conundrum was twofold. First, the club definitely lost money, and they were afraid of losing more. You see, they'd weighted the second half of their schedule for the 1870 season with a lot of home games against big-name teams from the East. In the middle of the 1870 season, they added seats to their grandstand in anticipation of big crowds for those games. But a lot of things worked against them. It was a really hot summer that year, they raised the price of a ticket from 24¢ to 50¢, some of the magic aura around the team had evaporated once they lost a couple of games, and a lot of people just lost interest in the team. Instead of crowds of 6,000 or 8,000 or 10,000, which were big crowds for that time, and which they'd gotten the year before, they got crowds of 2,500–4,000. So their investment in the ballpark didn't pay off.

Second, at the end of the 1870 season, there were so many teams that suddenly wanted to go professional and follow the Red Stockings model that they were bidding up the prices of players. A lot of the Red Stockings players were from the East Coast, and now they could go home and play and get more money than Cincinnati was going to offer them. When the Wright brothers decided to leave, the club directors felt there was no way they could field a competitive team or a team that would stand up to the high standards the Red Stockings had set, so they just said, "Screw it. We're not going to do it."

There was also one more minor but interesting factor. As I said earlier, the coverage of the Red Stockings in the Cincinnati newspapers was extensive and very detailed and extended to team business matters as well as to the games. At times, you'd think you were reading the official minutes of their business meetings. In one of these discussions at the end of the 1870 season, Aaron Champion, the president of the club, said, in reference to the way the Red Stockings had treated the opposition in 1869, "We were pitiless. We extracted every last penny that we could from the other clubs."

What Champion was referring to was this: When the Red Stockings went East early in 1870 before their first loss, they were still undefeated, they were the greatest thing in baseball history, and every club on the East Coast wanted to schedule them because the Red Stockings were drawing huge crowds. Well, Champion used the Red Stockings's drawing power to negotiate sweetheart deals by which the Red Stockings got much bigger cuts of the gate than normal. And they knew going into 1871 that they weren't going to get those deals any longer. Now they were going to be just another one of several really good teams, instead of being the one and only great team.

This was another indication that they weren't going to be able to make it work financially anymore, so they just threw in the towel. And, of course, they were under no obligation to keep the team going. Today, a major league team couldn't just quit. It's part of a franchised arrangement, and somebody else would step in to buy the franchise or move it to a different city. Back then there was no league—leagues hadn't been invented yet—and so the club leadership could do pretty much what they wanted to do.

It's interesting that you ask about Henry Millar. We did rely on him quite a bit because the paper he worked for, the *Cincinnati Commercial*, provided the most regular coverage of the Red Stockings of any of the Cincinnati papers, including the *Enquirer*. Millar's initials weren't on every game in the *Commercial*, but he covered most of the Red Stockings games, and he did travel with the team. He made the first big trip east to New York, and he went out to San Francisco with the team in the fall, so, yes, I guess you could say that he was baseball's first beat reporter.

A lot of claims, besides being the first professional team, have been made for the Red Stockings in terms of doing things first, and I personally think you have to be very careful in making such claims. It's very hard to trace firsts, and, if you pay attention, you'll often find several teams claiming to be the first to do the same thing. John Snyder, my latest coauthor, made a comment I really liked when we started the new book, called *Redleg Journal,* which is just about to go to press. John said, "We aren't necessarily going to believe anything previously published about the Reds is true." And I agreed with him because there's a lot of stuff published over the years that's just not right. Some of the fallacious things in print are not all that important, but the historian in you still wants to get it right, and especially when the matter is important.

For example, there's a lot of confusion about exactly how many games the Red Stockings won during the 1869 season and how many they won during their famous winning streak that lasted until June 1870. Erroneous accounts always pad win totals, and the confusion is completely needless as far as I'm concerned. All you have to do is go back to the original source, which is the Cincinnati newspapers, and the figures are right there. Harry Wright kept meticulous scorebooks, and at the end of 1869 and 1870 he released team and individual statistics and won-lost records to the newspapers, and the papers printed them toward the end of the year, in December of both years, as I recall. Perhaps part of the confusion comes from the fact that the Red Stockings did not have an official league schedule. They played against teams of widely varying caliber, and some of these games were considered to be official matches and some were not. The thing is, in the end-of-the-season summary that Harry supplied to the papers for 1870, he included only those games he considered to be official games, 57 games, and their record was 57–0. So right from the beginning in 1869, the number 57 was out there, and I can't figure out where along the line the number got screwed up. Some historians give a total of more than 100 straight wins up until they played New York in 1870 and got beat, but the actual figure was 81: 57 straight wins in 1869 and 24 more to start 1870.

It's a never-ending battle, and you'll never get it 100 percent right, but at least we're trying—we're making the effort. It reminds me of an old saying: "It's not what you don't know that will get you into trouble. . . ." If you don't know something, you'll say you don't know or you'll research it; you won't just make something up. To finish the saying, "It's what you are sure of that's *not* true—that's what gets you into trouble!" And a lot of times you fall into this trap because you believe that you have an impeccable, authoritative source and that you don't need to double-check him. And, to be fair, it's an almost impossible job because who has the time to double-check everything? Nobody. The point is, I think people who concentrate on a specific team are probably going to have better information just because they are more focused. Nevertheless, I make mistakes, and I've printed mistakes.

I did approach other publishers about *The First Boys of Summer*, but none of them were interested. I realize now that the nineteenth century is not a big topic for most publishers—they don't want to touch it. Plus, the publishers didn't know me. I was a first-time author with no track record. I'm glad things turned out the way they did, though, because the rejections steered me in the direction of becoming a publisher myself. And I must say that several of those publishers, especially Orange Frazer Press, were very generous in giving me advice on how to publish books. They clued me in on things like price points and how many copies to print in the initial press run. I was surprised to learn from Orange Frazer Press that it had printed only 6,000 copies of *The Cincinnati Game*: 3,000 in hardback and 3,000 in paperback. The books sold out and the publisher was very happy with that; and I was encouraged that those numbers, which I felt were kind of modest, could be enough to make a book financially successful. I felt that we could do something similar with the Red Stockings book. Anyway, after talking it over with my wife, Sallie, one night over a couple of glasses of wine—after probably one too many glasses of wine—I decided, "Hey, we can do this. If I do a lot of prep work and layout, and with John and me doing the writing, I think we can sell 4,000–5,000 copies of the book." So that's what we did; we published the book ourselves with a press run of 4,000.

I've learned that you are going to sell most copies of a book in the first year, probably within the first six to nine months. Although it took us a couple of years to sell out of the book, we did well enough in the first six to nine months that it gave me the confidence to go ahead and do the next book. And it turned out that the next book, the Crosley Field book, was the one that made our little publishing business work, because it sold really well and gave us a cushion to work with. Road West Publishing, as we named the business, is a niche publisher, and we have a fairly small geographic market to sell to. I'd say 90 percent of our sales come from an area encompassed by Louisville, Lexington, Indianapolis, Dayton, Columbus, and Cincinnati; it's a pretty manageable area that I can work myself. We have a distributor, Partners, out of Michigan, which specializes in the Midwest, because you can't do this without one. Even though there's mail order and the Internet, you still have to get your books into the bookstores, and you need a distributor for that.

One of the key issues for any publisher, but especially for a small publisher, is how many copies do you print? You have to print enough to make it worth your while, but you can really overestimate or underestimate how many copies you will sell and kill yourself either way. I remember John Baskin of Orange Frazer Press telling me, "No matter what Reds book you publish, you'll sell a couple thousand copies because there's that many Reds fans who'll buy any Reds book as long as it's not a total piece of crap." And I do think that's right. You've got a certain number of baseball book collectors, a certain number of people who buy books about Cincinnati, and a certain number of fans who buy every Reds book; and those people add up to a base you can build on. The rest of it is bringing in the people who might buy the book on impulse or as a gift, and to help reach those people, we have always put money into photos and illustrations and great covers. You usually have to cut a few corners somewhere on every project, but we never cut corners on our covers.

The first two books were paperbacks, but by the third book we had enough confidence to spend the extra money needed to do a hardback and think that we had a good chance to sell 6,000–8,000 copies and maybe even 10,000. At this point we are doing very well, and we've earned a reputation for producing high-quality books. On the other hand, I always say that we are just one book away from disaster.

Yes, I think the nostalgia factor was paramount in the success of the Crosley Field book. To a certain extent, book buyers tend to skew a little bit older, and the 50- to 60-year-olds in the Cincinnati area grew up going to Reds games at Crosley Field; so that's where all their best memories are. And the sterility of Riverfront Stadium made people long even more for a great old park like Crosley. The Crosley Field book was fun to do because Crosley was the ballpark I grew up on too. Richmond, Indiana, where I grew up, is only 65 miles from Cincinnati, and when I was in high school, my friends and I went to every Reds doubleheader at Crosley for a couple of summers in a row. And that's when they had six or eight doubleheaders a summer.

Crosley was a classic ballpark in the sense that it was a well-integrated part of its environment. It was located in an industrial, working-class neighborhood, and it reflected that environment. It was made of red brick and really didn't have much adornment or architectural flair of any kind. Much of Crosley's character came from its densely urban setting, and when all the buildings that surrounded it began to be razed around 1960, it became kind of bleak. As you know, Cincinnati is getting a new ballpark. When the developers initially entertained ideas for its design, they wondered, "Are there any elements of Crosley Field we can copy?" Well, the answer is, "Not many." I mean, these people have very fond memories of it, and I do too, but the truth is that Crosley Field had a very plain, very utilitarian design.

Ironically, the Palace of the Fans, the Cincinnati ballpark that preceded Crosley, or Redland Field as it was known then, was fresh and dynamic and so ornate as to be . . . well, palatial! Which one represents the city better? I don't know. The startling contrast between the two ballparks can probably be explained, though, by the difference between the two men who owned the ballclub when the two parks were built. Palace of the Fans was built by John Brush, who was a department store owner, and he probably had a keen sense of design and probably knew how to make things appeal to the eye. Crosley Field was built by a city water works commissioner. Garry Herrmann was a gregarious, popular guy, and I think he knew how to entertain the fans, but I suspect his sense of what a ballpark should look like was not nearly as imaginative as Brush's.

John Erardi and I had collaborated on the first two books, and at this point we decided to do something on the Big Red Machine. We knew that we'd have to cover the great things the team had done on the field, but we didn't want the book to be about those things. For one thing, the team's exploits were very well known already; and for another, if you concentrate on the hits, runs, and errors, game after game, season after season, they all begin to blend together and become meaningless after a while. No, John and I agreed going in that what we wanted to focus on was how the team had been put together. We decided to focus on Bob Howsam, the team's general manager, and Sparky Anderson, the field manager, as much as on the stars of the team: Rose, Bench, Morgan, and Perez. As a matter of fact, the book's subtitle is *How Bob Howsam & Sparky Anderson Built the Big Red Machine.*

Almost everybody we talked to for the book was extremely cooperative and generous with their time because all of them knew that their place in history is linked to that team. Dick Wagner, Howsam's assistant who presided over the team's downfall after Howsam retired, became the most reviled person in Cincinnati and was practically run out of town, but even he gave us three great hours. Dick was a great interview.

Howsam, though, set the tone of the whole project. He was a great interview too, but more than that, he paved our way with other people. There had been so much respect for him throughout the organization that all we had to do was drop his name, let people know he was on board and we'd spent a lot of time with him, and we were in. John got a great story from a scout that illustrates the respect that Howsam commanded. Howsam really loved his scouts, by the way, and really treated them well. There was a gas crisis in the 1970s, and some major league teams made their scouts start driving compact cars to save gas. Not Howsam. He wanted his scouts in big cars so they'd be protected in case of an accident. He was going to keep his scouts in the big gas guzzlers, high gas prices or not. Anyway, this Reds scout told John, "I'd be on a scouting trip in California, 2,000 miles away from Cincinnati, but when Mr. Howsam called me, I'd stand up in my motel room to talk to him on the phone. That's how much respect I had for Mr. Howsam."

I was the one who interviewed Sparky, and I went out to his home in Thousand Oaks, California. We did the interview on his patio, out behind his house, and after about three hours, Sparky said, "I hate to cut this short"—only Sparky would consider talking for three hours "cutting it short"—"but my mom went into the hospital last night. She's seriously ill, and I have to go see her." I couldn't believe it. Sparky didn't know me, and he didn't owe me one minute of his time, yet his feeling was he'd made the appointment and he needed to honor it. He very easily could have blown me off, and I would have understood.

Howsam and Anderson were the first two guys we talked to, and both said very early in their interviews, "You've got to talk to Ray Shore." Ray was the Reds's advance scout, and both Bob and Sparky trusted his judgment on players implicitly. Howsam liked to get input from everybody in the organization before making player moves, but in the end he usually deferred to Ray's judgment. So we knew that Ray was very important to the story too. I got Ray on the phone a couple of times, and I talked to him for an hour or so in a motel north of Cincinnati when he came into town working as an advance scout for the Phillies. Then he died about six weeks later from a heart attack. He never saw the book. That was sad, but his family saw it, of course, and it really meant a lot to them because Ray gets so much credit in the book for his behind-the-scenes work in building the team. His kids came to several book signings and presentations and introduced themselves because I'd never met them, and they ordered tons of books for all the nieces and nephews and cousins. That sort of thing—helping an unsung family hero finally get his due—is one of the unexpected pleasures of doing a book like *Big Red Dynasty*.

Perhaps the biggest surprise we uncovered while doing *Big Red Dynasty* was how few times the so-called Great Eight of Rose, Bench, Morgan, Perez, Griffey, Foster, Concepcion, and Geronimo actually played together. The idea caught our attention when we realized that it wasn't until early in the 1975 season that all eight guys were in the lineup at the same time. Griffey didn't really emerge as a full-time player until 1975, and Foster didn't really get into the starting lineup until Rose went to third base. And then, on the other end, Perez was gone after 1976. So it was a pretty short time period. Once we realized this, we asked Greg Gajus, a SABR member who loves doing that kind of research, to go back over box scores, and he was able to document that the Great Eight actually started together only 87 times during those two championship seasons, including postseason games. They get all the accolades, and they deserve them because they were the guys who won the two championships; and they will always be linked because of that, but they weren't on the field as a unit all the time, as people remember them being.

The other surprise had to do with Johnny Bench's clutch hitting in the postseason. Now, Bench did play a lot of postseason games, but even so he had a remarkable number of opportunities to bat in clutch situations. In five of those clutch situations, with the game on the line, he came through with a big hit, usually a home run, that either won the game or tied it or started the rally that won the game for the Reds. I don't know how many home runs Reggie Jackson hit in the postseason, but I do know that a lot of his postseason home runs did not come in clutch, meaningful situations, as Bench's did. Looked at from that perspective, maybe Bench should be called "Mr. October," not Jackson. However, I know that even though you're a Hall of Famer, if you are from Cincinnati, you're going to get "dissed," as they say, when you compete with Reggie Jackson and the New York Yankees.

We also tried in *Big Red Dynasty* to correct a misconception about the reason for the club's downfall in 1977. The popular notion attributes the Reds's demise to the trade of Tony Perez, but it was more than that. To begin with, the main reason the Reds traded Perez was to make room for Dan Driessen at first base. They felt that Driessen was ready and that they had to give him a chance to play. And in

1977, Driessen had a pretty good year in place of Tony. I mean, he put up Perez-like numbers: more than 90 RBIs and 20-plus home runs. It was a decent year, really one of the best offensive years he would ever have. But Perez was sorely missed in the clubhouse—there was no question about that. His absence left a huge void there. But there was also the sense that Sparky had lost a little bit of control over the guys; there was a lack of the overall team discipline that had been there before. This was partly because of the complacency that comes with success and partly because Sparky had backed off on some of the star players. He made it clear that he had two sets of rules, and he didn't apologize for it. He just didn't think he needed to ride Rose, Morgan, Bench, and Perez, and he didn't. Those guys were the consummate professionals, and they rode each other. On the other hand, the other guys were younger and hadn't strung together years of success as the stars had. Still, the double standard created a certain amount of resentment. And then, with the advent of free agency, the players were starting to get new leverage, and there was less loyalty to the club than before. So all these things added up to create some tension in the clubhouse that hadn't been there before.

But, ultimately, the thing that killed them in 1977 and 1978 was the fact that they just got lousy pitching. Even though they picked up Tom Seaver from the Mets, the overall pitching was lousy. It killed them. This brings up a point we ought to make here. Namely, the Big Red Machine always gets knocked for never having had any pitching, but every year from 1970 through 1976, which was the heyday of that team, they were significantly below the league ERA. Every season. When I say "significantly below," I don't mean they were a couple one hundredths under the league average, but a quarter or a half point under. Now, I don't think you say about such a team that they had no pitching. They had good pitching. This fact is obscured because the Reds didn't have a big hammer or two like the Dodgers and Mets, who had great pitching staffs during those years; but the fact is that the Reds had really good staffs, top to bottom. In 1977–78, the Reds were still scoring a lot of runs—I believe they still ranked first or second in the league in runs scored both years—but the staff ERAs ballooned, and that's really what did them in. The Perez trade hurt, but the lack of pitching hurt a lot worse, and that's the part that has been forgotten.

Howsam retired just before the start of the 1978 season, and if you ask him why he quit, he'll say it was because he was having very serious back problems and because he'd always planned to retire when he reached 60. I'm sure both of those things entered into it, but I also think Bob was starting to lose his enthusiasm for the game. When Howsam started out, a general manager could put a team together through player development and trades, and he could keep that team together for as long as he wanted. It was his choice as to how long a player stayed with the club because the players were treated almost like chattel. With free agency that all started to change. The old system wasn't fair to the players, but it was a much easier system for general managers to control. Howsam hated dealing with player agents, and he truly believed that free agency would be the ruination of baseball. I think the last straw for him was the Vida Blue case. Here was Howsam trying to figure out a way to circumvent free agency by making a big trade with Oakland to bring in a quality pitcher the Reds desperately needed, and then Bowie Kuhn voided the deal. Kuhn had some guideline about how much cash could be involved in a trade, and the deal violated Kuhn's policy because the Reds were to send too much money to the A's. They tried to restructure the deal but couldn't get it done, and I think that made Howsam feel as if there wasn't any point in trying anymore because he was no longer the master of his own fate.

After the third book, I explored the idea of doing a Pete Rose book, not a complete biography, but sort of an update that would focus on his life and troubles after the suspension. I've come to respect the judgments of some of the bookstore people around town, and I've often asked them what they thought about a certain idea for a book. That's what passes for my elaborate market research. Anyway, when I asked about the Pete Rose book, every one of them said they thought it was a terrible idea. Maybe they were wrong, but their unanimous skepticism scared me off the topic. I also toyed with the idea of the 1961 team and the 1990 team as subjects but, in the end, found neither team compelling enough.

The fourth book turned out to be a picture book, *The Reds in Black & White*, which got going when I hooked up with Mark Stang, who knew about a great collection of Reds photos from the first half of the twentieth century—the Steve Cummings collection—that was going up for sale in a big auction. I thought the photos belonged in some Cincinnati historical institution, and I tried to convince the historical society to purchase them, but it wasn't interested. So Mark and I decided that we would buy the collection ourselves—I've since bought Mark out, and I now own the collection outright—and then make a book out of the photos. It made sense because buying the rights to a couple hundred photos gets to be real expensive real fast, and we thought we could get our money back with one book.

The photos in this collection didn't cover the entire century, but I knew about another collection of Reds photos that had been taken by Jack Klumpe, a newspaper photographer who'd covered the Reds almost on a daily basis for the *Cincinnati Post* from the 1950s through the 1980s. So there was another 25 years of Reds photographs. Klumpe had donated his collection to the *Sporting News*, so I went out to St. Louis to talk to archivist Steve Gietschier about it. Five years earlier I'd visited St. Louis to look at this collection for the Crosley Field book, and when I looked at the photos the second time, I realized that nobody had touched them since I had five years before. Steve said, "Yeah, we really don't have the time to deal with them. They're still in the original boxes." It was obvious the photos were not a high priority with the *Sporting News*, so I offered to buy them, and the *Sporting News* accepted my offer. So now I had two great photo collections to take me all the way up to the 1980s, and I was able to fill the last two decades with photos from the Reds themselves and a few from the *Cincinnati Enquirer*. So that's how the photo sources for the book came together. Our model for the book was the Neal McCabe book of Conlon photos; we wanted our photos to look as good as those in McCabe's book, so we used an oversized format and expensive photo-grade paper like McCabe did to make the photos look as good as possible.

The book sold well, and Mark wanted to do the same thing with other teams. I didn't want to go out of the Cincinnati market, though, so I gave Mark my blessing to go on ahead on his own. He worked out a deal with Orange Frazer Press and brought out a similar book on the Cleveland Indians. It sold nicely too, and Mark has plans to continue the series.

The new book is an update of *Day by Day in Cincinnati Reds History*, which John Snyder and Floyd Conner did in 1983 with Leisure Press. I really loved that book, but what I wanted to do was a major upgrade of it, not just an update. The original book had been done rather inexpensively, and I felt that we could give the book a much better, classier presentation. I also wanted to use a year-by-year format because it makes more sense than a day-by-day format, and, coincidentally, John Snyder had reached the same conclusion. People don't remember that such-and-such happened on a particular day as much as they remember it happened in a particular season. On the other hand, dates are important, so we came up with the compromise of combining both formats—thus the subtitle *Year by Year and Day by Day with the Cincinnati Reds Since 1866.*

Redleg Journal, by the way, is a reference book, but it is also a history that tells stories. It contains vignettes of players and other prominent persons and about 50 feature articles on various topics, on everything from a history of the Reds Hall of Fame to an obscure 1918 betting scandal that involved Cincinnati players to the infamous 1957 All-Star game ballot box stuffing by Reds fans. The year-by-year format also gives us a chance to tell what's happening to the team chronologically, to explain why the team won the pennant if they won or why they finished second and not first and so on.

This book kind of got out of hand. Snyder's original "Day by Day" book had about 350 pages, and this one is twice as long. John's book didn't have much on the nineteenth century, and we really wanted to include the nineteenth century, in part because of my interest in the Red Stockings, and in part because the nineteenth century is so full of odd and funny and weird things that happened, apart from the Red Stockings. The book goes back to 1866 because that's when the Cincinnati Base Ball Club started, and I wanted to go all the way back to the very origins of the Reds. That's 135 years of Reds baseball history, and when you're going to devote three or four or five pages to each year . . . all you have to do is some simple multiplication to realize you're going to have a monster of a book! But I never did the math until it was too late. Here I was planning on a 400-page book, but it's actually more than 700 pages. It became a real editing and layout . . . some people might say "nightmare" . . . but I'll say "challenge." We missed our completion date by a year. We thought we'd get it out in 2000, but it came out in September 2001.

I always joke around that people are saying about me, "How many Reds books can that Rhodes guy do?" But there are more interesting Reds books to do. For instance, I'm thinking about doing a book that would be called "The Cincinnati Reds and the Small Market Blues." That's because I think the inequity between franchises is *the* major issue facing baseball. How do small market teams compete, and why can't major league baseball figure out a way to equalize revenues more fairly than it currently does? I'm not sure what I'll do next, but if I had to start on a new Reds book tomorrow, that's the book I'd do.

BASEBALL BOOKS BY GREG RHODES

The First Boys of Summer: The 1869–70 Cincinnati Red Stockings (co-
author). Cincinnati: Road West Publishing, 1994.

Crosley Field: The Illustrated History of a Classic Ballpark (co-author).
Cincinnati: Road West Publishing, 1995.

*Big Red Dynasty: How Bob Howsam and Sparky Anderson Built the Big Red
Machine* (co-author). Cincinnati: Road West Publishing, 1997.

Reds in Black & White: 100 Years of Reds Images (co-author).
Cincinnati: Road West Publishing, 1999.

*Redleg Journal: Year by Year and Day by Day with the Cincinnati Reds Since
1866* (co-author). Cincinnati: Road West Publishing, 2001.

14

LAWRENCE S. RITTER

With the demise of Ty Cobb in 1961, Larry Ritter realized that death was quickly silencing forever an entire generation of players from baseball's Golden Age (1900-1920). To preserve their stories Ritter spent the next few years interviewing dozens of Cobb's contemporaries around the country, and the resulting book of 22 monologues, The Glory of Their Times *(Macmillan, 1966), not only became an instant classic of baseball literature, but also virtually created the entire oral history book industry. The book also brought renewed attention to long forgotten heroes, who gave Ritter an inscribed silver tray in gratitude. Ritter collaborated with his good friend Donald Honig on* The Image of Their Greatness *(Crown, 1979) and* The 100 Greatest Baseball Players of All Time *(Crown, 1981); authored a juvenile history called* The Story of Baseball *(Morrow, 1983); and wrote a fine text for a book about his childhood hero,* The Babe: A Life in Pictures *(Ticknor & Fields, 1988). A professor of finance at New York University since 1960 and the author of a banking textbook now in its sixth edition, Ritter is currently working on a book about ballparks.*

PEOPLE CALL ME UP all the time to do baseball books, and I always say no. Almost always, anyway. First of all, I'm an economist and a teacher. I'm not a baseball writer. I lucked into *The Glory of Their Times.* I'm busy enough teaching my courses, grading papers, doing research, and keeping my textbook, *Principles of Money, Banking, and Financial Markets,* up to date.

Second of all, I don't generate ideas. Donald Honig generates ideas. He sits up there in Cromwell, Connecticut, and thinks up book ideas. He finishes one book and says, "What am I gonna do next?" He thinks of something. I don't. I've sat for days trying to think of an idea for a new baseball book, and I can't think of anything. So the only way I get to work on a baseball project is if somebody calls me up and asks me if I'd like to do this or that. Then I react. Usually I saw no because I'm too busy or because the subject doesn't interest me, but when John Thorn called me in 1987 and asked if I wanted to do the text for a picture biography of Babe Ruth, I said yes. I didn't hesitate a second. I knew that was what I wanted to do.

That's because Ruth was the first hero in my life. The first baseball game my daddy ever took me to, in 1931, Babe Ruth played in. He was the hero of every American boy when I was growing up. All the heroes of the 1920s and 1930s . . . Bill Tilden, Red Grange, Jack Dempsey . . . Babe Ruth towered over every one of them. You talk about today's heroes . . . Will Clark, Joe Montana, whoever . . . these people pale into insignificance compared to the hero Babe Ruth was when I was growing up. Babe Ruth was "BABE RUTH." So when John Thorn called about Babe Ruth . . . Wow! Fantastic! There was no hesitation.

When I worked on the book I lived across the street from the Ansonia Hotel where Ruth lived for many years. Every day I'd walk the streets that Babe Ruth walked, and I'd look at the Ansonia and at several other places where he used to live, all of which are only a couple of blocks away from here. I put all his addresses in the book in a parenthetical paragraph because it's so fascinating that they're all right here.

Every single day I wrote that book I'd wake up in the morning with Babe Ruth on my mind. I would go to sleep with Babe Ruth on my mind. I thought about nothing but Babe Ruth for five months. Nothing but Babe Ruth. My wife started getting worried. No matter what she did, no matter what was on TV, no matter what was going on, I was over there in the corner, with my word processor, living with Babe Ruth. I lived with him for months . . . every day, all day. I loved it! I thought he was the greatest fun, the greatest companion, the greatest guy to be around. I was immersed in him. I don't think I'll ever have that kind of experience again.

I think my Babe Ruth book is a good book. The reason I *know* it's a good book, actually, is I know the experience I went through in writing it. I don't care that Bob Creamer and Marshall Smelser did better research and have more facts in their books. I didn't do any real research; I just read all those Babe Ruth books you see up there on my shelves. Creamer is a hell of a writer, and I think that Smelser actually did a better research job than Creamer did, but my book is the best of the three because mine has the most love in it. I fell in love with Babe Ruth, that's all there is to it. There's so much love in that book that I know it has to come through.

Despite this, it's the worst-selling book I ever did. All my other books have sold very well. *The 100 Greatest Baseball Players of All Time* has sold about 50,000 copies; *The Image of Their Greatness* has sold about 70 or 80,000; and *The Glory of Their Times* sold way up there, about 225,000 copies. Even the children's baseball book I did sold about 30,000. And this book, the Babe Ruth biography, didn't even sell 10,000 copies. Unbelievable! Aside from the love in the text, the book has all those great pictures . . . from birth to death. Wow! We're not a reading country, I know; so look at the pictures! I love those pictures.

I don't think Ruth would have minded Maris and Aaron breaking his records. I think he would have cheered them along because he believed, I'm sure, that old hoary saying that "Records are made to be broken." All athletes are sad to see their records broken, but they realize it's inevitable. Someday somebody's going to hit in 57 straight games; it's inevitable. I don't think Ruth would have minded, but it would have been interesting to find out his reaction to a black man breaking his record. There's almost nothing written about Ruth's racial views, but I have a feeling he would have adapted very quickly. Babe was from Baltimore; he was a southern boy. Nevertheless, you'll notice in many of the photos in the book that Ruth has his arms around black kids as well as white ones.

I'm sure he slept with a lot of black women. I say that because he frequented every whorehouse he could find, and I'm sure he tried every variety of girl he could find also. This is instinctively knowable about George Herman. Not that it means anything, actually.

I think Ruth would have been fine as a manager if he'd had good players, and he would have had good players if he'd been manager of the Yankees. Through his own stupidity he just missed out on the Detroit job that Mickey Cochrane took. He could have had that job, and Cochrane took it and won two pennants with the Tigers in 1934 and 1935. Ruth was offered the job but didn't show up for a meeting with Tigers' owner Frank Navin. He went barnstorming in Hawaii or some place . . . said, "I'll see you when I get back," which pissed Navin off. So Navin hired Cochrane instead. Ruth wouldn't have had as good a catcher as Cochrane, but he would have come close to winning because that was a hell of a good ballclub with Tommy Bridges, Schoolboy Rowe, Hank Greenberg, and so on.

I think he should have taken the managerial job in Newark too, which the Yankees asked him to accept when he applied for the Yankees job. Newark had a fantastic team, the greatest minor league team that ever existed. He would have certainly won a pennant there, and he could have lived at home in New York while he was doing it.

That statement that "He couldn't manage himself, so how could he manage a whole team" was unfair. I think he was able to manage himself by that time in his life. He'd been married to Claire since 1929—he got married right up the street here, by the way—and he'd calmed down by 1933 or so. What's the big deal anyway? I've seen Earl Weaver up at the NY baseball writers' dinner, when he was regarded as the number one manager in baseball, totally inebriated. Casey Stengel lived a wild life in many respects . . . staying up all night and never getting any sleep. Babe Ruth would have been a perfectly good manager because I think a manager is only as important as the ballplayers on his team, and if he can maintain some sort of harmony on the club and keep his players on their toes over the long season, he'll be okay.

Actually, so far as technical baseball knowledge is concerned, you and I could manage if the players would only accept us. It's just that they wouldn't accept us. They wouldn't believe that we knew what we were doing. That element aside, we could manage as well as most. In the first place, we'd have a guy sitting next to us like Pete Rose had in Cincinnati who knows what it's all about, and so anytime we had a question we'd ask him what he thinks. Right? "Should we play infield in or leave 'em back? Should we steal or hit-and-run?" Many a guy's had somebody sitting next to him; this isn't unusual.

The Babe could have done all that bullshit easy enough, and I think as Babe Ruth he'd have had a pretty good shot at maintaining the players' morale, which is the really tough part of the job.

The impetus for me doing *The Glory of Their Times* was the death of Ty Cobb, who died in 1961. I was teaching then where I'm teaching now, at NYU. There was a historian who taught there named Herman Krooss who was an avid baseball fan. Herman Krooss and I and a few other people were having lunch a day or two after Ty Cobb had died, and Herman said, "You know, with Ty Cobb dying, Ruth is gone, Wagner is gone, Mathewson is gone . . . A whole generation of early heroes is gone. A generation that pioneered baseball in this country is dying out. None of the great, great heroes like Ruth or Cobb are left, but there are still some pioneers around. Somebody ought to take a tape recorder and tape their reminiscences because once they go there's nobody from that generation who's going to be left."

That stayed in my mind for weeks. It just hung in there. It's not like I started out the next day.

I had been divorced since 1952—I remarried in 1977 and now I'm in the process of divorcing again—and in 1961 I was single, living alone. I had a son, Steve, born in 1948, who was 13 years old in 1961, but he didn't live with me; he lived with his mother. Since I only saw Steve on weekends and summer vacations, my main problem with him was what to talk about. With children you talk about day-to-day things almost exclusively. You don't discuss the state of the world; you talk about what they did, what they're going to do, what we're going to have for dinner. And if you only have a kid on weekends, you don't know what to talk about.

But Steve loved baseball, as I did, so we often talked about baseball. I got the idea that maybe during vacations we could implement this idea of Herman Krooss's and get a tape recorder and go around and talk to the remaining elderly men who had played baseball around the turn of the century. So that's how it all began.

At the time tape recorders were just coming in, and I was not at all mechanically adept. The tape recorder I lugged around was a reel to reel type weighing about 25 pounds, a Tandberg, and I got a hernia carrying it around. Two hernias in fact!

I didn't know much about how to operate the Tandberg, so Steve operated it. We worked as a team. As soon as we walked into a house, I'd start talking to the man, and Steve would go look for outlets, survey the seating arrangements, and figure out where the best place to put the recorder was. Then he'd sit and operate it. I paid no attention to the tape recorder, which was good because the ballplayers soon forgot about it. Tape recorders were new then, but nobody objected to being recorded, not one person. And I think a lot of that was due to Steve's being so inconspicuous. So he was invaluable.

Nobody taught me how to do an interview, but I've been a teacher all my life, and interviewing is not unrelated to teaching. I'm used to talking to people, to communicating with them, to watching them to see whether or not we are on the same wavelength. And I'm used to doing my homework. Before I went to see anybody for an interview, I'd spend at least a day exploring their careers: checking who they may have known, who their teammates were, who they may have played against, what historic games they may have observed or been involved in.

At the start, in 1961, I wasn't thinking of a book, I was just interested in getting these old ballplayers on tape. I wasn't going to write them up. The concept of oral history was very new then. Columbia University had just established an oral history library about that time. So I didn't think about writing a book, but when I went to see these guys I couldn't say I was doing an "oral history." That sounds too pretentious. I'd say, "I'm doing a book."

Well, after I finished the interviewing, which took four or five years, I got a little tired. Geez, it was an awful lot of traveling. I was resting up, but I'd stayed in touch with most of these guys, and I started getting Christmas cards from them saying, "Where's the book? I'm not getting any younger. Where's the book?"

I started thinking, "My god, I have indeed made these pseudo promises to all these people that I'm doing a book, so I'd better do something about it."

So I got somebody to transcribe all the tapes, which was extraordinarily expensive, by the way. You have a six- or seven-hour interview, the transcript will be 60, 70, 80 pages of typing. Even a one-hour transcript could be 20 pages because the typist doesn't know what to leave out, what's bullshit, what's important. Typists type everything which, of course, is what they're supposed to do.

I worked up three of the interviews and started taking them to publishers. I took them to Prentice-Hall, Houghton Mifflin, and Holt, Rinehart, and Winston, and I got three rejections. They all turned it down emphatically. They weren't the least bit interested, so I put it away. I didn't do anything with it for a year. Then one day a book salesman from Macmillan came into my office at NYU. Book salesmen are always trying to get professors to adopt this or that textbook. They also want to sign up textbooks for their company to publish. He said, "What are you working on? What kind of textbook are you writing or would you be interested in writing?" I told him what I'd been doing, and he was intrigued. He said, "Let me take what you've got and give it to my trade book editor." He did, and I got a letter saying they were greatly interested and that Macmillan would give me a $3,000 advance to continue.

So, I traced a map of the United States and started pinpointing where these old ballplayers lived. It was hard, by the way, just to find out where people lived at that time because there wasn't a Jack Smalling and his book of ballplayers' addresses around then. It turned out that most of them had gone back to where they had been born and raised. So the first thing I did was find out where they were born by consulting the first encyclopedia, the one by Turkin and Thompson. Then I would go to the New York Public Library and look up these people in their hometown phone books. Usually a particular guy, say Sam Crawford of Wahoo, Nebraska, would not be listed, but his last name would be. So I'd call all the Crawfords in Wahoo, Nebraska, and sooner or later I always got a relative . . . a cousin, an uncle, and aunt, a distant relative. But they always knew where "Uncle Sam" was. "He doesn't live here now. He lives in Los Angeles now" . . . stuff like that. So then I'd go to the L.A. phone book.

I put pins down on my map of every guy who played before 1925, preferably before 1910, and was still alive. I got clusters of people. Here I would get eight people; there I'd get four, all within a 200-mile radius. This was particularly true of California, certain parts of the Midwest, and Florida. So I would choose those people who were clustered together because I could get to interview more of them on one trip.

I'd write them a letter saying, "I'm interested in doing a book"—I didn't really mean it—"Would you be kind enough to talk to me about the old days?" And I'd tell them that I'd be in their area during such-and-such week and that I'd call them. That way, when I called them they'd be expecting me.

There was a lot of traveling involved, and I traveled by plane. When I got there, I rented a car. And there were motel bills to pay. The traveling expenses were not only for myself but also for my son and often my girlfriend. The three of us were involved in this thing from beginning to end. Morality is a difficult problem when you've got a 13–14-year-old kid involved. I had to get two motel rooms: one for me and my son and one for my girlfriend.

It cost me a lot of money to do *The Glory of Their Times,* but I was able to afford it because I was single and I had a good income from NYU. I had child support payments to make, but that was the only call upon my income. And I live very modestly. I don't smoke. I don't drink. I don't go out to nightclubs. I don't even own a car— what would I do with a car in New York City? I don't spend a lot of money. So it was easy under those circumstances for me to spend money on the book. What it cost me was approximately $15,000, which I'd guess is equal to about $40,000 in 1990 dollars.

Nobody ever mentioned money to me, by the way, except Rube Marquard who started on the phone by saying, "Well, you're going to write a book? Now, you're going to get royalties from this, right? How much do you think this is worth to you, this interview?"

I said, "Well Mr. Marquard, I haven't any money, and nobody has said they'll publish the book yet, and to tell you the truth I've never thought about it, Mr. Marquard."

And then I heard somebody in the background—it turned out to be Mrs. Marquard—say, "Rube, stop that! Stop that right now."

And he said, "Aw, come on over."

I talked to Rube on a hot summer day, and we sat right in front of the air conditioner. My son put the stupid tape recorder right in front of the air conditioner too, and the air conditioner was fairly noisy. We were staying at Paul Volcker's house. Paul Volcker used to be chairman of the Federal Reserve Board, and we had worked together at the Federal Reserve Bank of New York. We had been old friends for years. That night Paul and his wife and son wanted to hear the tape of Rube Marquard. We turned on the tape recorder, and all we heard was that air conditioner going, "SHHHHHH." Couldn't make out a word of the conversation. I didn't know what to do. It was awful.

Finally, I really got my nerve up. I called Rube up and told him what had happened. He said. "Come over tomorrow. We'll do it all over again." And we did. I remember segments which I thought were very well put, and he said them the exact same way again.

One interview which was interesting but which I didn't print because the guy refused to let me print it was Billy Werber's. After he read his interview, he wrote me a letter saying, "If you print this, I'll sue you. I never said anything like that." Of course, he did because it was all on tape. He said he didn't like baseball, and he didn't like most baseball players. He thought they were uncouth, uneducated roughnecks. He had graduated from Duke, you know. And he didn't like baseball fans. Most of them were terrible people, and he recited a story about Babe Ruth being on his last legs and getting booed. On and on. It was a down interview, delivered with much vigor. I loved it! It was terrific to encounter it in the middle of all these guys saying, "I love baseball so much I would have paid them to let me play if I'd had to." And it would have really spiced up the book.

Werber was an insurance salesman, and I think on reconsideration he said to himself, "This won't be very good for my insurance business. This is the great American pastime, and I'll be saying these antagonistic things? I'd better cool it."

When I got the letter saying, "I'll sue you," I didn't argue with him. It's supposed to be his words; it is his words. I mean, the book doesn't say, "Written by Larry Ritter." It's in the first person. Rube Marquard says, "I did this, I did that." So I couldn't print it if Werber wasn't going to permit it.

About five years later I got a letter from Werber saying, "I have a very good friend who lives ten blocks away from you. He would love to get an autographed copy of *The Glory of Their Times* from you. It's his favorite book." And he added, "I really enjoyed it myself." I got a kick out of that letter.

Later Werber did his own book and published it privately. If he had gone with *The Glory of Their Times,* he would have gotten way more publicity, not to mention money. He would have done much better all the way around, even in his insurance business because it would have been a great topic of discussion.

The wives were mostly an interruption. They would come into the room during an interview and start to chit-chat. The ballplayer would be talking about something, and it would spark a recollection of the wife. But the recollection of the wife wouldn't be valuable. It would be something personal and trivial: "You remember when we lived in that apartment house three blocks from the ballpark, and there was this pretty girl living next door?" This sort of thing you can't use.

My girlfriend too, when she was there, would invariably pick up on something irrelevant and start to chit-chat: "How many children did you have back then? . . . "Oh, the girl went to such-and-such college; I know somebody who went there." You can't do anything with that sort of stuff, and it caused the conversation to veer off into detours. Finally, I barred her from the interviews. It was a ruthless thing to do because she enjoyed them. But she ruined an interview or two because she kept interrupting. She ruined what was going to be a great interview with Charley Jameison, a very good, .290-hitting outfielder for the Cleveland Indians back in the 1920s. Charley Jameison was earning his living in the 1960s as a street crossing guard, and she wanted to talk about that. She didn't understand the importance of the time element and of keeping people focused on the subject.

Whenever a wife came in, my heart would sink, and I'd say to myself, "Hope for the best." And I'd breathe a sigh of relief when she left the room because then I could get the old player's mind back to 1908 or 1910 or whatever. That's what I had to do: I had to get him living again in 1908, get him back in the ballpark, in the dugout. Then it starts to flow out of them. And you can't do that when the girlfriend starts talking about present-day stuff or the wife starts talking about who lived next door.

I did about seven interviews that didn't make the book for one reason or another. They were just bad interviews: my fault, their fault, the wife's fault. They weren't communicative; they didn't have anything to say. Not everybody has a good memory. One man I talked to was senile. I was lucky I didn't encounter more people who were senile.

In one case Heinie Manush's girlfriend came into the house, and this so embarrassed Heinie. He was from a generation where you didn't have a woman you weren't married to coming into your house and shouting something from the kitchen like, "Honey, we're out of coffee." He probably thought, "This means she half lives here, and here's this guy interviewing me, and this is terrible that he sees this." And Heinie cut the interview off practically. He stopped communicating, and I had to leave.

When the book was published, Macmillan gave a publicity party in New York. They flew everybody and their wives in for the party. Almost everybody came. A few had died, and a few didn't want to come, because of health reasons, but out of the 22 men in the book, I'd say 16 came.

We spent about four days together and had a good time. It was great publicity for the book too. Four of them were booked on the *Ed Sullivan Show*. They were supposed to interact with Ed on the show. But during the afternoon rehearsal Lefty O'Doul, who was having a wonderful time, started telling jokes and not listening to the directions of the director and Ed. This so upset Ed Sullivan that he banished them, and instead of being on the show they were introduced in the audience, which is something. Actually, we were all introduced, including me. They got on a lot of other radio and TV shows while they were in New York, so I think Macmillan felt they got their money's worth.

Mrs. O'Doul, unbeknownst to me, got contributions from all of them, and they chipped in and bought me that inscribed silver tray hanging over there on the wall, which they presented to me at a dinner on the last evening they were here. It was at this point that I finally started to realize the important role I played in their last years. When the book came out, their baseball lives started all over again. They were on the radio in their hometowns, and newspaper people interviewed them again. They were baseball heroes once more, and this continued until they died. I didn't understand it at first but gradually realized that *The Glory of Their Times* gave them all a new lease on life.

Almost all old-time ballplayers had some trouble adjusting to life after their careers were over. They didn't have any great pension plan like they do today. Many of them were not well off; some were but not many. So to be in the limelight again, to have the neighborhood kids come around and ask for their autographs . . . Wow! It was a big thing.

They liked autographs themselves, by the way. After I interviewed them, I'd give them a baseball and ask for an autograph, and it was always a little embarrassing. However, when they were here, damned if they didn't arrange themselves around a long table at the hotel where they were staying and start passing a stack of books around, each one signing on his own picture. They stuck a piece of paper in each book saying that this was Sam Crawford's book, for example. And Ed Roush would get the book and turn to his picture—they all knew exactly where their own picture was in the book, of course— and write, "To my pal, Sam Crawford, in memory of this and that . . . Eddie Roush." And then the book would go on. The next book Eddie would get would be Jimmy Austin's, and Roush would write: "To my pal, Jimmy Austin . . ." They went through this whole routine, so I thought, "I won't be embarrassed anymore about asking for autographs." They loved autographs themselves!

The income from *The Glory of Their Times* was quite substantial, but I didn't really need it because I had a good salary from NYU. Besides, I had textbooks which gave me royalties. Today the highest tax rate is about 33 percent. However, back in the 1960s and 1970s the highest tax rate was about 75 percent. I would have easily hit the highest tax bracket, so I would have given three-fourths of the royalties from the book to the government anyway. That didn't make any sense to me, so I distributed the royalties to everybody in the book, including Steve for handling the tape recorder and my girlfriend Barbara. Even though I barred her from the interviews, she still typed up many of the manuscripts. Everybody got one share, and I took two, for a total of 26 shares.

A lot of the men were able to use the money very much. I don't remember exactly how much each one got out of the whole business, but it was something like $10, $15, $20,000. They did very well for themselves. Billy Werber made the wrong decision. Even when they died, we had written documents as to who was to get their share in the future, and we went that way for one generation further. But then about five years ago I bought everybody out because the book-keeping got to be too much. I paid everybody $500 for his share. There wasn't much left anyway, and the bookkeeping was getting horrendous: three children and each gets a third of a third of a third.

I kept in touch with the men in the book almost all of their lives, and their deaths in every case was a very difficult experience for me because we were very close. For years I wrote to the wives who still lived. All the men are now dead. There's nobody still alive who is in *The Glory of Their Times*. There are a few wives remaining, but hardly any. They're almost all gone too.

I was interested in doing a sequel to *The Glory of Their Times*, and, in fact, I started doing one, started visiting people, but it wasn't the same. They all knew about *The Glory of Their Times*. Hardly any old ballplayers had not been given the book as a Christmas or a birthday present. Everybody I visited had read it.

So now I was a celebrity. I wasn't walking into the room anonymously as I had previously. I was now a celebrity, and we started talking in a more formal fashion. They knew their words were going to be seen on the printed page, and the interviews weren't as personal or as natural as before. It wasn't any good anymore because they were too impressed with the person they were talking to. After three interviews, I gave up. I said, "This is going to happen all the time. I'm sure of it."

I interviewed Lefty Grove, and he would have been great if he hadn't known I did *The Glory of Their Times*. But he was prepared for me. He came out with a bunch of notes he had written to be sure that certain things would be included. The only other person that ever did that was Al Bridwell, but that was different. Bridwell had written out on a yellow legal pad very laboriously his memory of the Merkle incident because he knew I would ask about it. He didn't refer to it though. He had it in case I didn't understand exactly what he said. He didn't know I would bring along a tape recorder. He wanted somebody to have the Merkle incident precisely as it happened. He ripped it out and gave it to me as I was leaving.

But now Lefty Grove had notes that he kept referring to. He wanted to be sure to mention this and mention that. So I gave the three interviews to Donald Honig, and he used them in his first book, *Baseball When the Grass Was Real*.

Baseball photos are great, and I love them. I'd never seen many photos of the players from the old days until I started doing *The Glory of Their Times,* when I started collecting photos to put in the book. What Donald Honig does in all his picture books is so valuable because he gives us pictures of people who otherwise would be just names: guys like Tommy Thevenow and Willis Hudlin.

I think photographs should have certain characteristics to be good pictures. My only objection to *The Ultimate Baseball Book* is that many of the photographs are too small. A photo should be at least a quarter page. I don't like postage stamp photographs. You can't see them well enough. With *The Ultimate Baseball Book* they made photos small in order to get a lot of guys in; I'd rather have fewer fellows and larger pictures.

Also, I think the face has to be seen very clearly. The face is the most important part of the body, and the eyes are the most important part of the face. The eyes are crucial. A lot of times the bill of the cap will throw a shadow across the face and obscure the eyes. Books often use a dumb picture like that; I don't know why.

Preferably, you should have pictures that have a little glint or a little star in the eyes. When Donald Honig and I worked on *The Image of Their Greatness,* Donald would lay out eight pictures of Roger Cramer, say, and I would always look for the same thing: clear face and a little glint in the eyes. I would always prefer a head shot if the picture had those two things. Donald would shy away from head shots because he wanted action shots. Actually, you need a balance, but if you can get an action picture that has the face too . . . Wow, that's the best.

I love baseball. I don't especially like baseball players, not the modern ones anyway. I like the old-timers, maybe because they were old men by the time I got to know them. They weren't competitive athletes anymore.

I think today's ballplayers are selfish babies. I think they're babied from the time they're six years old, and I think they grow up not accepting adult responsibilities. I think they're overpaid, although I think they should get what they're getting because that's what the market will bear. And why shouldn't they get it as well as the owners? But I still think they're overpaid. Lee Iaccoca is not worth $15,000,000, and neither is Will Clark worth $3,000,000. In my scale of values, neither one is worth that kind of money.

This big money has spoiled ballplayers today. It used to be that ballplayers got paid like factory foremen, and they could relate to the fans. Now they can't relate to the fans. They don't have the same problems as we do. And they're spoiled sexually, as well as financially. They behave like 20-year-old kids in the Navy on shore leave. Everything is too easy for them, and they have no sense of responsibility, most of them, even to their wives or families.

I don't like the owners either. I think they're greedy plutocrats who have very little real love for the game. Actually, the ballplayers have a lot of love for what they do, but they have no knowledge of anything preceeding them, no sense of history. They've heard of Babe Ruth, but they don't know much about him. They certainly don't know who Tony Lazzeri was. They've never even heard of him.

No, I don't like today's players, nor do I like the owners. I don't like the commissioners. I don't like the umpires. It's the *game* that I love.

That's why I can't write the kind of romantic, romanticizing things that Bart Giamatti wrote or Roger Angell can write. As you read Roger Angell pieces, you see he enjoys going down on the field and meeting players and schmoozing with them. He likes to go to the front office and talk with the owners. He likes all that stuff. I wouldn't do that if you paid me. I don't much like those people. But I love the game. The game is so beautiful to watch, and today's players, whom I don't care for, do such wonderful things on the field, that it transcends the people involved and makes it all endlessly fascinating.

BASEBALL BOOKS BY LAWRENCE RITTER

The Glory of Their Times. New York: Macmillan, 1966.

The Image of Their Greatness (co-author). New York: Crown Publishers, 1979.

The 100 Greatest Baseball Players of All Time (co-author). New York: Crown Publishers, 1981.

The Story of Baseball. New York: William Morrow, 1983.

The Babe: A Life in Pictures. New York: Ticknor & Fields, 1988.

Lost Ballparks: A Collection of Baseball's Legendary Fields. New York: Viking Studio Books, 1992.

Leagues Apart: The Men and Times of the Negro Baseball Leagues. New York: Morrow Junior Books, 1995.

The Babe: The Game That Ruth Built. Kingston, NY: Total Sports, 1997.

15

DAN SHAUGHNESSY

The Boston Red Sox have inspired more literary writing than any other major league baseball team; and no one writes about the damned darlings of all of New England, their tortured fans, and beloved Fenway Park with more passion, verve, and understanding than Dan Shaughnessy. Born in 1953 in Groton, Massachusetts, Shaughnessy graduated from the College of the Holy Cross in 1975 and two years later became the Baltimore Evening Sun's *beat writer covering the Baltimore Orioles. He later covered major league baseball for the* Washington Star *and moved on to the* Boston Globe *in 1981. He covered the Boston Celtics for four years and began covering the Boston Red Sox in 1986. A sports columnist for the* Globe *since 1989, Shaughnessy has been named Massachusetts Sportswriter of the Year seven times and five times has been voted one of the country's top-10 sports columnists by the Associated Press. He has written two basketball books:* Seeing Red: The Red Auerbach Story *and* Ever Green: The Boston Celtics, *as well as four books about the Boston Red Sox.* At Fenway: Dispatches from Red Sox Nation *was named a finalist for the 1996 CASEY Award, and his newspaper story about the night Roger Clemens fanned 20 Seattle Mariners was anthologized in the fourth volume of* The Fireside Book of Baseball. *Shaughnessy is currently writing the text for an illustrated book about spring training and makes his home in Newton, Massachusetts, where he lives with his wife, Marilou, and their children Sarah, Kate, and Sam.*

LET ME START by saying that today, September 11, 2001, is a terrible, terrible day. Our country has been attacked by terrorists, and thousands of people, perhaps tens of thousands of people, are dead or injured from the plane crashes into the two towers of the World Trade Center. Events are still unfolding, and we may well face even more attacks. Who knows.

Baseball and the Boston Red Sox have always been a big part of my life, personally and professionally, but I think now it's totally inconsequential what the Red Sox are up to. This is a Pearl Harbor kind of day in our nation's history, and baseball's the furthest thing from my mind and everybody else's. I would expect that there won't be any baseball today, maybe not for a while, and there certainly won't be any baseball today in New York. I don't see how they can do anything in New York for a while. So, baseball means nothing under these circumstances.

Nevertheless, I know that you've traveled a long way to see me, so I'm willing to go ahead with the interview . . . even though we are both pretty distracted. I also know that you'd prefer to do this someplace private and quiet, instead of the cafeteria of the *Boston Globe*, but I have to be near a television. This is just too important.

Why did I decide to become a baseball writer? Well, it's a long story, and we should probably start at the beginning.

I was the youngest of five children, and I was born in 1953 in Groton, Massachusetts, about 40 miles northwest of Boston. Groton is a very small town of about 4,000 people. It just so happens that Peter Gammons, who becomes important to my story later on, grew up there too. His dad taught at the Groton School; I went to public school there.

My brother Bill was quite a good baseball and basketball player. He played varsity baseball in the seventh grade, and he was a star throughout his scholastic career. By the way, Bill's daughter, Megan Shaughnessy, is a professional tennis player. She was the twelfth seed in the U.S. Open. She beat Venus Williams two months ago. So the Shaughnessys are a very athletic family. Bill himself played baseball at Nichols College and in the Cape Cod League, a summer league for the best college players, but he got drafted by the U.S. Army after college. He played a lot of ball in the army, but he was too old for pro ball by the time he got out.

Naturally, I looked up to my brother Bill. I went to all his games, served as the bat boy whenever I could, hung around him and his teammates all the time; and that's how I really became a baseball fan, by watching him.

I remember that in 1962 I caught onto an appreciation of big league ball for the first time, even though the Red Sox weren't very good. I was eight years old at the start of that season, and for the next six or seven years I knew everything about baseball. I knew all the rosters of all the teams. I was fanatical. I collected baseball cards and even baseball coins. Salada Tea made plastic baseball coins with players' pictures on them—there were cardboard sheets you would stick the coins in—and I had those coins. I lived for that stuff. And I was a big reader of baseball too. I subscribed to *Sports Magazine*, and I went to the library and read every baseball book that was available. There wasn't a lot of product back then, but the librarians knew me and would let me know whenever something new on baseball came in.

I really got deep into it. Of course, I liked basketball, football, and hockey too, but baseball was the one. And I played it nonstop—played three years of Little League. I narrated my own imaginary games in the backyard, and I kept standings in my dice game—played the regular 162-game season too. It was complete immersion. I knew more then than I know now in terms of who plays third base for the Minnesota Twins.

Baseball was *the* most important thing in my life, and it was disappointing that the Red Sox were so bad. They were historically out of it in those days. Boston, Kansas City, and Washington were usually the bottom third of the 10-team American League. So that was depressing.

Of course, in 1967 they wound up playing the St. Louis Cardinals in the World Series. That was the Impossible Dream season, and that is still the greatest sports experience as a fan I've ever encountered. I was in eighth grade going into ninth during that season, and it was an indescribable thrill to see them not only be competitive, but also win the pennant in the greatest pennant race of them all.

So I had all the background, and I think going to my brother's games developed in me a reporter's instinct because I'd come back home and talk to my parents about what I'd seen. After a while, I knew my parents were going to want me to tell them what had happened at my brother's games, so I learned to report at an early age. Nineteen sixty-seven was also the year I really started reading newspapers. The *Boston Globe* made a push to the small country towns around that time, and it was a big thing for me to get a great daily paper. I was able to read guys like Ray Fitzgerald, Cliff Keane, and eventually Peter Gammons in the early 1970s, and that was very helpful.

The first writing I did was for the high school paper, which was sort of a joke since they only put out three or four issues a year. My senior year, the local paper, called the *Public Spirit*, a weekly that covered five or six of the apple towns out there, asked one of the faculty members for the name of a student who could cover sports at Groton High School. My friend turned it down but said, "Maybe Dan would like to do it." The faculty guy asked me and I said okay.

They paid 15¢ an inch to write the school paper copy. My byline was "Lancer," which was John F. Kennedy's code name in the Secret Service. So it was Groton High School Sports by Lancer. I used a pseudonym because I was playing on a lot of the teams I was writing about. I also covered girls sports like softball and field hockey. I got a lot of names in the stories, and I wrote in longhand. I'd take it down to Mrs. Martin in Chicopee Row for her to type up, and the next week the story would appear in the paper. At the end of the month I'd make $20 or so because I made the stories really long. At 15¢ an inch you have to write long! In my senior yearbook, under my name where they predict your future occupation, it says "journalist," and my dad thought that sounded like a good idea. I think he actually put "journalist" down on one of my college applications.

I was very active in high school. I played three years of varsity basketball—mostly on the bench—and three years of varsity baseball—mostly playing. And I ran varsity cross country one year. I was also class president my last two years. I worked at an ice cream stand in town, and I was an altar boy. In short, I was the kind of kid who never got into trouble because I was too busy to get into trouble.

I went to Holy Cross in 1967, and I was nervous about being from a small town; I thought all the other kids were smarter than me, more sophisticated, all that jazz. The *Holy Cross Crusader* was the college's once-a-week newspaper, and I think they went through applications looking for students who had journalism backgrounds in high school. I got an unsolicited letter from them in my mail box saying, "We're the school paper; come to our first meeting if you want to." I hadn't planned on joining the paper, but I thought I could do one activity, so I went to the meeting and joined up.

I went to fall baseball tryouts, and I was doing pretty well. But the paper had stuff for me to do right away, so I stopped playing baseball and never went back. I might have been able to make the team, but I would have been very marginal at best at the college level. And right from the start, I was intrigued with the writing. They put me on freshman football, and in my first story I wrote that the freshman football team was in a rebuilding year. Well, a freshman team pretty much is always in a rebuilding year, if you think about it. But I really liked working for the paper, and I became very involved with it.

My sophomore year they started letting me do some varsity games, and back then Holy Cross was still playing a big-time schedule: Syracuse, Boston College, Villanova, Temple, Army, Navy, Air Force. The sports editor got married four or five weeks into the fall semester, and he appointed me to take over the job, which was a big responsibility. I took it very seriously, and it was a very challenging assignment, just putting out the paper once a week. Some of these kids today put out college dailies, which is amazing.

At Holy Cross there was no college credit and no pay; there was just the practical experience. In the next three years, I spent as much time working on the paper as I did my academics, which proved to be a smart decision because not one of my future employers ever looked at my transcripts or ever checked to see if I'd actually attended Holy Cross. But they did look at my clips. And I had clips. I was an English major because Holy Cross didn't offer a journalism major, or even any journalism classes. It was my sophomore year when I said, "This is what I want to do with my life." And it was helpful to know that so early in my college career. The fact that I was at a small school where there weren't a lot of other kids who wanted to do what I was doing was helpful too.

I was really reading the *Boston Globe* in those days, and it had an all-star lineup working there. Ray Fitzgerald, the great columnist, was there; Gammons was in his heyday; Bob Ryan was doing the NBA; Will McDonough was on football; Fran Rosen had hockey; Bud Collins was there. You had all those Hall of Famers working there at the same time; it was a tremendous cast.

The *Globe* had student correspondents at the colleges it covered that were not right in Boston: Dartmouth, Providence, U Mass. If a school had athletic interests for its readership—and Holy Cross did—it would have a correspondent. Again, when I was a sophomore, the guy who was the *Globe* correspondent was graduating the next year, so I asked him if I could take over for him when he left. He said he'd call the *Globe* and ask. The sports editor of the *Globe* said, "Sure. Great. I won't have to call the school's SID [sports information director] and ask him to find a new kid. That's one less thing I have to do." So that was my entrance to the *Globe*. As the *Globe*'s correspondent, I'd call just about every day with a paragraph about how football practice went; and, occasionally, if Holy Cross played Villanova, say, and the *Globe* didn't send a staffer, I was allowed to write a little game story. I think I had 10 bylines for the *Globe* during my junior and senior years.

When the *Globe* writers came to Holy Cross to cover a big game, I tried to be as helpful as possible. I'd get coffee for them, and I'd run around and get interviews for them. I also solicited their help. I'd show them my writing and the school paper, and I'd ask for critiques. I tried to be aggressive without being pushy . . . tried to let them know "I'm out here, and this is what I want to do." Fortunately, those guys were helpful. They were very generous with their time and very encouraging, especially guys like Jerry Nason, a wonderful old sports editor at the *Globe*.

After my junior year at Holy Cross I tried to get the summer intern job at the *Globe*, but I got turned down. It's a great program and very competitive. However, the paper was going to let me be a part-time night hawk during the summer. A night hawk answers the phone, gets coffee, takes scores, stuff like that. And I was excited about that. Then Dave Smith, who was the sports editor at the time, called me in and offered me a job covering a new amateur basketball league that was going to be called the BNBL, the Boston Neighborhood Basketball League. This was in 1974 during the busing crisis, when there was a lot of racial tension. The city wanted the kids occupied, so it started this program to keep them busy, and the league was going to be sponsored by the city, Coca-Cola, and the *Globe*. Part of the sponsorship of the *Globe* was to cover the league in the paper.

Kevin Dupont, a Boston College guy who was my age, was supposed to have taken the job, but he decided to go to Europe at the last minute. I'd been bothering the staff enough that they thought of me when he turned the job down. I did the BNBL the summers of both my junior and senior years, and I turned into a monster. I drove *Globe* pool cars around all night to find these neighborhood games, and there was more BNBL in the paper than there was Red Sox. I was totally pushing it all over the place. And, again, I was trying to be aggressive without being pushy, and I tried to let everybody know that I was really serious about making sportswriting my career. And I think that went a long way.

Kevin Dupont, he comes into my story a lot too—he was one of the ushers at my wedding—Kevin was a stringer for the Associated Press at Fenway Park, so when he left for Europe I got part of that gig too. When I went over to Fenway Park to string for the Associated Press, I got seven bucks a night, plus all the food and beer I wanted. It was great—the best deal ever. There are no elevators in Fenway Park, and the old guys didn't want to have to walk up and down the stairs, so I'd do it for them. I'd go onto the field and into the locker rooms, get some quotes, go back up to the press box, type them out, and give them to the old guys. It didn't even seem like work. I'd get to sit in the press room and listen to guys like Billy Martin and Calvin Griffith tell stories. And I was there in 1975 when Fred Lynn and Jim Rice were rookies and the Sox wound up going to the World Series, which had the famous Carlton Fisk game. That was a great summer!

I graduated from college on May 23, 1975. The BNBL had ended, but the *Globe* kept me on doing high school sports. There were four divisions of high school sports, and we had Kevin Dupont, Lesley Visser, and myself doing Divisions 2, 3, and 4. We were all the same age, and we had all just graduated from college. It was one of the greatest high school teams ever assembled, we all thought. That was $35 a day, three days a week, which seemed pretty good to me, since my part of the apartment I shared only cost me $81 a month. I did that for about two years.

Actually, it was a scary time for a guy like me. It was post-Watergate, and a lot of people wanted to get into this business. A lot of females and minorities were coming in, and with affirmative action, white guys just out of college were not a desired commodity. It was a very difficult period for me, but I was assembling a lot of *Globe* clips.

Occasionally, somebody wouldn't show up for work, and the paper would let me do a side bar on something bigger, like the New England Patriots. And once in a while my story would be on the front page of the sports section—that was pretty cool—and I started to get assignments other than high school sports. But I was not on the staff, and I had no benefits, so I was applying to newspapers all over New England. The *Worcester Telegraph* twice offered me a bureau job, and my dad said to take it because it was full-time and it had benefits, but I turned it down because it wasn't sports.

And, of course, I got turned down a lot: by the *Glouster Times*, the *Salem News*, the *Providence Journal.* I've got a drawer full of rejection letters. I'd write anywhere—Newark, Camden. Somebody told me to write to the *Milwaukee Journal,* and I did. I spelled *Milwaukee* incorrectly on all the stuff I sent, so it's no wonder no one wrote back. I remember going up to the *Salem News* because I'd met the daughter of the sports editor at a party, and she told me I should go talk to her dad. The guy totally "big-timed" me. He said, "You might be ready for us in a couple of years." I thought, "Geez, what do I have to do!"

By the spring of 1977, I was then two years out of college. I was 23 years old; I'd written 400 stories for the *Boston Globe,* most of them small pieces about 11-year-old basketball players; I'd been a stringer for the Associated Press; I'd written for magazines that wouldn't pay so I had to chase them down; I was still bartending at the Harvard Club . . . and so I was starting to feel like a failure. I was also feeling a little guilty about having gone to Holy Cross, which is an expensive school. My dad never made more than $14,000 a year, as far as I could figure out from looking at his tax returns, and Holy Cross cost $4,600 a year when I attended.

I was not feeling so hot, but a lot of people in the business were encouraging, told me to stick with it. And some of them said, "Don't take that bureau job at the *Worcester Telegraph*—you'll never get out of there if you do. You like sports and you're good. Stay with it." Again, I keep bringing up names like Ray Fitzgerald, Bob Ryan, Peter Gammons, Leigh Montville . . . those guys were great to me, and they were all looking out for me.

Things started coming to a head for me in 1977. Dave Smith, who was the sports editor at the *Globe* then, called me into his office and said, "Look, Dan, we can't keep you here for 10 years as a part-timer for $35 a day." Then he basically told me that when high school sports were over, I was pretty much going to have to move on. See, they worry about you when you get into your midtwenties. You become part of their conscience, and they don't want you hanging around without benefits. They know it's not good for you, that it's detrimental to your career; plus, there are new young kids that need to be doing that beginner's stuff. So I intensified my search, and I remember going to the post office with stacks of envelopes containing my resume, my references, and my 10 best clips.

My break came when Peter Gammons told me to apply to the *Baltimore Evening Sun*. Gammons had gone over to *Sports Illustrated,* and when he was down in Florida working on a cover story about the rookies of 1977—Bump Wills, Richie Dauer, etc.—he ran into Mike Janowski, a sportswriter for the *Sun*, who said, "We have two guys cover the Orioles, but one of them, Phil Hersh, has left, so we have an opening." So I applied, and pretty quickly I got a letter from Bill Tanton, who was the sports editor of the *Sun*. He told me that he loved my stuff but that he was going to hire somebody else. Bill had had his eye on Mark Purdy a long time and had been waiting for an opening to hire him; but after Bill rejected me, Purdy turned the job down.

This was during the Final Four in Atlanta when Al McGuire and Marquette won it. Ray Fitzgerald called me and said, "I saw this guy from Baltimore, Bill Tanton, on a plane. He's gonna call you tomorrow and offer you a job." "Ray," I said, "I already talked to the guy, and he said I was his second-best choice." "Well, he wasn't drunk, and he told me he was going to offer you the job. Be home tomorrow."

So the next day I stayed home and waited by the phone. When I had to go out for some food, I had a friend come over and man the phone until I got back. Later that afternoon, Bill did call, and he said, "I've never hired anyone over the phone before, but I want you to come down here tomorrow."

I flew down the next day, wearing a corduroy suit, and when I got to Baltimore it was boiling hot. Bill picked me up at the airport, showed me around town, explained everything, brought me back to the newspaper, and said, "I can tell you really love this job because you haven't asked me about money yet." The *Sun* had a four-year scale, and he started me at the two-year scale, which was $273 a week. I thought I was a millionaire. Then he said, "In two years, you'll be at the top of the scale, $400 a week." I thought, "That's $20,000 a year!" I couldn't believe it.

The next day I took my father out to lunch, which was something I'd never done before. We sat down in a place not unlike this, and he said, "Something must be up. You're either getting married, or you got a job." When I told him I'd just been hired by the *Baltimore Evening Sun*, he was thrilled. I was a little worried about what my mother would say because I was the last kid at home and people in my family didn't move out of the area much. But she was okay with it, and they were both very supportive.

Lesley Visser and Judy Foy threw a going-away party for me at a tavern on Massachusetts Avenue, and they invited all my family and friends. My parents were so impressed that all these older people like Ray Fitzgerald, Leigh Montville, Gammons, and Bob Ryan had come to the party for somebody like me who was just a kid. It was really cool.

Anyway, I drove to Baltimore with one of my sisters and two friends in the dead of night, and I started to work at the *Sun* on April 11, 1977. The deal was, I would just do tennis and local desk work for the first half of the baseball season, and then I would take over the Orioles at the All-Star break. I started covering the Orioles on June 23 during a road trip to Cleveland, and I remember being on an elevator with Brooks Robinson, who couldn't have been nicer to me. He asked me how old I was, then said, "You're really going to enjoy this."

Right away I got a call from Phil Itzoe, the traveling secretary, who's still with the team. He said that I should come up to Billy Hunter's room because Hunter had just taken a job with the Texas Rangers. Hunter had been the third-base coach for the Orioles for a thousand years, but I didn't even know who he was. So I went up to Hunter's room with the two other writers who were following the team, I talked to him, wished him well, and wrote the story. I had Itzoe, a team official, read the story to see if there were any mistakes in it. He said, "No. It's great." That's something I would never do now—ask a team official to approve one of my stories.

I was on the road with the Orioles for the rest of the year, and I ended up doing the 1977 World Series too. I was at Yankee Stadium when Reggie Jackson hit three home runs in one game, and I also went to LA. I did such a good job that the paper had me do the Orioles by myself the next year. At 24, I was one of the younger guys to ever take over a team for a legit paper. So I covered them from the very first day of spring training; I was their guy. The Orioles won 90 games that year, but that was bad for them. We finished the year in Detroit, and I had a flight booked from Detroit to Boston immediately after the game because I knew there was going to be a playoff game in Boston. And I made it for the game. I was there. It was a great year for me, despite the Red Sox losing the playoff game.

In 1978, Dave Smith left the *Globe* as a sports editor and went to the *Washington Star*. Vince Doria, the assistant sports editor under Dave Smith, replaced Dave and had a hiring, so I applied for the job. I had good clips now, and everybody at the *Globe* knew me, but they hired Mike Madden. Then, wouldn't you know it, Dave Smith offered me a job to write baseball for him at the *Washington Star*. The guy who wouldn't hire me to do high schools at the *Globe* now wanted me to be his baseball writer. I asked him, "Dave, how come I was no good in Boston and now I'm great?" But I was just kidding, because I had proven myself. I had done the job for a year and a half at the big-league level, and I knew I would be in demand. I was young and single and good, so I was a good candidate.

My father was against the move because he felt the *Baltimore Evening Sun* had done a good thing for me—it had rescued me, really—and he felt I owed the paper some allegiance. But Dave was offering me more money, $491 a week, whereas top pay at the *Sun* was $400. Plus, I figured, "It's D.C., I can't go wrong taking a job there." And I had a lot of faith in Dave too. So I went over to the *Washington Star* in the spring of 1979 and was its national baseball writer for three years, pretty much up against Tom Boswell, the baseball guy at the *Washington Post.*

I had a great time in Washington, but Dave Smith left the *Star* in 1981 and went to the *Dallas Morning News,* which was a big blow to me. And then, to make matters worse, my paper went out of business during the baseball strike that year. There I was, the baseball writer in Washington, D.C. . . . there's no team in the D.C. area, there's no baseball anywhere, and now there's no paper. So it was time to go.

I never got a good offer from the *Washington Post.* The staff were actually pretty insulting. They offered me some dreadful sports business writing job. I'm not sure now if they actually even offered me the job, but it was nothing I had any interest in whatsoever. I wanted to stay in the area because I liked it; I had a condo there, I was set up nicely there. But they didn't really try to get me, and it was their big mistake. I'd been writing baseball for five years, and I was still only 28. And single. Sports editors love guys like that! And I was out of work with no disgrace.

Actually, it was great in a way because I was getting offers from all over the place. It came down to LA or Chicago, but LA never made a firm offer, so I was all set to take a job with the *Chicago Tribune.* Then Vince Doria offered me $600 a week to take a position at the *Globe.* Now I really had a difficult decision to make. Boston wasn't a baseball job; it was doing takeout pieces. Chicago was a baseball job, and it was more money too, but it was still an excruciating decision because I wanted to go home.

In the end, I took the *Globe* job for less money and less prestige. It worked out for the best, though, for both parties. The *Tribune* ended up getting the god of baseball in Chicago, Jerry Holtzman, and was much better off hiring a guy like him, who really knew Chicago, instead of a kid like me, who didn't know the town. And it worked out well for me because I was able to go home, and I finally had a real job with the *Boston Globe.* I started at the *Globe* in September 1981, so it's been . . . wow . . . 20 years as of right about today!

I did takeouts for a year, and in 1982 the paper asked me to do the Celtics, which was a great beat, because Larry Bird was just coming into his prime. I was the beat guy for four years, and Larry won the MVP award three times. There was that great Lakers final that the Celtics won in 1984. Every game was a sellout—Michael Jordan was a rookie; Magic Johnson was doing his thing. I replaced Bob Ryan, who was a legend, but it was the perfect time to be covering the NBA, and it worked out really well for me.

In 1986, Peter Gammons left the *Globe* again to go back to *Sports Illustrated,* so the *Globe* asked me to do baseball. Basketball was great, but I had to do baseball. I wanted to do it. It's the same in Boston as in St. Louis: the baseball writer has the most visibility and prestige of any sportswriter in town. People in both towns just care more about baseball than any other sport. And, I wasn't that popular with the Celtics. I was always kind of a wise guy, even though they were a great team. We were in the Sacramento airport on a West Coast road trip when I learned that I was going straight to Winter Haven, Florida, for spring training, as soon as the road trip was over. After I got off the phone, I went over to a group of players just sitting around and said, "Well, guys, as soon as this trip's over I'm going on baseball." And Larry Bird said, "I'll pay your way if you go now."

Despite Bird's offer, I finished the trip with the Celtics, returned home briefly, went to Winter Haven for six weeks of spring training, and then opened the baseball seasons with the Red Sox in Detroit. By this time I was married; my wife and I had two baby girls, who were one and two years old; we were in the middle of changing houses; and I did 14 straight months of the NBA and baseball because the Red Sox wound up going to the seventh game of the World Series. It was a tough time for my wife, but I was really kind of hitting things in stride. I was covering the Celtics when they were the big thing, and then I was covering the Red Sox when they came back after being terrible for years and years. It was a historic year, 1986. Clemens started the season 14–0, went 24–4, was named MVP of the league, and won the Cy Young Award; the Red Sox got Don Baylor, and Jim Rice came back and had a good year again. All this great stuff was happening, and the Red Sox mattered again. It was like catching lightning in a bottle.

I wasn't the beat man. I was a complementary guy to him. Gammons had created the Sunday baseball page, which is the most read page in the *Boston Globe,* and I wrote that from 1986 through 1989. I also wrote columns on the team during the week and occasionally game stories, and I started doing radio and TV because I was covering the Red Sox. Consequently, I became very identified with baseball.

In 1989, Frank Deford started *The National* and offered me a job with that paper. He wanted me to cover the American League and Peter Pascarelli to cover the National League. It was double my salary and a five-year contract. I thought, "This is a slam dunk. I've got to do this." My boss, Vince Doria, told me why I shouldn't leave the

Globe, and then *The National* went after him. He went over to *The National,* and then he tried to hire me! Leigh Montville left the *Globe* to replace Deford at *Sports Illustrated,* so the paper wound up having a column open. Don Skwar, who was the assistant sports editor under Doria, moved up, and he asked me and Ryan to do the column. So I could either go to *The National* for a lot more money, or get a small raise and be a columnist at the *Globe.*

Once again, I chose to stay at the *Globe* for less money. I became a columnist in 1989, and *The National* folded one year later. It would have owed me four years of money, and it paid all the salaries it owed. There weren't many five-year contracts. There were a lot of twos and threes. Frank kind of overextended himself with me early on, so I think the staff weren't that disappointed when I said no.

I've been a columnist since 1989, and it's worked out well. I've never really been tempted to leave since then except for the time *Sports Illustrated* offered me a job in 1995. That one went to the wall. I was close to leaving because it was more money and less work and no relocation. It was the ultimate sportswriting position. In the end I didn't take the job because I didn't think I would have been a good magazine writer; plus, I like the daily charge of writing a column. Something happens, we react to it, and it's in the paper the next day. It's on your doorstep. Your neighbors know what you're doing. And I think I'm better suited to being a big fish in a small pond, and at *Sports Illustrated* you're kind of invisible. Sure, you have a national audience—12-year-old kids in Nebraska are reading you—but now, with the Internet, everybody is reading you anyway. So I'm glad I stayed. Every time I've stayed, it's proven to be better for me. I've very much attached myself to the Red Sox, and I've become identified with the team. That phrase used to refer to the tremendous fan base here, the "Red Sox Nation," I invented that. And "The Curse of the Bambino" . . . I didn't invent that phrase; a book editor did, but it's become associated with me, and I know that it will be in the first line of my obituary because a book with that title just refuses to die.

I wrote my first baseball book, *One Strike Away,* at the end of the 1986 season, and I wrote it in six weeks. It wasn't that hard to do because I'd been writing parts of it, the profiles in the book, all season long. And, of course, I didn't do anything else for those six weeks. I got very sick when I finished the book. I'd been going hard for 14 straight months, covering the Celtics and Red Sox championship seasons, and then, after I'd spent another six hard weeks on that book, my body just gave out. I've had this Cal Ripken Jr. running streak going since 1983. I've only missed four days in all that time, and one of those misses came after I finished that book and got so sick.

I only got to do the book in the first place because Peter Gammons turned it down. The book started out as a collection of profiles. That's what the publisher originally wanted because there were so many players on the Red Sox: Bruce Hurst, Wade Boggs, Roger Clemens, Jim Rice, Oil Can Boyd.

I signed the contract in something like June, and there was a clause in the contract that said if they made it to the World Series, the advance would be $5,000 more than otherwise. That was really huge for me, and all they had to do was make it to the World Series. I started writing the profiles during the season, but then the team started winning and kept winning and kept winning. As they got better and it appeared that they were going to the World Series, we changed the whole concept and made it into a book about what the whole season was like.

It almost ended up being the year they finally won it all, and I had all the profiles and the stuff about what a great season the team had had. Then they didn't win, and it became a different kind of book again, a book about the most agonizing failure you could imagine. It didn't sell very well; in fact, it is by far my poorest seller. It didn't perform at all. People were depressed about what had happened, and they didn't want to read about it. Ironically, it's experiencing a huge surge now. People like it now, and it may get reprinted by a local group. I think it should get reprinted because it's a very tidy recap of those unfortunate, unforgettable events.

That book had a great title too. The funny thing is that the publishers picked that title when the Red Sox beat the Angels because Boston was "One Strike Away" from losing to California but came back and won the ALCS. And then it went the other way on them: the Red Sox were "One Strike Away" from winning the World Series and wound up losing to the Mets. I remember the book's editor wanted to change the title. He thought "One Strike Away" was too negative. He wanted to use "Rise Up and Fight Again," from Chaucer's *Canterbury Tales*, which would have been the worst title of all time! Can you imagine the *Canterbury Tales* . . . "Rise Up and Fight Again"! No, I think "One Strike Away" was exactly what we needed, and that's what we used. Looking back on it, I'm happy with the book, even though I never made any money on it besides the advance, and I had to sue the publisher to get the second half of that. It was nasty, not a good first experience at all.

My second baseball book, *The Curse of the Bambino*, came out in 1990. You might not know this, but I've added to it twice, and the updated paperback versions are everywhere. The first time, I added a chapter about the horrible 1990 playoffs when Clemens came unglued on the mound out in Oakland. And the second time, I added a chapter about all the bad stuff that's happened since then through the 1999 playoffs against the Yankees. I'll probably wind up adding to it again because bad stuff just keeps on happening. Pedro Martinez said this year, "Bring back the Bambino; I'll drill him in the ass"; and he never won another game! It's unbelievable. The beat just goes on and on.

As I said before, the title of that book was not my idea but that of Meg Blackstone, who was an editor at E. P. Dutton. Meg grew up in Oyster Bay, Long Island—John Lennon bought the house she grew up in—and she was a child of privilege. She went to Yale and is a very brilliant person. Her grandfather Arthur Whitfield Davidson was a house painter in Dorchester. He used to throw beer cans at the TV and say, "It's the curse of the Bambino!" whenever things went wrong for the Red Sox. So Meg grew up with this idea that the Red Sox gave away the best player in history, and as a consequence, bad things have happened to the Red Sox ever since. She's a casual baseball fan—she can't tell you what the infield fly rule is about—but she is very brilliant and always carries around this idea of her grandfather's about the reason behind the Red Sox's bad fortunes.

She was on an airplane in 1988 with her husband heading for a summer home in Maine, and her husband was reading a copy of the *Boston Globe*. He read my stuff in the *Globe* and said to her, "This guy here has a pretty good way with words. Why don't you ask him about your baseball book idea?"

So she wrote me a letter, dated August 8, 1988—8/8/88—I remember stuff like that. She introduced herself, told me about the idea, and said to please call her if I had any interest. I called her and we talked; she offered me a decent amount of money, and I agreed to write the book. But the title was all her idea.

The idea of *The Curse of the Bambino* was to basically write a black history of the Red Sox, to tell the story of the Sox getting rid of Babe Ruth and then having all this bad stuff happen to them after that. It's somewhat comical, but that's basically what it is: a black history of the team.

As I was writing the book in 1989, the Red Sox flirted with success that year. I thought, "If they win the World Series this year, I'm screwed!" And it was possible because once a team gets into the postseason, anything can happen. You can't take that chance and say, "Well, they're not gonna win the whole thing."

Fortunately, for the purposes of the book, they didn't make the playoffs. I finished the book, and it came out in the spring of 1990. And 1990 was a good year for it to come out because a lot of goofy things happened that year. They did make the playoffs and then imploded with that horrible Clemens thing in Oakland.

The title is very catchy and has become a monster really. Out-of-town writers and broadcasters and commentators love using it to explain why bad things happen to the Red Sox. It's become part of the language around Boston, and I take a lot of pride in that. For instance, Joe Kerrigan gets hired as the manager of the Red Sox, and the first thing he says is, "This is my chance to break the curse."

Do I believe in it? I don't know. Yeah, strange things happen to the Red Sox, but I don't really think it's because Babe Ruth is looking down saying, "You traded me, so now suffer the consequences." Nevertheless, it has become part of the permanent lore of baseball, like the Babe's Called Shot and the Billy Goat Curse of the Chicago Cubs. I'm kind of proud of that and proud, as I said before, that the phrase will be the first thing in my obituary. And I know that when I die they will still not have won the World Series, so the phrase will still be out there in use.

I'm also proud that the book has lasted so long. It's not *Tuesdays with Morrie*, which is the king of longevity for books, but it's been around a good while now, and I get a kick out of being able to go into a bookstore in LA or Chicago and still see it on the shelves. And it still sells around Boston and is being read by the next generation. It's on some of the high school reading lists around here, and parents come up to me all the time and tell me that their kid did a book report on it for school.

The Red Sox, God bless them, they certainly do everything in their power to keep the book going. For example, there's a souvenir shop across from Fenway, and the guy who runs it carries my books. I do book signings there all the time. I was signing books there before a game against the Yankees this summer, and a guy came over and said, "I want two *Bambinos*. Sign one to me, but don't sign the other because I'm going to tear it up as a curse-breaking ritual during the game." And that turned out to be the night Mike Mussina perfect-gamed the Red Sox. That was the night! It's unbelievable, you know. You can't make this stuff up.

Oh, yes, Red Sox fans have definitely become pessimistic. If you're in the stands at a playoff game, you'll see it for yourself. If things are going good, it's quiet there because they're constantly afraid of the other shoe dropping. They don't have that confidence and "We're Number One!" swagger that fans of other teams have. Instead, they carry around a Calvinistic streak of self-doubt, and they don't expect good things to happen. And because of 1986, all bets are off. You just can't imagine how losing that game affected people here. I mean, people were opening up bottles of champagne and waking up babies, and then. . . . You just can't lose that game. It's impossible. You can go to games all your life and not see a loss like that: a two-run lead, two outs, nobody on, bottom of the 10th. We figured the odds of losing in that situation, and it was something like 274–1: four straight guys reach base and three straight guys score with two outs in the bottom of the last inning.

The players all start off saying they don't believe in the curse, and some of them get ticked off about it, but a lot of times later on I think it does get into their heads a little bit. It's just that some are better than others at disguising it. One thing is for sure: the guy who throws off the curse is going to be some kind of big hero. Dave Henderson almost did it, and he was the perfect guy to do it because he didn't give a damn about anything. That's why he performed so well in the postseason. If you ask Dave Henderson today what the athletic highlight of his career was, he'll tell you it was scoring four touchdowns in a high school football game. He's just that kind of guy. He never felt any pressure, and that's why he was able to step up to the plate and hit home runs without worrying about 80 years of history. He just played.

Do I think rooting for the Red Sox would lose some of its luster if they ever won? Absolutely. It happened to the Phillies. I was there when the Phillies won in 1980 after a hundred years of losing. They used to be special, but now they're just the Phillies.

If the Red Sox won, their fans would have no reason to live anymore. You wouldn't be able to complain about them in the wintertime. We'd love to try, no doubt about it, but winning would definitely change the dynamic around here. The Red Sox would lose their mystique, definitely.

The great thing about our fans here is that they are such intelligent fans, and readers. They don't want boosterism, but they're very passionate. They want depth and don't mind sarcasm. And they're legion, and they're spread across the board demographically: old, young, black, white, male, female. Everybody is a Red Sox fan. I see this passion in my e-mail. If I write a story about something other than the Red Sox, I get nothing. But if I write about Carl Everett or Dan Duquette, I get inundated.

Yes, it would be ironic if leaving Fenway is what finally gets the Red Sox over the hump, and a lot of people have suggested that until they get out of Fenway and stop building teams for the place, they won't win because those teams do poorly on the road.

The team identity has changed somewhat lately. No longer do teams have slow right-handed sluggers who can't get around the bases, but they still play station-to-station baseball. They don't run; defensively they're usually weak; and they never have teams based on speed, defense, and pitching like the old Dodgers, Cardinals, or White Sox teams. They're Clydesdales who play station-to-station baseball. And some people think left-handers can't win here because the bullpen wall is so close in right field. So, yeah, there's some thought that leaving Fenway might help them eventually win.

Obviously, I love Fenway Park, and I've written a lot about the place. I've put in a lot of time there. I've heard all the stories about the place, and I've done a lot of research about it. And I'm always trying to learn more. There are people who know more about the place than I do—groundskeepers, scoreboard operators, people like that. But it's a very special place to me. Outside of the house I grew up in and the house I now live in, it's the place I'd most like to spend an afternoon. And I'll just be emotionally devastated when the Red Sox leave Fenway Park. The silver lining in that scenario is that I think I'll be dead by the time they manage the construction of a new stadium. They move so slowly around here that I know my kids are going to be able to get through high school and Fenway will still be in use by the Red Sox. And I like that.

Even if I hadn't grown up here, I think I still would have been a big baseball fan because of the family dynamic I spoke of earlier: my brother being a good athlete and all that. Even if I'd grown up in South Dakota, I would still have been immersed in baseball by the time I was 9 or 10 years old. I'm sure of that.

What growing up a Red Sox fan did was equip me to do what I do. If I had grown up in Sioux Falls, I couldn't do what I do. We're very provincial here in Boston, and I have more institutional memory than even Bob Ryan, who's older than me. Ryan grew up in New

Jersey; he's *only* been here since 1967, you know, *only* 34 years, so he doesn't count. This is the way we think about such things here. If you didn't grow up with it, you can't quite get it. I did grow up with it, and it's wildly helpful to me. And I could not have the same appreciation of what people go through nor could I write with the same sarcasm about it if I hadn't grown up here myself. And that's why it's good I didn't go to Chicago. Even in Baltimore, which was a good place to live and work, it wasn't the same. This is where I belong; and the *Globe* readers, they're my people. I'm one of them.

The book I'm working on now is going to be another collaboration with my good friend Stan Grossfield, who did the photos for our picture book about Fenway. It's going to be a book about spring training, and it will be published by Houghton Mifflin, a local publisher, which also did our Fenway picture book. The spring training book is going to be a generic book in the sense that it's not just about the Red Sox.

What book would I write if a publisher gave me carte blanche to write on any baseball subject I wanted to write about? I've already written them; it would be these two: *The Curse of the Bambino* and *At Fenway*.

At Fenway is my favorite because a lot of my best thoughts about baseball, the Red Sox, Fenway Park, and being a fan are in that book. It's a hard book to summarize for somebody, but I look at it as a kind of love letter to Fenway Park. I was afraid it wouldn't hold together because it's kind of all over the place, but it holds together okay.

And, you know, when the Red Sox finally do win the World Series, I'm going to write that book. Houghton Mifflin is talking about putting me on retainer just so I'll be on board to do that book. If they really keep me on retainer until the Red Sox win the World Series, their attorneys will probably have to keep giving me money for a long, long, long time. You gotta love the Red Sox!

BASEBALL BOOKS BY DAN SHAUGHNESSY

One Strike Away: The Story of the 1986 Red Sox. New York: Beaufort Books, 1987.

The Curse of the Bambino. New York: Dutton, 1990.

At Fenway: Dispatches from Red Sox Nation. New York: Crown Publishers, 1996.

Fenway: A Biography in Words and Pictures. Boston: Houghton Mifflin, 1999.

16

JOHN THORN

A highly respected baseball historian and a consultant to several magazines and institutions, including the National Baseball Hall of Fame Library, John Thorn is one of the most familiar names on the contemporary baseball literature scene. He founded and is president of Professional Ink, a sports book production company, responsible for (among other fine books) a successful challenger to Macmillan's Baseball Encyclopedia, *the massive and exhaustive* Total Baseball *(Warner Books, 1989). As the former publications director of the Society for American Baseball Research, Thorn also founded and edited the society's most attractive publication,* The National Pastime *(1982–89). Among the best of the Thorn baseball books are: the seminal study,* The Relief Pitcher; Baseball's New Hero *(E. P. Dutton, 1979);* The Armchair Book of Baseball, I *and* II *(Scribners, 1985, 1987), two in a series of "Armchair" anthologies edited by Thorn;* The Hidden Game of Baseball *(Doubleday, 1985) in which Thorn provides a lucid explanation and history of baseball statistics; and the* Sporting News *pictorial,* The Game for All America, *named one of 50 notable books of 1988 by the American Library Association. A 1968 graduate of Beloit College (WI) and a member of the World Baseball Hall of Fame's board of directors, Thorn lives and works in Saugerties, New York.*

I WAS BORN in 1947 on Alexander Cartwright's birthday on April 17 in Stuttgart, West Germany, in the British-occupied sector where my parents had come as war refugees from Poland as Jewish refugees. I stayed in Germany until the age of two and a half, at which point we sailed for the New World . . . or, rather, a visa came in. I'm told my parents applied for visas to Australia, Argentina, and the United States, and whichever one came first, that was the country they were going to. The U.S. visa came first; otherwise I'd be Juan Thorn writing about soccer.

We arrived here in the fall of 1949, went to Ellis Island, and were

processed as immigrants. I spent my first night in the New World in
what was then called the Broadway Central Hotel on Broadway and
Third Streets. I didn't connect any of this until much later, but the
Broadway Central was formerly known as the Grand Central Hotel,
and that was where the National League was founded in 1876. So
reconstructing all this years later, it's clear that I was hearing voices
like Joan of Arc being told to save the honor of France. I too had my
mission all spelled out from a very early point.

I came over knowing no English but speaking German as well as
any two-and-a-half-year-old boy would. My parents were poor, and
both had to go to work. I was put into a nursery school situation
where I was made the butt of much ill-tempered humor because I
couldn't speak English . . . such as being tied up as the Indian in
"Cowboys and Indians." So it became clear to me in my third year
that I'd better learn how to become an American quickly because I
wasn't having much fun.

Somewhere in my fourth year, in the summer of 1951, I discovered baseball cards. By then I was already speaking English of
course. The passion with which the older kids on the street were
flipping baseball cards really intrigued me. The idea that there was
a competition, that whoever got a "leaner" or closest to the wall
would take the other kids' cards, was extremely attractive. And I
learned to read from the backs of baseball cards and from the backs
of cereal boxes, like most kids. I'm blessed (and cursed) with a near-
photographic memory so that if I read the stats on the back of a
card, I could just spit 'em back out. I didn't have to study them. So
for a while I was regarded as the boy marvel of my neighborhood. I
also became an avid, avid fan and became passionately involved with
the Brooklyn Dodgers. So baseball was my quick fix on becoming
an American. It also gave me an area of utter independence from
everybody in my family. My parents scarcely knew what bat and ball
games were, nor did they care. And, for whatever reason, I deter-
mined it was important for me to carve out an identity that had nothing to do with my history or my parents.

When it was time to go to college, I picked Beloit College in Wisconsin, not knowing that that was the college attended by William
Hulbert, the founder of the National League. I went to graduate
school in English literature at Washington University in St. Louis. I
had in mind to be a professor at the college level. I completed the
course work but declined to write the doctoral thesis because I realized that I was looking forward to the West Coast reports on how the

Mets had done against the Padres much more than I was to reading about Ben Johnson and John Donne. This was the summer of 1969. So my thesis on Herbert—that's George Herbert, not Ray Herbert—never materialized.

I went back to New York and, with the recommendation of one of my college professors, got a job at the *New Leader,* which was an old left political magazine that kind of had hardening of the arteries and had become new right over the years. I worked there for three years and made no money, but I learned a great deal about publishing and learned to love books and magazines not only as things to read but as objects with aesthetic qualities of their own.

I went from there as a freelance editor to a small book publisher named Hart, where I rose precipitously to editor-in-chief, mostly from a lack of there being anyone else ahead of me.

While I was there, we had a dry spell, and Harold Hart, the 72-year-old publisher, came to me and said, "Look, I've got 60 pages of a baseball book. I know you like baseball, and I've got nothing much for you to do for the next six weeks. Why don't you write more stories in this vein—you'll get your regular salary—and we'll make a book for kids." And he said, "You and I will share authorship on this."

So I finished the book, writing very much to order, writing in a style that would match the existing material. And I thought I was writing a book for kids. When the book, called *A Century of Baseball Lore,* was done, Hart said, "We can't promote a two-headed author. You be the writer." I, being young and naive, said okay, and I've regretted it ever since. I've always regretted that move because my name is on a book one-quarter of which was not mine. It was in the can already, had been written over the period of 1950–1955. The style of that book, which I had to follow, is very antiquated and archaic. It's the *Cosmopolitan* magazine style of baseball . . . lots of exclamation points, lots of italics, lots of verbal indications of "jaws dropped" and "eyebrows raised." It's quite horrendous. But then Hart decided that the book was wonderful and that if kids were going to like it, what's the difference between kids reading about baseball and adults reading about baseball? So he issued it for adults, as an adult trade hardcover book.

It received a scathing review from Jonathan Yardley in *Sports Illustrated,* which just mortified me, and I felt the injustice of it keenly because he said something to the effect of "This book is written in a style that's for children." I felt like calling him and saying, "Yes!

That's right. I thought I was writing a kid's book. It wasn't my decision to bring it out as an adult book."

To top it all off, I received no royalties, just my salary, and the
book sold 120,000 copies. So that book is not my favorite child,
though I'm looking at it more kindly than I used to. I'm 42 now and
I was 26 then, so I guess I'm finally giving myself a break.

I left New York City to write the "Great American Novel" and
failed. I realized, "Gee, I'd better get back to what I know, and I'd
better write another baseball book." When I tried to get a contract
for *The Relief Pitcher,* I found it was convenient to have written a
120,000-copy seller.

My baseball career owes a lot to having started in this offhand way.
Moreover, I wrote *A Century of Baseball Lore* in Hart's offices, which
were on Third Street around the corner from Broadway where the
Grand Central or Broadway Central Hotel was. And while I was wrap-
ping up the book, the Hotel collapsed in a heap of rubble. No cause
. . . it just collapsed. Killed a couple of derelicts staying in this old
SRO (single room occupancy) hotel. And I thought later on that
that was very symbolic . . . more of a piece with my "astrological"
view of life. I have very little appetite for occultism, but it's hard to
ignore these particular concurrences.

The Relief Pitcher was another mistake, in the opposite direction, in
that I had no idea who I was writing it for. I wrote it for myself, I
guess. I think it's a pretty good book, and over the years people have
come to view it as an important book because it contains a lot of
research that was never done before by anybody else and has not
been duplicated since. If you want to know about the rise of relief
pitching and how it got to be where it is today, you've got to start
with that book.

All the same, it's written with a fairly turgid style and with a SABR
researcher's type of zeal, although I didn't know what SABR was
until the book was nearly completed. That was a book with no audience in mind, and as a result it found no audience. I think it sold
4,400 or 4,600 copies.

It's not an entertaining book. It's a castor oil type of book—"read
it; it'll be good for you"—and there are a lot of books published like
that, mostly self-published works, like *The History of the Three-I League*
or *Japanese Players in Vancouver, 1921–1923.* These books are written
from the heart—I admire the hell out of them—but as someone
who's become a professional at this, I know you'd better have in
mind a reader. If you're writing just because you've got to get it out

of you, well, then, get it out and then get on with some real writing—because real writing involves communicating, and if there's not someone out there you want to communicate with, then you're just masturbating.

This type of self-expression is the individual equivalent of the support group. It's not what I'm about any longer; however, I do have in mind a work which I will publish myself if nobody else will. That's a book on the rise of baseball from 1820–1900. It's my hobby interest, and I don't give a damn who reads it. That's one I have to get out, but I have no illusions about it being a popular success. I will try to make it entertaining, but I'm writing it for myself because I know a great deal about the subject that is not in print anywhere, and I'm frightened that I'm going to die without getting my research, 10 years of it already, into print.

My next book was a children's book called *Baseball's Ten Greatest Games,* which I still really like. I had to make it accessible to 12-year-olds, so I aborted my romance with the semicolon, and I made sure that if I was going to use a two-bit word I put it in a context where the meaning could be divined. I was conscious of a 12-year-old reader, but I figured I'd rather have that 12-year-old stretch a little bit and reach me than go for the lowest common denominator.

I regard that book as a signal success because I wanted it to cross over from children to adults and it did. It's the only book to my knowledge which was adopted by the Junior Literary Guild as a main selection and by the Book-of-the-Month Club for adults because neither knew if it was an adult book or a children's book. It was also an experimental work in that it was the first time a baseball book had been written not only in the first person but also in the present tense. So I had some fun with that one.

After *Baseball's Ten Greatest Games* I did *Pro Football's Ten Greatest Games* and *The Armchair Book of Baseball.* In fact, I did a series of "Armchair" books: *The Armchair Quarterback, The Armchair Mountaineer, The Armchair Aviator, The Armchair Angler, The Armchair Traveler.* That series was one of the bigger scams in publishing in that I got people to pay me to read. I simply devoured the literature in a field I really had an interest in, read 10 pieces for every one that was included, and created anthologies that had little introductory bits that were peculiarly mine. I used those introductions to do things that I thought were either entertaining or meaningful or supplied in some cases neat counterpoint to the pieces that followed. So there's a personal cast to all the "Armchair" books that's carried through those introductions, and I have a feeling of identification with them that ordinarily an anthologist might not have if all he did was pick the pieces and say, "This was published in 1943 by *Colliers*."

I don't think I'm a terrific writer. I think I occasionally wind up writing something that's well phrased, that's effective, that's nice. But I'm not in a league with my betters. There are better writers than I am. For a page or two, though, I can hold my own. I'm content to think that in my chosen form, whether it's the "Armchair" introductory pieces or the captions in a book like *The Game for All America*, I'm as good as anybody. Over the length of a book, there are people who write better than I do. No question about it.

But I've got some important books, some books that will not discredit me before my family in my *New York Times* obituary. *The Hidden Game of Baseball*, for example, was a thing worth doing, and I think it gets better every year.

It's very humorous to me that because of that book I'm now referred to in the press as a "Sabermetrician," as a statistical pundit, which I'm not. I do love math, aesthetically. Math is beautiful, and if offers something of what baseball offers. Mathematics offers an ideal world and provides a form of escape for a lot of people who wear different colored socks and put pens in their shirt pockets and look like misfits. But they hear the music of the spheres when they're involved with their math, and the same is true with the baseball nut. SABR has any number of these people whom some of us find comical, but that's my brother, that guy. I'm just *this far* away from being the baseball nerd myself.

The appeal of baseball, like that of mathematics, is that it is under a bell jar, that it seems like a perfect world containing justice and swift retribution. We like to think that the worst team does not win, that the team that makes the critical error in the field or the base-running blunder in the ninth will suffer. If not that day, then surely another. But baseball's not as perfect as mathematics because you get quirky results. You get the Mets winning in 1969; you get the Mets winning in 1973, quirkier yet. So there's the joy of surprise as well as the beauty of the order, the regularity, the predictability. Baseball is beautiful, math is beautiful, but I'm not a mathematician. I'm a baseball writer and a baseball fan, and I love baseball's history more than I love its math. And, frankly, I can get as sick of sabermetrics as the next guy. You start telling me about offensive efficiency records and secondary averages . . . my eyes can glaze over just as people's eyes glaze over when they read about some of the stuff Pete

Palmer and I have put forward in *The Hidden Game of Baseball* or *Total Baseball.*

The reason I like Palmer's system of linear weights, which we expounded in *The Hidden Game,* so much is that it's theoretically appealing. It's not just jerry-rigging a combination of one average with another and saying, "Let's award two points for this and three points for that, and four points if you had an MVP season . . ." That stuff I find very tedious and amateurish and not worth reading. You've got a lot of people self-publishing this type of stuff . . . some of it good, but most of it truly awful. Sabermetrics is not brain surgery; you don't need to be certified. Anybody with a printing press can be a menace. And Gresham's Law will eventually operate: there'll be so much bad sabermetrics out there, that people will toss out the good sabermetrics with the bad.

You know, *The Hidden Game of Baseball* was a forerunner of *Total Baseball,* and the way it came about is interesting.

David Reuther and I came up with the idea of doing an encyclopedia to combat the Macmillan encyclopedia in 1982. We think the term "encyclopedia" for the Macmillan book is just dead wrong; it's not an encyclopedia. There's nothing to read. It is a big fat record book. And it's a marvel of its kind, one of the great books in the history of baseball publishing, although I think the 1969 edition remains the best edition.

But I thought there was a void. I liked the old Turkin-Thompson encyclopedia where there was stuff to read as well as the records, even though their records were very sketchy and didn't begin to hold a candle to Macmillan. But Turkin-Thompson was dying; it was fading from the moment Macmillan came into being. And it was a shame because Macmillan was not totally supplanting them; Macmillan did not seek to compete with them on the prose level.

I had the idea that we could come up with an encyclopedia that offered different kinds of records and a more analytical approach to the game, a sabermetric approach to the game, as well as have articles on topics like the Negro Leagues and Japanese baseball. If you want to find out about such things and you don't know the literature, you don't know where to go. I thought it'd be great to have something like the Turkin-Thompson mix of prose and stats, only larger.

We proposed this idea to Simon & Schuster. They thought it was great. Peter Schwed, the senior editor, said it was one of the best proposals, if not *the* best, he'd ever seen. They called us in and gave us the dog and pony show with all the executives there, and they offered us $120,000, which was a mammoth amount of money in 1982. But they said we had to do it in nine months so they could bring it out in the spring of 1984. And we thought, "It's possible we could do it by killing ourselves, but it's also possible we might not do it." Now, Simon & Schuster has something of a reputation for being litigious. And we knew that if we took half of the advance money and spent it on producing the book, paying writers and getting Pete's data base in gear, and then we didn't make our deadline, we'd have to give back the money we'd already spent, and we'd all go bankrupt. We thought the personal risk was too high, so we declined that offer.

Instead we scaled the book down to become *The Hidden Game of Baseball,* which had something of a records component but was basically a writer's book. We sold that to Doubleday for less than half of what we turned down from Simon & Schuster, but we knew we could produce that in the time allotted. And we thought, "Well . . . maybe someday."

And you can imagine how hard that was. I had never received more than $15,000 for a book, and here I'm offered $120,000 and I have to turn it down! It was a personal crisis! You turn down money like that, you don't know if you're ever going to see it again.

But David and Pete and I tried it again with *Total Baseball,* an even larger concept. Sabermetrics had grown even further in the years between 1982 and 1986, when we proposed the project to Warner Books, and so to reflect that growth we included stats like Runs Created, Total Average, Clutch Hitting Index, Park Factor, and Pete's linear weights measures like Batting Runs, Stolen Base Runs, and Fielding Runs. And, of course, *Total Baseball* has 700 pages of articles on just about everything you can imagine, so I think we did finally produce the most complete baseball encyclopedia ever . . . really, the first complete one.

The Game for All America is a book I take some pleasure in. That was a book I didn't cook up. The *Sporting News* wanted to do a book called "A Day in the Life of Baseball," and they were supposed to have Gannett and Fuji for sponsors. Gannett was going to send their photographers out and shoot baseball all over the country on one day, August 17 or whatever. But Gannett backed out. So the *Sporting News* had some photos they had commissioned—they had tons more in their archives—and I got a call from Dick Waters, who said, "Listen, we've got 10,000 photos here, and we want to make a book. What's the hook? What do we do with this?"

I said, "Why don't we make it a sentimental look at traditional baseball. We can use those photos to point up all the various things that baseball means to America and Americans. And we can use as a title 'The Game for All America,' which is the title of Ernie Harwell's poem that ran in the *Sporting News* back in the Eisenhower years."

I gave them some sample chapter titles, and Ron Smith did a great job pulling the photos together. They slapped them on boards and left holes for me to fill. That's the way the book was done. I didn't select the pictures. I'd have to look at six photos and say, "What am I going to say that'll unify these six?" It was a jigsaw puzzle and quite a challenge. I'm pleased to think that I brought off some really nice effects with some of these captions that bring together disparate pictures and find things that are common to all of them.

It's a book that you buy for the photos if you buy it at all, and the writing is incidental. Yet my feeling about the book is that, in fact, the photos are by and large Kodak snapshot quality. They're not wonderful photos; there are some, but a lot of them you could have taken yourself in your backyard. I think what holds that book together—if it holds together at all—is the writing, and it's odd to think of it because you don't buy that book for the writing. So it's both a regret and almost a secret pleasure of mine that I've written quite a good book that nobody reads. I was proud that the book was exhibited in Moscow as a good portrait of America and Americans.

SABR, of course, has been very important to my career. In 1981 I had a *Sporting News* assignment to cover the SABR convention in Toronto, and I met so many weird and fascinating people that within a year I was not only an avid member but I'd also started a new publication that would be somewhat more accessible, somewhat more visually appealing than the *Research Journal*, which Bob Davids had masterminded so well over the early years. The *National Pastime* was created as a membership growth vehicle for SABR, and it worked marvelously. The organization went from 1,400 members to 4,200 in a span of nine months, and a lot of that growth had to be chalked up to the *National Pastime*. There's no other reason for it; the organization had already been in existence nearly 10 years, and it gained 10-15 percent per annum. And here you have a growth of 300 percent! I was really pleased to think that the joys and pleasures of SABR were going to be communicated to a wide audience. I was disappointed that the charge that Cliff Kachline, the executive director at the time, and I led out of the trenches . . . you know, "Come on, guys, let's go get 'em" . . . was not followed by the troops. Members of the executive board were queasy about making this organization for the masses. There's still a sense of SABR of the "True Cross," that if you're not a resercher, then you don't deserve to belong to SABR. Some people like to belong to exclusive organizations. Me, I like to belong to inclusive organizations. I think SABR has great things to offer to 100,000 baseball fans. Maybe not a million, but 100,000. To achieve that kind of growth, however, there has to be dedication within the organization to go out and achieve it, to do the things necessary to grow, to promote, to spend some money on growth. The will wasn't there, so the vision that Cliff and I had for SABR kind of withered on the vine.

The *National Pastimes* were a tremendous boon to me personally because, in putting those issues together, I made a lot of friends. I wrote to people I didn't know like Harold Seymour. I thought his books were wonderful. In fact, it was Seymour and Larry Ritter who made me realize that a baseball book could be more than just funny stories about Rube Waddell. Fred Lieb's books are great, but they are *baseball* books. Harold Seymour's books are not *just* baseball books anymore than Ritter's are. They're books about America. They're serious books, they're important books. So here I was all through the 1980s writing to, speaking with, and eventually becoming friends with people who were formative for me, whom I idolized, if I'd idolized anybody.

Editing the *National Pastime* was a great experience because it leaned upon my *New Leader* experience where I edited, rewrote, proofread, pasted up, did everything. The *New Leader* was a letterpress operation, and I really learned the business from top to bottom, so that I was able to put the *National Pastime* together on my living room coffee table. There are a lot of headaches involved in self-publishing, as you know, but it's a very rewarding feeling to have something in your hands that started as an idea I had while shaving. And while it contains the contributions of many people who've written for it, a magazine is essentially informed by one vision, and that's the editor's vision.

SABR also showed me the joy of the obscure. It's the archeological impulse in baseball . . . Indiana Jones in baseball. It's people blowing away the dust and digging in there with their trowels where nobody really cared to go in years past, with the possible exception of guys like Ernie Lanigan or Bill Haber, who'd be looking for new major leaguers or Tris Speaker's lost doubles. I think it's great that these guys are driven by things the world would label picayune or inconsequential. They've marched to the beat of their own drum. They've decided what's important; they didn't let somebody else decide for them.

I can call Frank Phelps, and he goes down to his local library or the county courthouse and does research to find out whether Fred Chapman, a pitcher in the 1880s, really did make his debut at age 14; whether he was, in other words, younger than Joe Nuxhall. Why should we care? It's only because we think it's neat, we think it's interesting, we think it matters.

And we also have this proprietary sense that all SABR researchers have: yes, you share your results with the community, but the find is yours! Bill Haber's find is his, always his! If I read 1860 newspapers, and I find a first name for a guy who's never had a first name in any of the reference books, that's my find, and I'm tickled. Or if I find a new major leaguer, which I did a couple of weeks ago, he's my major leaguer. He exists only because I resurrected him, after he was unknown for the last 110 years. And this is a source of enormous pleasure.

I'm on the board of directors, but the idea for the World Baseball Hall of Fame was Bruce Prentice's. He was the one who created the Canadian Baseball Hall of Fame, another idea had while shaving. Bruce and I and Joe Vellano and Dave Durgy shared a condo for a weekend in Lake Placid two winters ago. Why were we in Lake Placid? You're going to love this: to do a re-creation of baseball on ice as played in the 1860s!

But anyway, Bruce came up with the idea of having a Hall of Fame to honor the baseball stars of all nations, stayed up through most of the night making notes, and the next morning he told us the idea. We all immediately thought it was great.

Why am I interested in being one of the founding fathers of the World Baseball Hall of Fame? Well, for one thing, I like starting ventures . . . like the *National Pastime* and Baseball Ink, my publishing company. I like identifying niches in the marketplace. There was a niche, a void for us to occupy, for example, with *Total Baseball*. Nobody was doing anything like that. Macmillan was not tending its own garden very well, and there was also nobody coming out after them, so I did.

The National Baseball Hall of Fame is a wonderful institution run by a lot of terrific people, and we could not hope to do better than

they have done: which is celebrate the game of baseball as it is played by the U.S. major leaguers and, historically, the Negro Leaguers.
But I don't see them or anybody else doing what we have in mind,
which is building a Hall of Fame to celebrate the baseball heroes
and exploits and experiences of other lands, other countries, other
cultures. The World Baseball Hall of Fame will recognize both amateur and professional baseball figures from around the globe,
including those people who have made important contributions off
the field to the spread of the international game.

You know, in Finland they play a game called "pesapallo," which
is a combination of an ancient folk game called "King Ball" and
baseball. Some Finn, I forget his name, came back from a trip to the
United States in 1919 or so and joined the two games, and now it's
the national game. They have stadiums, they have teams, they have
uniforms, the whole bit. It's hot stuff. Their pitcher stands alongside
the batter and kind of bloops the ball up into the air, the batter hits
it and runs, and otherwise it's pretty much like baseball—which to
me is fascinating because this relationship between the pitcher and
the batter is precisely the one that existed in American baseball
before Jim Creighton, a pioneer pitcher, decided, "Well, why should
I just lay it in there for 'em? Let me make it tough. This might be
interesting!"

Being a historian, I know that baseball didn't start in North
America, and that the first attempt to bring baseball from America
back to Europe was in 1874 when the Boston Red Stockings and
the Philadelphia Athletics visited England. I also know that the first
around-the-world tour in 1888–89, the Al Spalding and his Chica-
gos vs. All-Americans tour, pretty much failed: baseball did not take
off internationally even though the Spalding Company continued to
publish their guides in various languages to give the impression that
baseball was spreading like wildfire. Knowing all this, I think it's
great that 100 years after they tried and failed, it's now really ready
to take off.

We think of baseball as a traditional sport, as an adventure in
archaism, but it's the growth sport too. It's "what's happening,
Baby!" in 1960s lingo. Baseball is the fastest growing sport in the
world.

Looking at baseball spread around the world, how it's taken different shapes, and how it's all coalescing now with baseball becoming a medal sport in the Olympics for the first time in Barcelona in
1992, and knowing what I know of baseballs' rise and its history in

our country; it is a source of fascination for me to see it happening all over again, in other countries except now I'm alive for it! So, yeah, I want to be part of this.

Secondly, I guess I'm a genuine sap. I believe the stuff I write about baseball being a means of promoting international brotherhood. I believe in baseball being a language which not only permits boys and men to speak together but permits nations to speak together when diplomats haven't a clue. I think the world needs baseball; it needs some kind of common language. Esperanto: why did Shaw champion Esperanto? For the same reason I'm championing the World Baseball Hall of Fame: to break down barriers.

I really like the idea of baseball spreading around the world, and I think it's not suited solely to the North American and Latin American temperaments. I think it's a game for the whole world. I wrote that in *The Game for All America,* and I believe that. Spalding was right; he was just ahead of his time.

We believe that baseball in the Olympics is just the opening shot. We believe we're going to see professional teams competing, one country against another, and we're going to have a true "World" Series by the end of the decade.

Right now I am looking at the possibility of going to the Soviet Union this summer with my two older sons on an exchange program to a summer camp 40 miles south of Moscow where my boys would play baseball with Russian boys. And then Russian boys from that camp would come over here and play ball here. Who woulda thunk it?

The ways in which this connects with my personal background are pretty fascinating. That old left magazine where I got my start, *New Leader,* was the official organ of the Socialist party in this country for 50 years. When there was a split in the American Socialist party in 1948 between those who were pro-Stalin and those who were anti-Stalin, the *New Leader* crowd went with the anti-Stalinists, which made them turn progressively toward the right, by definition. So I was involved almost daily in the affairs of the Soviet Union and Eastern Bloc, deeply concerned with Khrushchev's speech about crimes of the Stalin era, the oppression of dissidents, the rewriting of Communist history. I was a budding Sovietologist. After leaving the *New Leader,* I interviewed at the *New York Times* for a job with the "News of the Week in Review," and at *Commentary,* and at *Time.* That was going to be my career, not baseball writing. And it's just lovely for me to contemplate my old paths crisscrossing themselves: baseball, the Soviet Union, politics.

I dropped out of college for a year in 1966–67 to join VISTA, working on an Indian reservation in Montana and in a ghetto in south Philadelphia. I had spent several months of the previous summer working in eastern Kentucky, teaching in Appalachia. So having a social conscience is not unprecedented for me. It's not as if my notion of international brotherhood and peace and goodwill as developed by baseball comes from nothing. It comes from something and, in fact, it comes from something that seems almost as occult as my sharing Alexander Cartwright's birthday; and spending my first night at the Broadway Central Hotel; and going to Hulbert's college, Beloit; and having the hotel fall down while I was writing my first baseball book. It's pleasing to look on your life and think that there are some things that are all of a piece, and that maybe you're headed in the right direction. So the World Baseball Hall of Fame is a nice fit for me. It makes sense. Will it go or not? I don't know. We'll see.

BASEBALL BOOKS BY JOHN THORN

The Relief Pitcher. New York: E. P. Dutton, 1979.
A Century of Baseball Lore. New York: Galahad, 1980.
Baseball's Ten Greatest Games. New York: Four Winds Press, 1981.
The Armchair Book of Baseball, I (editor). New York: Scribners, 1985.
The Hidden Game of Baseball (co-author). Garden City, NY: Doubleday, 1985.
The Armchair Book of Baseball, II (editor). New York: Scribners, 1987.
The National Pastime (editor). New York: Warner Books, 1987.
The Pitcher (co-author). Inglewood Cliffs, NJ: Prentice-Hall, 1987.
The Game for All America. St. Louis: Sporting News, 1988.
Total Baseball (editor). New York: Warner Books, 1989.
The 1990 Baseball Annual (co-author). New York: Warner Books, 1990.
The Whole Baseball Catalogue (co-author). New York: Simon & Schuster, 1990.
The Official Major League Baseball Record Book (editor). New York: Simon & Schuster, 1991.
Treasures of the Baseball Hall of Fame. New York: Villard Books, 1998.

17

LONNIE WHEELER

A professional journalist while in high school, Lonnie Wheeler graduated from the University of Missouri School of Journalism and later won numerous awards for his newspaper sports reporting. He co-authored The Cincinnati Game *(Orange Frazer Press, 1988), a history of the Cincinnati Reds so original and spectacular it redefined the baseball team history, and wrote* Bleachers: A Summer in Wrigley Field *(Contemporary Books, 1988), which* Booklist *called "a minor sports classic." Wheeler's latest book, a collaborative autobiography of Hank Aaron called* I Had a Hammer, *exceeds the usual parameters of its genre in depicting the subject as a direct descendent of Jackie Robinson in the continuing struggle for racial equality in baseball. A frequent contributor to the* Christian Science Monitor, *Wheeler resides in New Richmond, Ohio, and is currently at work on a biography of a well-known political figure.*

I CAN HARDLY remember *not* knowing and caring about baseball. For some reason my first recollection of baseball is a silly question I asked when I was about four years old. I was sitting in the den with my father, watching a Cardinals-Phillies game on TV. Rather than ask my father who was already in the room, I got up and walked into the utility room to see my mom who was doing some laundry. I said, "Mom, what's the Cardinals' first name? The Phillies' first name is 'Philadelphia'; what's the Cardinals' first name?" There I was, living in St. Louis, to make it all the dumber.

That's all I can recall that would suggest that I ever lacked an awareness of baseball because I can remember my teachers in first and second grade commenting about how much baseball I knew. I didn't think anything of it; I thought everybody followed baseball the way I did. Later on in grade school, I was talking to a friend who visited one summer around the time of the All-Star Game, and in the course of our conversation I realized that he didn't understand the difference between the National League and the American League. I didn't think he was stupid, but I was astounded that somebody wouldn't know the difference between the two major leagues. It was beyond my comprehension, like not knowing how many fingers are on your hand.

My dad was not a huge fan, but he rooted for the Cardinals. He liked to talk about the old Gas House Gang Cardinals, and I enjoyed listening to him talk about something he really enjoyed talking about. I read a lot of baseball when I was a kid. I read and reread *My Greatest Day in Baseball,* a book of first-person accounts by numerous Hall of Famers, and fiction-wise I was addicted to Clair Bee's "Chip Hilton" series.

I loved to play and was a pretty good curveball pitcher, but I peaked at 13 and was washed up by the time I was 16. We moved to Kirksville, Missouri, a town of about 15,000 people, when I was 16 so that my dad could open a ladies' ready-to-wear clothing store. The high school there didn't have a baseball team, but the town did have a daily newspaper where I got my start in journalism while I was still in high school.

The *Kirksville Daily Express* had one sportswriter, and he was a high school kid. Having grown up reading the St. Louis sports pages, Bob Broeg in the *Post-Dispatch* and Bob Burnes in the *Globe-Democrat,* I could tell that Kirksville's sportswriting wasn't what I was accustomed to reading. I guess I thought I could do better than this other kid, just by imitating what I'd read in the St. Louis papers. I wasn't intent on replacing him; I just thought maybe they'd let me do some sports reporting too. I went over to the paper and told the editor what I had in mind. He handed me a story the other kid had done about a double-header the local college baseball team had recently played and told me to rewrite. I rewrote it in a very straightforward wire-service style, and it must have been an improvement because, after he read it, this editor looked up at me and asked, "Have you ever *done* this before?"

He hired me immediately and must have fired the other kid because he didn't stay on; something I didn't concern myself with at the time but which I feel a little guilty about now. Anyway, that's how I became the sports editor of the *Kirksville Daily Express* at the age of 17. I wasn't really a sports editor; I just wrote stories about the local high school and college teams and turned them in, and I knew nothing at all about design, makeup, layout, editing, and so on. Nevertheless, within a year's time the paper sent me to St. Louis for a convention of sports editors. I bought a pinstriped suit and went down to St. Louis to rub elbows with a bunch of seasoned middle-aged sports editors. I can't imagine what they must have thought of me, but that was my first taste of the big time.

I don't recall having any ambition to become a journalist before I was hired by the *Kirksville Daily Express,* but once I started working at the paper I knew that journalism was going to be my career. After high school I went to the University of Missouri without even consid-ering any other colleges because Missouri had one of the best jour-nalism schools in the country and was only 90 miles away. During the summers I interned at the *Cincinnati Enquirer* and the *Miami Her-ald,* and when I graduated in 1974 I took a job as assistant sports editor for a paper in Anderson, South Carolina; primarily because I had a thirst to live and work in the South. I'd always been intrigued by distinctive places, places with a sense of place and character, and I felt that the South had a stronger sense of place than any other region in the country. And Anderson was a good place to write sports because it was close to Clemson University, which meant we covered ACC basketball, and fairly close to Athens, Georgia, which meant we covered SEC football. We had minor league baseball in Anderson, and we were close enough to Atlanta that we provided some coverage of the Braves.

Incidentally, I had my first contact with Hank Aaron my first year in Anderson when I was assigned to do a three-part series on him. This was just after he'd broken the home run record. I did the series without really interviewing him. At first, he said he'd talk to me, but then he managed to keep his distance. Before the games he'd walk off to sit on the rolled-up tarp down the right-field line because he knew I couldn't follow him there, nor could the other reporters. Back then I didn't know how to take his behavior, but now, having done a book with him, I realize how weary he'd become with all the questioning and all the hoopla and I understand that he was just trying to politely remove himself from all of it.

After two years I left Anderson and sportswriting and went over to the *Clarion-Ledger* in Jackson, Mississippi, where I did a sort of roving, "way of life" column about places in the state three or four times a week. I'd go in cold, snoop around all day, and then write a column about the place where I was. This job really scratched my profession-al itch, satisfied my curiosity about southern places, but it became very tedious after about 16 months, so I moved on. I went back to the *Cincinnati Enquirer,* where I'd interned, and took a job there as a feature writer.

After I'd been at the *Enquirer* for about two years, I moved over to sports again in an effort to get a column. I thought doing a column was the only way to write with liberty for a newspaper, and I'd been told that sports was the best avenue to take to get a column. I bided my time doing mostly general assignment and some longer feature stories, and filling in for beat writers and the regular columnist, Mark Purdy, on his days off and during his vacation. I didn't particularly enjoy working like that, going in every day and having no idea what my assignment would be . . . having no autonomy whatsoever . . . but I stayed with it because I was led to believe that I was next in line to take over the column. However, when Mark Purdy left and the column opened up, it was given to someone else, so I turned in my resignation to become a freelancer. Fortunately, things have worked out for the best.

I thought I'd be able to freelance for out-of-town newspapers as well as magazines. I figured other papers would be interested in the availability of a guy like me, who knew the business and the Cincinnati teams, to cover the local sports scene so that they could save all the traveling expenses connected with sending a reporter here. I wrote to every pretty good-sized newspaper within a 200-mile radius of Cincinnati . . . Louisville, Lexington, Columbus, Indianapolis, Cleveland, Toledo . . . and was taken aback when I didn't get even one response. I had much better luck with the *New York Times*—I wound up doing a lot of work for them and with the magazine market. Within two years I could see that I was going to make it as a freelancer.

I also did a number of pieces for *Ohio Magazine.* I was recruited by that magazine's senior editor, John Baskin, who was always on the lookout for good writers to hire. Writing for John was a terrific experience, and I learned a lot from him; particularly, how to compile research, which is something, oddly enough, I hadn't really learned in the newspaper business.

It was Baskin, by the way, who came up with the idea of doing a baseball book in conjunction with Cincinnati's bicentennial. John and I and a couple of others decided to put up our own money and publish the book through John's small publishing company called Orange Frazer Press. Originally, *The Cincinnati Game* was supposed to be a collection of new essays written by me, and I had a list of about a dozen topics; however, once we really got into the material, the book evolved into something much bigger than we had envisioned, and it became a much more sweeping comprehensive book.

The turning point in the expansion of the book came when I was doing research for a chapter that was supposed to be about the Reds's best teams. That chapter developed into a decade-by-decade Reds history which included categories not only on best and worst teams, but also on managers, players, anecdotes, and whimsical oddball things. It was 80 pages long by the time I finished it. When I turned it in, Baskin said, "This is a book within a book. We've got to cut this down and restructure the book." So at that point we redefined our concept and basically started over. John got more involved, started doing some of the writing himself, and kept accumulating more and more material. He'd come up with files on things like "tobacco," "brawls," "superstitions," and just about any other human aspect of Reds history you can imagine.

I wrote the majority of the book, including the essays, which utilized my strength: putting things into perspective; but John wrote a good bit of it, and it was really his vision and energy which made *The Cincinnati Game* so unique. John approached the book as a non-fan. He knew next to nothing about baseball, and he was proud of the fact he'd never been to a major league baseball game—I don't know if he's been to one yet. Of course, in doing the research for the book he learned a great deal about baseball and especially about the Reds. John really got caught up in the personalities, particularly those of the nineteenth century players who were great characters. He also became a fan of Lee Allen, who wrote a history of the Reds, because Allen had a grasp of character, and John, as a writer and journalist, also is very sensitive to character and is interested in it.

I knew going into *The Cincinnati Game* that the Reds have a special place in baseball history for a number of obvious reasons; first and foremost because they fielded the first professional team in 1869. However, in doing the book I realized that the team is special in ways I hadn't understood. For instance, I hadn't realized how consistently the Reds have been connected to innovation in baseball; we did a whole chapter on baseball origins and firsts involving the Reds. It was also remarkable to discover how many of the game's top executives have had a Cincinnati connection. We're talking about Harry Wright, Garry Herrmann, Ban Johnson, Judge Landis, Larry MacPhail, Happy Chandler, Bill DeWitt, Gabe Paul, and on and on. I don't think any other franchise has had this connection to the baseball braintrust. It's one of the reasons, I think, baseball has ingrained itself so deeply on the consciousness of the city.

The Cincinnati Game is primarily a Reds team history, but as the title implies, the book is not exclusively about the Reds. Cincinnati has always had a unique blend of professional baseball and outstanding amateur baseball, and it's amazing how many major league players the area has produced over the years, particularly the west side of town, which is the hot bed of amateur baseball in Cincinnati. Probably the most compelling explanation for the inordinate number of major leaguers Cincinnati has produced is simply that the city accepted baseball wholeheartedly from the very beginning and didn't buy into the attitude held by many people in the early days that baseball was a profession for rogues, rowdies, and neer-do-wells, but not decent, educated people. Cincinnati is considered a conservative, laid-back town nowadays, but back in the nineteenth century Cincinnati was a rowdy, beer-drinking town, and the people embraced baseball, rough edges and all. Baseball has simply been an important part of the culture in Cincinnati for as long as anybody can remember.

A key element of the book is the design, and Baskin and Brooke Wenstrup, a woman he worked with at *Ohio Magazine,* put in untold hours doing very tedious, intricate work on the book's graphics that a large-scale publisher wouldn't even contemplate doing because it wouldn't be cost effective. We spent the better part of two years preparing the book, and John estimates that the three of us spent close to 10,000 hours on it. It's very unlikely that another team history like ours will ever be done because I don't think any three people will put in that much time for so little return. Financially, it doesn't make sense.

The Cincinnati Game was tremendously fun to do—it was also grueling—but we didn't make any money on it to speak of, for two reasons. First, the book was expensive to produce because of all the graphic effects and also because of its oblong shape. We knew the shape would be costly, but we wanted it for its effect; that is, we thought the material lent itself extremely well to a horizontal treatment, and we have numerous two-page spreads in the book.

Second, although the book got some great reviews—Dick Miller in *Sports Collectors Digest* called it "the best baseball book ever published"—the local newspapers practically ignored it. And that really hurt. When we finished the book, we were very optimistic that it would sell. Not only was the book timely in respect to the city's bicentennial, but there also hadn't been a Red's history in a long time. We were satisfied with the wordsmithing we put into the book, were convinced that in terms of its literary quality it was the equal or superior to anything of its kind. We thought the book's whimsy would be a selling point, and we knew that it was a very appealing book to look at; in fact, in design it's unparalleled. We thought we had all the bases covered. We thought, "How can anybody not notice this book? It's all there between one set of covers."

I think one reason the local media pretty much ignored the book was that it was produced locally by local people. There's a certain certification that comes when somebody from the outside, especially New York, recognizes Cincinnati, whereas if the recognition comes from within it doesn't seem to count. I'm convinced that if somebody from New York had produced the same book we did, the reaction would have been much different. For instance, certain parts of *Eight Men Out* were filmed here, and that got front-page treatment over and over. Granted, a movie is newsworthy because it reaches a lot of people. Still, the fact remains that while *Eight Men Out* deals effectively with one episode in Reds history, the 1919 Black Sox World Series, *The Cincinnati Game* accomplishes one hundred-fold what the movie does in terms of reporting about Cincinnati and Reds history. In fact, I don't think any of the other numerous books and products about Cincinnati that came out during the bicentennial gives you more information about Cincinnati or a better sense of what the city is and has been than *The Cincinnati Game*, despite its being a baseball book.

In the middle of working on *The Cincinnati Game* I took about nine months out to write another book, about the Cubs and Wrigley Field, called *Bleachers*. I wanted to do *Bleachers* for two reasons. First, as I said, I have this thing for places, and I'd seen the Cubs play on TV often enough to know that the Wrigley Field bleachers, with all those wild shirtless fans and their idiosyncracies, was probably the most unique place in baseball. I thought it would make a great book to spend a season in those bleachers and then write about the experience. And second, I thought that with *Bleachers* I could write about the most neglected aspect in all of baseball literature: the fans. With all the extant literature that tries to get at "the essence of baseball" and at what baseball means to our society, I'm amazed that the fans have been almost completely overlooked, because the players have very little to do with determining baseball's place in America. The fans create that, not the players. Baseball is part of our consciousness, and that consciousness is not a player consciousness, it's a social consciousness, a public consciousness. We devote an enormous amount of our time and resources to baseball, and that's where you see the hold baseball has on our society, through the fans. The consciousness of the fans is where baseball resides. I wanted to get at that, and I thought nobody personified this phenomenon any better than the Cubs fans who inhabit the bleachers in Wrigley Field.

The Cubs finished last in 1987, the year I was there in the bleachers. Some people thought that was a bad break for me and the book, but I didn't, precisely because I wanted to experience a typical Cubs season: a promising beginning followed by a slow slide into mediocrity. One of the best definitions of Cubs fanship I heard that summer came from a guy I met in the bleachers whose claim to fame was that he was in divorce court the same day as Ernie Banks. He said that being a Cubs fan is like getting married for a second time: "Hope wins out over experience."

The interesting question, given the Cubs' history and their image as "lovable losers," is "If the Cubs ever *do* win a World Series, will 'Cubness' be destroyed?" I don't think it will. Cubs fans are proud of the fact that they've stuck with the team even while it has been losing, but they don't relish losing. They want the Cubs to win. It's just that they feel their suffering and loyalty is an extra validation of their right to celebrate when the team does win.

What would destroy the Cubs phenomenon would be the desertion of Wrigley Field for a new stadium in the suburbs. With all of its romantic, special qualities—its ivy-covered walls, its huge obsolete scoreboard, it's inner-city location, its bleachers, and, until recently, its absense of lights—Wrigley Field has been and still is the most pertinent of all factors in "Cubness." Cubs fans love the ballpark as much as they love the team. And if the Cubs ever abandon Wrigley Field, I'm convinced the Cubs will become just another team.

You know, I thought *Bleachers* also had all the ingredients to make an impact in the market. First of all, there was the enormous popularity of the Cubs. Second, the book got very positive reviews, and I was able to plug it on *The Today Show*. And third, *Bleachers* was timed right too. It came out in 1988 when Wrigley Field was getting lots of national attention because it was finally getting lights. With all this going for it, I thought the book really had a chance.

The problem was that the publisher, Contemporary Books, didn't have the mechanism with which to promote it. I'm not a celebrity, and they weren't going to send me around the country on an author's tour like they did Joe Garagiola whose book, *It's Anybody's Game,* came out the same year. To compound the problem—and this is only my presumption—Contemporary's East Coast distributor was apparently not very enthusiastic about the book. I guess they didn't understand the Cubs phenomenon, and, I assume, their lack of enthusiasm led to the decision to print only about 8,000 copies of the book rather than the 20,000 they were originally going to print. The lesson I learned with *Bleachers* is that if you want a book the publisher is going to get behind and really publicize, there's got to be a name involved. There are others who deserve a similar status, but I can think of only three or four writers who can sell baseball books just because their names are on the covers. If the rest of us are going to do a book that will crack the market, we've got to get involved with somebody the publisher and the big chain bookstores will promote. My agent, David Black, and I arrived at this conslusion at about the same time, and that's one reason we wound up doing *I Had a Hammer* with Hank Aaron.

David saw a little note in the newspaper that quoted Aaron as saying he might leave baseball because he was becoming disillusioned over the game's treatment of blacks, and he thought Aaron might have something to say. Of course, I was extremely interested in working with Aaron, but it was a real longshot because I had never done a collaboration; and although I had written two baseball books I thought had merit, hardly anybody knew about them.

We got a break in that we hit it off right away with Aaron's agent, Alicia Berns. I had been thinking of doing a book on Satchel Paige, who was from Mobile, Alabama, the same as Aaron. My interest in Paige and the fact that I was very interested in Aaron's background growing up in Mobile, the most southern of southern cities, struck a chord with Alicia, and she went to bat for us with Aaron.

When David and I first met with Aaron, in Milwaukee, I had a terrible case of the flu. On any other day I wouldn't even have gotten out of bed, but this was my big chance and I had to go. I remember feeling so weak that just dragging my luggage through the airport terminal was an ordeal, and I had to lean up against the wall to rest every 30 or 40 feet. When David opened the door to our hotel room, I just kind of fell into the room. But we had a nice conversation with Aaron at lunch, and soon after that the lawyers started hammering out a collaboration agreement. I met with Aaron a few times after that and did enough interviews with other people to write the proposal which David sent to about 20 New York publishers. Three of them got into the bidding seriously, and, after having done two quiet books, it was pretty heady for me to see them express that level of commitment.

I always thought that when you did a collaboration you went up to a cabin with the subject and talked for two weeks straight; that turned out to be a complete misconception. I met Aaron many different times for a day or two or a week at a time, and usually away from Atlanta, where he makes his home, because he has too many distractions when he's home.

Aaron has an image of being reticent and aloof, but when he's relaxed and with somebody he trusts he's very amiable and open. One of the main things I realized in doing the book is that, as much as Aaron is misunderstood as a person, he was also misunderstood as a player. It's ironic that the home run record defines Aaron because he wasn't really a home run hitter. Home runs were a by-product of the way he hit; they were his residue. When Aaron first came up, he was a line drive hitter, who hit off his front foot and hit a lot to right field. He was such a good contact hitter early in his career that people thought he would make his mark by being the next .400 hitter. Nobody imagined that he would break a home run record. When the Braves moved to Atlanta, Aaron changed his hitting style and became more of a conscious home run hitter to suit the needs of his team and the nature of the Atlanta ballpark.

If he had stayed in Milwaukee and hadn't changed his hitting style, there's a realistic chance Aaron would have been the first player since Ty Cobb to reach 4,000 hits. I don't know if he would have exceeded Cobb, but through the first half of his career he was on a brisker pace to reach 4,000 hits than Pete Rose was at the same point in his career; and Aaron was as good a player as long as Rose was. There's every reason to believe that, if base hits had been his concentration, he would have, at least, reached 4,000 hits. It's pretty amazing to think that the all-time home run leader might, under different circumstances, have been the all-time hit leader.

People sometimes try to diminish the home run record because Aaron played nine seasons in Atlanta Stadium, which is a home run ballpark. But they forget that he played 12 seasons in Milwaukee County Stadium, which was not a hitter's park and certainly not a home run park. When he left Milwaukee, Aaron had hit more home runs on the road than at home.

The one raw statistic that really impresses me though is Aaron's total bases. To accumulate a lot of total bases you've got to get a lot of hits and you've got to get power hits; in other words, you've got to be a good all-around hitter. Aaron is so far ahead of everybody else in total bases it's almost unimaginable. If you take each player's total bases and line them up one after another, 90 feet for a single, 180 feet for a double; Aaron is more than 12 miles ahead of the nearest challenger.

It's a cliché to describe somebody as a "complete ballplayer," but that's what Aaron was. I talked to a lot of his former teammates, and they never brought up his home runs. They always wanted to talk about other facets of his game, about how fundamentally sound he was in every aspect of the game.

This was the point Aaron's teammates brought up in favoring him over Willie Mays, to whom Aaron was often unfavorably compared. Eddie Mathews, for one, said that nobody ever ran on Aaron because he would always throw to the right base or hit the cutoff man, while the Braves had a standing rule to run on Mays because he continually threw to the wrong base.

The rivalry with Mays is still a sensitive subject for Aaron, in large part, I think, because the press and the public's preference for Mays had a lot to do with racial stereotyping. You see, in the early days of Aaron's career, he was described as "slow-talking" and "shuffling" and was referred to as "Step-'n-fetch-it." Essentially, those are euphemisms for "nigger." It's true that Aaron wasn't highly educated or sophisticated when he came up to the big leagues, but neither was Mays, who came from the same type of environment in Alabama that Aaron came from. The difference was that Mays had that bubbly personality, he had Leo Durocher constantly gushing about him, and, to put it bluntly, he was more entertaining. The white press and the white public back in the early 1950s loved a black person if he was an entertainer, but if a black ballplayer didn't entertain people, then he was just another nigger.

The discrimination inherent in the public's perception of Aaron can also be perceived if you compare Aaron's image to Joe DiMaggio's. Aaron was the consummate ballplayer who seemed to perform effortlessly . . . he did everything smoothly and seemed to glide after balls in the outfield . . . and off the field he was very quiet and unobtrusive, just like DiMaggio. This style created a mystique about DiMaggio, and he became an icon for it; Aaron became ignored because he didn't entertain as he was expected to, or worse, he was depicted as being lazy and slow.

DiMaggio was the player Aaron should have been compared to, but most often it was Mays. Willie's playing first, in New York, and, second, on both coasts, made a tremendous difference in the amount of publicity he received compared to what Aaron received. Aaron didn't mind being quiet though. He didn't crave the publicity that Mays got; but on the other hand, he didn't appreciate the fact that this difference in publicity contributed to his being underestimated as a ballplayer. He never felt he had to take a back seat to anybody as a ballplayer. He's not a boastful guy, but he'll tell you flat-out that he was a better hitter than Mays.

This is not to say that setting the record straight about his playing accomplishments was Aaron's motivation for doing the book. That was something I thought was incumbent on me to do since *I Had a Hammer,* the last book Aaron will ever do, will represent him in history. Aaron was interested in doing the book for an entirely different reason, which was made explicitly clear to me one day when he asked me if I thought he'd made anything of himself, if he had done anything with his life. Beside revealing some humility, that question showed me that Aaron doesn't put his life in the context of baseball; otherwise the question wouldn't have made any sense at all. Obviously, in a baseball sense he has done great things with his life, and he has records to prove it. But Aaron wasn't talking about baseball, and his question showed me that he sincerely puts his life in another context: what good has he done for the world, particularly for his race? That's the question he asks himself. He wants to do some good, and he saw an opportunity to do some good through the book by calling attention to what baseball has and has not accomplished in racial matters. People assume that the issue is pretty much over now, and he wanted to make it clear that it isn't.

In the book we touch on the current racial situation in baseball, but our principle method of conveying that message was just to tell what his life and career were like, to show what he went through. Everybody knows that Jackie Robinson went through hell in 1947, but people assume that after Robinson broke the color line everything was hunky-dory; they assume that the hurdle was cleared by the mid-1950s, and it wasn't. Blacks couldn't even stay with whites in spring training in the early 1960s, 15 years after Jackie Robinson broke in. Aaron himself, along with two teammates on the Jacksonville, Florida, team and two players on the Savannah team, integrated the Sally League in 1953, a very traumatic thing to do since the Sally League was in the deep South. You can talk all you want about racial prejudice, but it doesn't have any impact unless you dramatize it with examples. That's why we included the hate mail Aaron received. And that's why the stories about the discrimination Aaron faced early in his career, in Milwaukee, and even in Atlanta in the 1970s . . . stories that hadn't been reported before . . . were so vital to the book. I don't think people will be all that surprised to read in the book about Aaron's feelings because he's more or less been the spokesman in recent years for racial equality in baseball, but I do think they will be surprised to understand the depth and scope of the discrimination and hatred he encountered. I know I was.

Because of his desire to improve the racial situation in baseball, Aaron was committed to the book, and he was eager to talk. Ironically, the last thing we talked about was what first comes to mind whenever anybody thinks of Aaron: the home run record. It just wasn't what the book was about. It's not what Aaron is about. We set out to do a book that had some pertinence beyond baseball—which is something I hope applies to all of my books.

BASEBALL BOOKS BY LONNIE WHEELER

Bleachers: A Summer in Wrigley Field. Chicago: Contemporary Books, 1988.
The Cincinnati Game. Wilmington, Ohio: Orange Frazer Press, 1988.
I Had a Hammer. New York: Harper Collins, 1991.
Stranger to the Game: The Autobiography of Bob Gibson. New York: Viking Penguin, 1994.